'Brilliant, provocative an
book you need to read this

'If the Lovin' Spoonful taug... ...g, it's that it's
difficult to try and tell a stra..g.. about rock and roll.
Luke Haines not only tries – he succeeds'

John Niven

'Haines takes a dyspeptic approach to music history in
Freaks Out. Dividing pop sheep from out-there GOATS
with spite and guile, it's part SCUM manifesto, part insane
hot or not list'

Sunday Times

'A waspish eccentric guide to rock n roll misfits from the
1950s to today'

Telegraph

'[A] very funny and incisive book'

★★★★ the *Sun*

'A customary mixture of [Haines] hostility, panache and
gags'

★★★★ *Record Collector*

'Haines is a genuinely funny nuisance, and he can write. Like all unabashedly opinionated curmudgeons with a sincere love of art and a healthy sense of acerbic humour, Haines is often right and often wrong, but he's almost always entertaining'
Big Issue

'*Freaks Out* is wickedly entertaining, it is the kind of manifesto we might all like to write, choosing heroes and villains that others may vehemently disagree with, but Haines' phrasing, justifications and the sheer out-there choices he makes make for a unique read'
Louder Than War

'Acerbically entertaining but utterly sincere and, yes, righteous'
★★★★ *Shindig!*

'Rip-roaringly funny ... there's so much to love within these pages'
Blitzed

'An expert stylist, Haines acquits himself nicely to the various genres of writing, although it's never at the expense of his trademark humour. Make no mistake, *Freaks Out!* is one of the funniest rock books in recent times'
Penny Black Music

FREAKS OUT!

*Weirdos, Misfits and Deviants –
The Rise and Fall of Righteous
Rock 'n' Roll*

Luke Haines

NEB 024 PB

First published in hardback in the UK in 2024
This paperback edition published in 2025 by Nine Eight Books
An imprint of Bonnier Books UK
5th Floor, HYLO, 103–105 Bunhill Row, London, EC1Y 8LZ
Owned by Bonnier Books, Sveavägen 56, Stockholm, Sweden

@nineeightbooks

@nineeightbooks

Hardback ISBN: 978-1-7887-0934-7
eBook ISBN: 978-1-7887-0933-0
Paperback ISBN: 978-1-7887-0935-4

All rights reserved. No part of this publication may be reproduced, stored in a retrieval system, or transmitted in any form or by any means, without the prior permission in writing of the publisher, nor be otherwise circulated in any form of binding or cover other than that in which it is published and without a similar condition including this condition being imposed on the subsequent purchaser.

A CIP catalogue record for this book Prelimis available from the British Library.

Cover design by Alex Kirby
Typeset by IDSUK (Data Connection) Ltd
Printed and bound in Great Britain by Clays Ltd, Elcograf S.p.A

1 3 5 7 9 10 8 6 4 2

Text copyright © Luke Haines, 2024

The right of Luke Haines to be identified as the author of this work has been asserted in accordance with the Copyright, Designs and Patents Act 1988.

Every reasonable effort has been made to trace copyright-holders of material reproduced in this book. If any have been inadvertently overlooked, the publisher would be glad to hear from them.

www.bonnierbooks.co.uk

For Becky, Mercy and Fred with love

Gooble, gobble,
we accept her
we accept her
One of us
One of us.

'Freaks' – Tod Browning, 1932

Gabba Gabba
We accept you
We accept you
One of us.

'Pinhead' – Ramones, 1977

CONTENTS

Brief glossary		ix
Foreword	Do not proceed until you have read this	xi
CHAPTER 1	We are 'A Puppet's Facade'. You are not (Eight reasons to love the Doors)	1
CHAPTER 2	'Limp, you bugger, limp'	15
CHAPTER 3	Crowded trousers	29
CHAPTER 4	How Elvis's quiff knocked out Johnnie Ray	35
CHAPTER 5	The psychedelic dawn of Hank B. Marvin and the Shadows	47
CHAPTER 6	How the Beatles ruined everything for everyone ever	63
CHAPTER 7	Weasel-faced dunces – how I might have killed Steve Peregrin Took (We have to talk about Steve, Part One)	75
CHAPTER 8	Mick Farren ruined my marriage	85
CHAPTER 9	Mad Bob from Margate	93

CHAPTER 10	Psychedelic Morris Men	101
CHAPTER 11	Something entirely fucked up	111
CHAPTER 12	Male Genius Myth Buster – (Thomas Chatterton teenage rampage)	115
CHAPTER 13	The Fall can no longer be Freaks	121
CHAPTER 14	Australians in Europe	129
CHAPTER 15	Never work	137
CHAPTER 16	The children with Xs carved into their heads	147
CHAPTER 17	Gary Glitter was my Big Bang	161
CHAPTER 18	Freaks don't wear shorts, they wear leotards	171
CHAPTER 19	Dismantled teenage rock 'n' roll Pope	183
CHAPTER 20	The Greatest Photograph of the Twentieth Century	191
CHAPTER 21	Lou, John, Sterl, Mo Tucker and me	201
CHAPTER 22	The three Fs	211
CHAPTER 23	We have to talk about Steve, Part Two	217
CHAPTER 24	Weasels (slight return)	227
CHAPTER 25	In the future nobody will be famous for fifteen minutes	237
CHAPTER 26	The empty seat on the bus	241
CHAPTER 27	Fifty dead Taylor Swifts	247
CHAPTER 28	Billie Eilish is alive and kicking – and she's gonna make us all freaks, baby	259

Epilogue	267
Discography, bibliography, miscellany	273
About the author	303

Brief glossary

Rock 'n' roll: In this book, rock 'n' roll will refer to all pop music created from the 1950s onwards, regardless of previous or accepted genre. For example, Elvis will be referred to as 'rock 'n' roll', as will Kylie Minogue, the Beatles, the Carpenters, et al. Rock 'n' roll will also refer to an attitude and may also be applied to various pre-enlightenment sects that may crop up in the text. Remember: rock 'n' roll is a deadly serious business. It is also very funny.

* * *

Freak: An unusual or unexpected event: 'a freak accident'. An anomaly. A person, or animal, with a physical abnormality perhaps appearing in a circus sideshow (archaic). One who is over-enthusiastic: 'a sports freak'. *Verb*: to behave in an irrational way perhaps under the influence of illegal drugs: 'that motherfucker totally freaked out'. *Noun*: a deviant. A 'head' (archaic slang). An individual with a highly evolved attitude. One who wears their Freak flag high.

The followers — this book is not for you.
The salt of the earth — this book is not for you.
The worthy — this book is not for you.
The ideologists — this book is not for you.
Hedonists and bohemians — this book is not for you.
The middlebrow — this book is not for you.
The highbrow — this book is not for you.
Dilettantes — this book is not for you.
1970s middle school RE teachers — this book is not for you.
The England football team (women's and men's) —
this book is not for you.
The litanists — this book is not for you.
Gatekeepers — this book is not for you.
Gamekeepers — this book is not for you.
(Not even for the poachers . . .)
The curators — this book is not for you.
The left, the right — this book is not for you.
The list-makers — lists are for shoppers not rockers, and
this book is not for you.
This is not a list — this is a manifesto, and
this book is for . . . the Freaks.

FOREWORD

Do not proceed until you have read this

I got lucky: I was born a Freak. Too precocious for state school and too lazy for academia. Both of these ideal qualifications ran through me like a stick of rock ('n' roll). I had natural Freak chemistry. Comedians have funny bones. I have Freak bones. An adolescent as the wan light of punk rock blinked over suburban late '70s/early '80s Britain, mixing it up with early Genesis, ELP, King Crimson, Yes, the Shadows and Pink Floyd. They were all punk rock to me. Dudes with deviant hair. Wild-eyed kids from Freecloud. All conjuring up a blitzkrieg of noise that sounded even better in a darkened bedroom. My parents didn't dig pop music too much. My dad once shared a flight with the Rolling Stones in the mid-'60s; his verdict: 'They could've done with a wash.'

My mum and dad's modest collection of around thirty elpees consisted of vanilla crooners: Vince Hill, Matt Monro and cosy MOR titans: Big Val Doonican and the Ray Conniff Singers. My mother felt that Frank Sinatra was a bit too gauche. There were some musical soundtracks and some light classical (also for some reason Tchaikovsky's 'Liturgy of St John Chrysostom', a terrifying choral piece). Among the 7-inch singles – in particular, 'Hello, Dolly!' by Louis Armstrong, 'Little Green Apples' by Roger Miller (both great) – skulked a couple of proper rock 'n' roll records: 'She Loves You' by the Beatles and 'Hey Jude' (note the lost five-year gap). Ma and Pa insisted that the B-side of the 1968 smash, the hard overdriven Panza rock 'Revolution', was suffering from a 'manufacturing fault'. 'Hey Jude' on the other side was deemed to be 'correct', and also a 'big hit in the dancehalls,' according to my mother. These rock 'n' roll types were not the kind of people my parents envisioned in their precious only-child's future. These pop musicians would not last ten minutes in the Debenhams sale and most probably hadn't even thought about their pensions. These young people were Freaks.

I don't and never did look down on my mum and dad for their perceived 'straightness'. They were both born five years before the outbreak of the Second World War, and my mum into a strict naval Edwardian patriarchal family. By the mid-1950s they were already married, by the '60s in their fourth decade. Technically, by the standards of the day, old, or at least middle-aged. I always feel a pang of sympathy whenever I hear some hipster going on about their parents' cool record collection of Bowie, Zeppelin and Dylan. Too easy, man. Just too easy.

FOREWORD

'What is on your badge, Haines?' My RE teacher, an idiot buzzard, Mrs Barnyard, called me up in front of the class.

Imperiously she peered over her glasses and read my lapel badge mock slowly. 'I'm a Blockhead.'

'Hmm,' she muttered, puffing up to her full height of 4 foot 10, about to unlock the safety on a mustard gas cloud of ignorance and pleased with the few giggles she had scored from her audience of eleven-year-olds. 'I'm a Blockhead . . . that just about sums you up.'

I was, of course, only briefly chastened. Soon I came to realise that not only was I proud to be wearing my 'I'm a Blockhead' badge but it was also the first time I'd ever held my Freak flag aloft. Whether Mrs Barnyard (and all of the 1970s Mrs Barnyards) ever realised that Ian Dury would soon come to be recognised as not only one of the UK's leading Freaks but one of the country's finest poets remains unknown.

By the 1980s, Freak job opportunities in rock and pop were plentiful. Not just because of the punk revolution, but due to three decades of freakery bubbling away in the pop-culture-stew. You could seemingly do anything: Dress up as a pirate, channel the Glitter Band and the Burundi drummers *and* become the most avant-garde teeny-bop idol in history (Adam and the Ants). You could be a visionary poet backed by a bunch of avant-garde brickies, or a visionary poet backed by a bunch of actual brickies. You could even be Kevin Rowland and become a pop star.

In the 1980s, signing on the dole was all the rage. All the Freaks hated Thatcher and Thatcher hated the Freaks.

FREAKS OUT!

Some sort of mad authoritarian accord had been achieved. As the country was pillaged by Thatcherism, God's finest weirdos thrived. Proud to be signing on, proud to never want a job, unconvinced that there was any dignity in labour. I was eager to get in a band and join the bone-idle crusade. I spent the latter years of that decade lolling around in the lower depths of the indie charts with all the other 'benefits arrive on Thursday' bands hoping one day to underachieve as much as, say, Dinosaur Jr. (best record: 'Freak Scene').

By the mid-1990s, I was in a more successful rock band. At the vanguard of outsider-dominance (alongside Pulp and Suede). The weirdos were taking over. Pulp even had a song about it, 'Misfits' (they had an earlier album called *Freaks*), but the signs were ominous: All-purpose politics 'guy' Tony Blair was about to become Prime Minister. *Loaded* magazine gave rise to the low-level dreams of regional estate agents. Football, which had successfully marginalised itself in the '80s, and in my mind, like smallpox, had been pretty much wiped out, was on the rise again. And then: Britpop – Simple Jack in the form of a bunch of Herman's Hermits tribute acts. Heralded at the time by complicit media goons and assorted useful idiots, now correctly derided as a disastrous navigational error on the ship of fools. The 1980s dole generation feeling emasculated by Thatcher became 'lads'. Football, Blair and Noel Gallagher were the axis of evil against us.

I have been fighting this war since I first drew breath. In the reckoning of the first quarter of the twenty-first century the time has arrived, for this is no straight History of Rock

FOREWORD

and Pop. This book is not for straights. I have deliberately striven for an imbalance. This book is for the unbalanced individual. Groupthink has been abolished and only free-thinking rules. If your favourite artist has been left out or derided, then get out of my tent, man.

My attitude to rock 'n' roll is the same as Bill Shankly's attitude to football. To paraphrase: 'Rock 'n' roll is not a matter of life and death, it is more important than that.' With one addendum: 'Rock 'n' roll is also utterly ridiculous.' Bear that in mind when reading this book. Onward, groovers.

CHAPTER 1

We are 'A Puppet's Facade'. You are not (Eight reasons to love the Doors)

The horror of a first band – of all first bands.
How the early '80s fell in and out of love with Jim Morrison.
The high magick of the Virgin Prunes, and the future maxim:
'Getting sacked is all part of being in a band.'

The dreaming is better than the waking. The eve of success is better than the success. Failure is inevitable and, inevitably, failure is at least the equal of success, and at worst, depending on the quotient of the failure, then the failure is likely better than the success. Right now, it is the dreaming. I am still asleep. It's 1982, I am fifteen years old, I have already been a 1982 teenage provincial punk. You'll read about it later. Right now, I want to be in a band. More than anything. That's it. Band or bust. 'Wake up!' as Jim Morrison quite rightly said.

I didn't really do the imaginary band thing; where you make up a band name and a logo, painstakingly draw the logo of your imaginary band over your school exercise books or your khaki rucksack as you dream up your imaginary band biography. Most important in the preliminaries for your *imaginist* band is to work out the cool things that you will say in imaginary interviews. Well, I did do that last one, but that was a few years later, when I was in a band called the Servants. The Servants spent the interminable (yet strangely quite enjoyable) five years or so of our existence practising our good quotes and waiting for people to interview us. The two times in those five years that we were interviewed, my well-rehearsed pearls didn't make the cut. In 1982 I went straight from really wanting, needing, to be in a band to actually being in one.

My cousin Rob had a drum kit. Rob's parents – my Auntie Molly and Uncle Bill – had a bit of money. Rob's dad was a self-made builder. Very 1970s: big house with home extension, big boisterous family. Big bouncy 1970s dog. Self-made. Post-war. Working-class-done-well. Throughout the 1970s Rob and my other older cousins had everything that I wanted: acres of Scalextric track, and mini-garage forecourts lined up with little Scalextric cars, armies of Action Men, bags of Lego; air guns, plastic Evel Knievels and die-cast metal UFO interceptors. Then later: records, LPs: everything by Bowie, Led Zep, ELP, the Nice, T. Rex, Bob Dylan. Then even later: the Clash, the Stranglers, Joy Division; instruments, tape recorders, synthesisers and an electric guitar. Finally, Rob got a drum kit. I was jealous as all hell.

Rob and I listened to the same music apart from a six-month departure when I went behind enemy lines and flirted catastrophically with plastic punk. I soon came back

WE ARE 'A PUPPET'S FACADE'

to our main obsession: the Fall. I had gathered important intelligence when I was out in the field; that the Fall were better than anything else. Rob agreed. So we formed ... an experimental duo. Yes, we did.

I had an Arbiter Gibson Melody Maker copy that my dad had worked overtime to pay for.[1] Rob had his massive drum kit that his dad hadn't worked overtime for. Rob got better on the drums, and I tried to write songs. We borrowed Rob's brother's massive British-engineered Cat Octave synthesiser that spat out cool white noise when it felt the climatic conditions were acceptable. We also found an old two-track reel-to-reel tape recorder in the garage and we learned to make crude overdubs and create tape 'experiments'. It was all crap. Precocious crap. And it was all great. Precociously great.

Rob must have sensed that we weren't about to secure that dreamed-of Peel session as a teenage 'experimental' duo, and one Saturday afternoon when we were making a racket in his bedroom two strangers turned up.

Gavin and Jayne were very cool. Jayne was one of the 'sought-after' girls. Rob knew some girls at this point; I did not. I knew Jayne from being in the year above me at school – the kind of cool girl that all the teenage boys had hopeless fantasies about knowing. Pre-Raphaelite curls, a budding actress and a great piano player. I also remembered Gavin, who was also in the year above me

---

[1] To my eternal regret I smashed this excellent but cheap guitar up in early Auteurs days in a fit of frustration.

in school and was a bit of a lad. Gav and Jayne were now at sixth-form college. Jayne had been playing in a 'punk' band with Gavin and a bass player called 'Bug' (there was always someone with a name like Bug who had a bass in the provinces in 1982). Bug only wanted to do Jam and Stranglers songs. Gavin had other ideas.

Sixteen-year-old Gavin Ridley – nearly seventeen – was an 'ideas man'. I knew this because Jayne solemnly told us that Gav was an 'ideas man'. I'd never met an 'ideas man' before. Come to think of it I hadn't met too many sixteen-year-olds (nearly seventeen) either. The only older teenage boys I'd met usually came on the end of a Doc Marten boot that was making contact with my ribcage as I lay on the tarmac outside the science block. Gavin had the balls to get up to a microphone and make a noise that sounded to us a lot like singing. None of us questioned whether Gavin could actually sing. Gav had his eye on being Pete Murphy or Pete Burns (this was pre 'You Spin Me Round' Dead or Alive era Pete Burns), or, *say it with hushed breath*, 'one of the Virgin Prunes'. More importantly, Gavin had one clear vision: his hair. Gavin spent more time thinking about hair than any person I'd ever met. My own hair was going through a crap transition, as ever; the punky spikes had grown out and I was in danger of looking like someone from the Alarm. Gavin had strong ideas about what I should do with my hair. Ideas that involved crimpers and backcombing. Ideas that could make me look even more like someone from the Alarm. Uh-oh. Gav had strong ideas about what everyone should do with their hair. He had a

WE ARE 'A PUPPET'S FACADE'

lot of ideas. Gavin was the first truly charismatic person I'd met; he was very other, and fearless. I liked Gav a lot. He was . . . An Ideas Man.

We start practising most weekends. We get better, and better. I manage to write some songs and Jayne has bits of music that we learn to graft on to other bits that I've written, and Gav does his Pete Murphy/Guggi-out-of the-Prunes impression on top of it all, tosses his long black hair around and pouts, and does a pretty impressive version of a frontman.

None of us have ever really thought about the idea of frontmen. Who thinks about frontmen at sixteen? Luckily we have a guide: the early 1980s are all about the Doors. Danny Sugerman's fabulous teenage love letter to Big Jimbo Morrison, *No One Here Gets Out Alive*, has just been published.

In the decades to come, the Doors will become hopelessly unfashionable. Off-trend. Passé. Terminally uncool, even. Sure, they are loved by French people, Euro hippies, female students, and me. But in my future travels around the kingdom of rock 'n' roll I am always struck by the yawnsome loathing they draw from the serious rock fan (I have yet to meet a music journalist with a good word to say about Jimbo). Some would lay the blame at the feet of Oliver Stone's excellent 1991 biopic, taking particular aim at Val Kilmer, who played Jim as a monstrous, drunken scallywag confused visionary (a good thing). Others may say that Doors' teenage manager, original biographer and John the Baptist to Morrison's Jesus, Danny Sugerman, can take a portion of the blame, along with good old Ray 'Manzo' Manzarek, for separating Jim Morrison like split mayo, tossing the man aside and spending the best part of their lives reinforcing their very own myth of Morrison: Dionysian God of Rock (see also Sugerman's terrifying autobiography, *Wonderland Avenue*). For me, I think that Jim knew that he would fall foul of taste, when he sang the fateful Willie Dixon line, 'And the men don't know what the little girls understand,' back on the Doors' eponymous 1967 debut album.

What the twenty-first-century Doors fan needs is some kind of cut-out-and-keep riposte to the haters. I offer up eight reasons to love Big Jim:

1) 'The Lizard King'. Jim Morrison was not only a Freak King, he was a Lizard King. The Doors denier likes nothing more than to invoke the Lizard King clause. That is to say that because Jim Morrison thought that the spirit of Native American Indians had squatted in his body (or something), he was rubbish at pop music. This is a ludicrous argument, pop stars are meant to be 'taken over' by Native American Indians. It's what pop stars do – ask Adam Ant. Nul points for the Lizard King argument.

2) 'Leather Trousers'. For some reason Jim Morrison is held up as a nitwit by Doors deniers for wearing leather trousers. Very few people can wear leather trousers and get away with it. Bowie didn't wear 'em, Marc Bolan didn't wear 'em, and the Velvet Underground didn't wear 'em, because they knew

WE ARE 'A PUPPET'S FACADE'

they couldn't get away with it. Only four acts have got away with wearing leather keks: the Beatles (in Hamburg), Gene Vincent, Lulu and Jim. Morrison was the king of leather trousers.

3) 'Jim's Poetry'. Befuddlingly, your serious rock fan thinks that Jim couldn't write lyrics. The case for the defence presents Jim's 1970 state-of-the-nation address from 'Roadhouse Blues': 'Well I woke up this morning, I got myself a bee-er . . . the future's uncertain and the end is always near.' The case for the defence rests. If that doesn't work, I would (seriously) offer up Geezer Butler and Iggy Pop – as I often do – as favourite say-what-you-see-and-don't-edit visionary lyricists. If that doesn't work, well you just don't *know* rock 'n' roll, so you should definitely read on.

4) 'The Celebration of the Lizard'. The Doors' unfinished much-unloved folly; a kind of freeform tone poem experiment in rock theatre. The Doors denier will fall about laughing at the mere mention of this. All you need do is stare at them, straight-faced, and slowly repeat: 'It's a freeform tone poem experiment in rock theatre.' You then follow up by swigging from a bottle of 'hard liquor' and bellowing, 'Wooh, awlright, love my girl.' That's what Jim Morrison would have done.

5) 'Miami'. On 1 March 1969, Jim Morrison was arrested at a show in Bible-Belt Miami for drunkenly exposing himself. All evidence shows that Morrison was teasing the audience but didn't – shock and awe – actually expose himself and show them Little Jim. The

FREAKS OUT!

Miami incident and the unresolved threat of serious jail time hung over Jim until his death; it is a sign of how seriously 'Amerika' took the threat of the Doors upon the youth of the nation. The Doors didn't really do 'humour', another perceived slight against their detractors. The crux of this is that the Doors existed in the blessed pre-irony age of rock and, scoff all you like, but Morrison literally and metaphorically lived his life teetering over the edge.

6) 'Ray Manzarek's Continued Organ Bothering'. Much like Ray Manzarek's wearing of open-toed sandals, 'Ray Manzarek Keyboard Pest' is hard to defend. Best change the subject.

7) More importantly, the Doors had the tunes. If your average Doors denier (they are extremely average) can honestly deny that 'Light My Fire' ain't a Polaris rock missile then they can pull me up by my leather trews and give me a big Lizard King of a wedgie.

8) Finally, you'll never score with a honey by banging on about Little Feat or *Trout Mask Replica*, but take your woman back to your cabin in the Hollywood Hills and serenade her with 'The Crystal Ship' and you'll have the moonlight drive of your life. The men, you see, don't know what the little girls understand. God bless you, Big Jim.

'What college do you go to?' asks Gav. Strangely, we've never broached this. Jayne laughs.

'He's still at school,' she shoots, somewhat cruelly.

WE ARE 'A PUPPET'S FACADE'

'Huh?' queries Gavin, then he shrugs his shoulders, and gets on with his Pete Murphy act. I'm an outsider in my own band. I lag behind the other three by an all-important twelve months. They're all at college, I'm still a fucking school kid waiting to take my O-levels. A year is a lifetime when you are fifteen. This bugs me out. It doesn't seem to matter much to Gav though – he's an idea's man, remember?

Gavin brings his friend Craig along to rehearsals. Craig is nineteen. He's already a local legend. (Remember, this is Portsmouth in the early 1980s – it's a tough place to be anything, let alone a 'local legend'.) Craig Morrison is boisterous, loud, and arty.[2] He's dressed like Gavin Friday. Full make-up. Dreads. Leather trousers. He's already notorious at art college, a highly talented precocious visual artist and something of a prodigy. He has absolutely no musical ability. He was in a band with Gav's older brother, called rather excellently Bedlam 1573; they made one demo tape. Craig was naturally the frontman. Naturally he sings like Charlie Chuck. None of which stops Craig joining in with our rehearsal. Craig seems to be thinking of himself as a 'vibes' merchant. Our Guy Stevens perhaps. He has brought along his fucked-up Woolworths' electric guitar with only a couple of rusty strings left on it. He proceeds to plug it into a music centre and then goes entirely mental. This is a very impressive display. Craig

---

[2] Craig Morrison goes on to become a designer of much renown, with his latex bug bags. He also works on the visual side of electronic industrial duo Meat Beat Manifesto.

FREAKS OUT!

is throwing himself around the room for five full minutes of screaming and sweating.

'I can't actually play the guitar,' says Craig cheerfully, picking himself off the floor, as if we need help identifying this. 'I just knock out rhythms on the fucker.' Yep, you do. I'm learning a lot. Very quickly.

'What are you gonna call yourselves?' asks Craig, who now seems to spend a lot of time at our rehearsals. Craig has an instant entourage. Everyone wants to be around Craig Morrison. Especially Gav. Gav is a kind of apprentice Craig. I'm smart enough to notice how hierarchy can evolve, and I've somehow avoided being a component in the hierarchy. It turns out that I'm the best of all of us at writing songs (I can make something sound like it's a 'song' even if it isn't). Sure, the bar isn't that high, but I'm at least the one setting it. So I don't have use within the hierarchy (which, as most hierarchies do, operates a random generator deciding who will be the next figure of fun). I have a use as the provider of 'songs'.

'A Puppet's Facade,' says Gav, in answer to Craig's question of what name we should choose. Rob and I make faces of the 'a fucking puppet's fucking what?' type at each other. Craig, being another Virgin Prunes,[3] Dead or Alive, Bauhaus fanatic, thinks that A Puppet's Facade is a great

---

[3] It can't be overstated how important the Virgin Prunes were at this time. The last time I saw Gavin was at a Sleaford Mods show at Camden's Electric Ballroom. 'This better be good,' he said. 'The last time I was here was for the Virgin Prunes and that was the greatest show of my life.'

name. Craig and Gav are very wrong about this. Tragically so. Some sort of vote is taken and it's three against two. Jayne, Gav and Craig. Against Rob and Me. We are A Puppet's Facade. This is not good. Another lesson learned: democracy doesn't work in pop groups.

We have already played at a few parties. People think we're pretty good. 'You sound a bit like Magazine!' says a hip partygoer (it's 1982). We don't, we sound like . . . A Puppet's Facade. Good grief.

We have a 'proper' gig on the horizon. We are going to be playing at the local sixth-form college Battle of the Bands. 'Is this good?' I ask Gav. He doesn't seem to know. He has to think about how long he will crimp his hair for. Apart from the name (which I will try to only repeat when necessary as of now), I like all this. I'm embracing my own weirdness, my inner Freak has long been inside me and now it's starting to come out. Rob has noticed my newfound confidence. You see, I'm the de-facto band leader, I'm the fucker who writes the songs. We start getting better. And college kids talk about us like we're cool. And we are. Okay, it's not difficult to be the coolest people in Portsmouth in 1982/83. That we know we are the coolest people in Portsmouth obviously means we're not the coolest people, of course. People think we're getting a bit aloof. Which we are. That's the point, right? We win the Battle of the Bands competition – four hours' free time in the local recording studio. Well, of course.

There are dark rumblings. Has 'success' gone to our teenage heads? Yes, of course it fucking has. Everybody

FREAKS OUT!

seems to want to get rid of Jayne. Apparently she wanted to 'dress as a cat' for our next show.

'She wants to dress as a fucking cat!' says Gav. Craig thinks this is a wild transgression too far. Gav and Craig seem to make lots of executive decisions. Craig isn't even in the band, he is sort of leader of some kind of nebulous fan club. The thing is, Jayne hasn't yet even 'dressed up as a fucking cat', she has only so far expressed a desire to 'dress up as a fucking cat' (I was not witness to this heinous crime). Wanting to 'dress up as a fucking cat' is a sackable offence in the new Gav/Craig Puppet's Facade politburo hard line. I like Jayne. She's loads more talented than Gav and Craig, and it all seems a bit awful. But I do get a frisson of teenage power. Ugly and mean. They, Gav and Craig, have made the decision, I get railroaded, and they make out that, as the songwriter, I need to 'sign off' on it. Like a mad teenage Roman Emperor, I give Jayne the thumbs-down and she is puppet toast. 'Well,' I reason to myself, 'it's all part of being in a band – getting sacked.' I'll think this more than once over the coming decades.

We record our demo, with our new bass player, Saul, and our new keyboard player, Mark – Mark looks exactly like a 1967 Micky Dolenz, so he is immediately in – we are now a gang of boys. Walking it and talking it. We are the New York Dolls of the suburbs of 1983 Portsmouth. You may know us by our name – we are . . . A Puppet's Facade. Except we're not. We are now called – marginally better, marginally worse – Imperial! Once Jayne got sacked, Gav

WE ARE 'A PUPPET'S FACADE'

and Craig conveniently forgot that A Puppet's Facade was their name and blame it on the blameless Jayne.

Everyone who hears our recordings really likes them. The problem is that we don't really have anywhere to play. Everyone is really young. Craig is nineteen, Gav seventeen and I'm still only sixteen. We don't know how to get gigs, outside of sixth-form colleges, and besides, there are very few places to play in Portsmouth at this time. Unless you want to battle it out with a bunch of off-duty sailors. This happens a few times and we crumble. We are not exactly the Cockney Rejects. We are too much of a bunch of softies for the School of Hard Knocks.

There is only one thing to do. Record another demo. This will be the thing to launch us into the stratosphere of pop. So into the same studio we trot again, with borrowed money and time. We are a hardcore gang of dude rockers now. No girls wanting to dress up as fucking cats can stymy our shimmy. Four hours later we're done. Six brand new songs. Ready to change the world.

The new demo is not as good as the first one.[4] It sounds muddy and sludgy. Jayne is missed. And something else is missed; it all feels a bit stale. We have effectively fucked up our second album. It's 1984, I'll be going to art college in September, the same art college that Craig is about to leave for: London Central Saint Martins. The summer is a

---

[4] One of the songs from this second demo tape gets re-tooled with entirely new lyrics ten years later and becomes 'Bailed Out' on the Auteurs first album, *New Wave*.

bit of a moper. We don't do band things any more, it's all got slow. I want to do something different. I reckon I could be a better singer than Gav. We decide to do one more gig. A farewell gig, upstairs in a Portsmouth pub. Astonishingly, we sell tickets to this preposterous farewell gig. Even more astonishingly, we actually sell quite a few. Gavin seems quite sad about the whole thing. Me too, really. We have effectively done it all in just over a year. The whole band cycle: formation, hierarchy, early success, sacking, hit first album (well, demo), disillusionment, botched second album (demo), farewell gig, mild acrimony. If we could have grown beards we surely would have done so.

Everything that happened over the preceding paragraphs and pages will inform everything else that happens in the subsequent pages. It is the framework for everything. The axiom of the accepted rock 'n' roll arc. Every record mentioned (with a few noted exceptions). It's all there within the latticework and in the angles of that very framework that we will disassemble, looking for the Freaks.

They are everywhere.

CHAPTER 2

'Limp, you bugger, limp'

Walton-on-Thames in the 1960s.
Gene Vincent in the '60s in Walton-on-Thames.
From Portsmouth, Virginia, to the Isle of White for Gene.
From Walton-on-Thames to Portsmouth, Hampshire, for me.

I was born in a two-up two-down rented house in Walton-on-Thames, in God's own county of Surrey on 7 October 1967. My mum worked at the American Embassy as a secretary in London and my dad tried to get jobs in a graphic design studio. Then I was born, and my mother became a housewife for a while and my dad worked for the Navy, doing the graphic work on the design of Polaris submarines.

Walton-on-Thames is not what you think it is. You think it is full of stockbrokers, long driveways, hedges, the Rotary Club infiltrated by Freemasons, the Round Table, executive four-wheel drives, lynchings at the golf club. It isn't really any of those things. It is a town in Surrey, 18½ miles from the centre of London. It could be any other town centre in the UK, but for a small theatre: the Walton Playhouse.

In 1967 – the year I landed – the Walton Playhouse became known as the Walton Hop. The Hop had a pop lure for the Surrey Kids; two of the Beatles lived nearby as well as a whole load of other pop stars. All pooled up and living it up in the surrounding stockbroker belt. Maybe one night the Fabs would turn up at the Hop. Maybe not.

In the mid-1970s you would have found a teenage Jimmy Pursey there, miming to Bay City Rollers records.

'Hold up, who's that driving up in the Rolls-Royce? Is it John and Yoko?' No, I'm afraid not. I'm afraid it's novelty hit maker Jonathan King. The Walton Hop was where you'd find Jonathan King, preying upon underage boys. In 2006 I wrote a song about King and the Hop:

> *All kids want to go backstage at the Walton Hop*
> *Have a whiskey and Coke no need to prove your age at the Walton Hop.*
> *I was craning my neck to see who got out of the Roller*
> *One of the Beatles or a local DJ*
> *Jumping the queue to get a specially signed photo*
> *One for me, one for you – luv Johnny Reggae*

Walton-on-Thames is an outer perimeter type of town. The cool but trash 1973 Hammer Horror picture *Psychomania* was filmed there, starring Nicky Henson, Beryl Reid and George Sanders in a terrifically un-frightening Hells Angels-in-a-pact-with-Satan flick, deliberately maxing out

'LIMP, YOU BUGGER, LIMP'

on their machines, man, to achieve eternal life. Walton-on-Thames is not referenced in the film. *Psychomania* was the last film George Sanders appeared in before he took his own life.[1]

The Nashville Teens also hailed from Walton-on-Thames. The Teens were fantastic. They had a massive hit with 'Tobacco Road' in 1964. Just prior to that the Nashvilles (as no one has ever called them) acted as Jerry Lee Lewis's backing band at the Star Club in Hamburg. Their performance was captured masterfully on tape one night and released as *Jerry Lee Lewis Live at the Star-Club*. It is unarguably the greatest live album ever recorded. To say that Jerry Lee and the Teens are smokin' hot is a disservice to fire. That Walton-on-Thames does not seem to merit a mention on *Live at the Star-Club* is a disservice to nothing much at all. Walton-on-Thames is just a kind of nearby town.

Jimmy Pursey, when he had stopped miming to Bay City Rollers songs at the Walton Hop, formed the excellent and wildly misunderstood Sham 69. Sham's masterpiece 1978 concept album, *That's Life* – essentially the day in the life of a Herbert – was written while staying at the Walton Boathouse hotel. Once again, there is no mention of Walton-on-Thames.

---

[1] George Sanders. Actor, singer, 1906–72. On 23 April 1972, Sanders took his own life by gulping down five bottles of Nembutal. He left two suicide notes. The most famous of the two read: 'Dear World, I am leaving because I am bored. I feel I have lived long enough. I am leaving you with your worries in this sweet cesspool. Good luck.'

FREAKS OUT!

Nick Lowe was born in Walton-on-Thames. To my knowledge, he has barely acknowledged Walton-on-Thames, let alone written a song about the place.

The Unlimited Dream Company, 1979, is one of J. G. Ballard's strangest novels. It is a fever vision of a crashed air pilot who becomes a nightmare Pied Piper, seducing town folks and turning them into feathered flying bird people. The book is set in the Surrey village of Shepperton, Ballard's home for much of his life. Walton Bridge does get a mention. It's nearby, you see.

Oh, and Gene Vincent was holed up in Walton-on-Thames for a few weeks or so in late 1969. Nearby to me.

Walton-on-Thames is the perpetual nearby kind of town. I guess I'm a nearby kind of motherfucker as well. I don't mind that. You can see much more by standing nearby than being at the centre of the storm. If you are born somewhere as non-plussed by itself as Walton-on-Thames, you have to make the most of what you have. You don't get the rock 'n' roll leg up that you get if you are from Manchester, Sheffield, Leeds, Glasgow or Liverpool.

As no one had written anything much – in a rock 'n' roll sense – about Walton-on-Thames, I thought I should make amends. So in 2013 I wrote a psychedelic children's album called *Rock and Roll Animals*, featuring Nick Lowe as a badger, Jimmy Pursey as a fox, and Gene Vincent as a cat. All living in the 'magic town' of Walton-on-Thames and fighting off their nemesis, the Angel of the North: Antony Gormley's appalling public art-statue-come-to-life and the embodiment of all that is unrighteous.

'LIMP, YOU BUGGER, LIMP'

So what was Gene Vincent (the real one, not the cat) doing in Walton-on-Thames in the winter of 1969?

Rock 'n' roll, pop music and, let's face it, all modern culture got its first big break in the summer of 1955 when twenty-year-old sailor Vincent Eugene Craddock decided to take his $900 bonus and buy himself a fuck-off Triumph motorbike. Craddock got drunk and on returning to Norfolk (Norfolk, Virginia) naval base crashed his bike into a barrier, crushing his left leg horribly in the process. A lucky break for world culture, not so much for Eugene Craddock. The prognosis was amputation. Like all the greats (Charles Hawtrey, Zsa Zsa Gabor), Eugene refused the offer of being legless – although later being legless was very much his modus non operandi – and spent a prolonged sojourn in Norfolk military hospital with his leg in a brace for a year. The leg never healed, and Eugene Craddock developed brittle bones and constant weeping sores. And for ever pain.

It's okay, we can stop referring to Eugene Craddock as Eugene Craddock soon, as Eugene Craddock is just about to see Elvis perform on a live radio show (bottom of the bill beneath the Louvin Brothers and Hank Snow). All historians of rock will tell you in great detail about Elvis's considerable achievements between 1954 and 1955. As this is not a history book, we'll just take it as a given that every single time that Elvis gets out of bed from 1954 until March 1958, when he joins the Army, it will be the catalyst for some major spinning of the world's changing axis – and that is exactly what happens. As soon as Eugene Craddock claps

FREAKS OUT!

eyes on the future King of Rock 'n' Roll he knows what he has to do: he has to become Gene Vincent.

Eugene reaches out to the show's producer – the manfully named Sheriff Tex Davis – and plays him some of the songs that he has been strumming on his guitar during his convalescence, including one called 'Be-Bop-A-Lula':[2] The Sheriff likes what he hears and gets Eugene a gig supporting rockabilly 'Blue Suede Shoes' main man, Carl Perkins. Big Carl likes what he hears as well, and by 1956 Eugene Craddock has signed to Capital Records. In a moment where all the cosmologies align, Craddock self-actualises by switching his names around, losing the 'Eu' and becoming Gene Vincent. Holy fucking shit.

Chaos magick takes over; Gene puts together a backing band – the Blue Caps – a potent brew of the amateur and the genius. The Genius being 28-year-old Cliff Gallup,

---

[2] Just like the grail, the cup used to catch Christ's blood on the Cross, there are many stories regarding the provenance of 'Be-Bop-A-Lula'. According to Blue Caps drummer Dickie Harrell, Gene and Sheriff Tex bought the song off a guy called Donald Graves for $25. The more accepted version is that Graves and Gene were both in the Portsmouth naval hospital in Virginia, Gene recuperating from his motorcycle accident. Graves apparently used the phrase 'Be-Bop-A-Lula' and Vincent wrote the song around it. Sheriff Tex Davis certainly received a cut of the royalties. Davis also claimed that he wrote the song with Vincent after listening to the 1925 Dixieland jazz number 'Don't Bring Lulu'. 'Be-Bop-A-Lula' also bears similarity to 'Be-Baba-Leba', a big hit on the R&B chart for Helen Humes in 1945. Gene would certainly have heard this record. The provenance of the Holy Grail is foremost in importance. The provenance of 'Be-Bop-A-Lula', unarguably the real grail, is of interest, but does nothing to diminish the song's split-atom godhead power.

the hands-down greatest guitar player of the rock 'n' roll era. The amateur element being fifteen-year-old drummer Dickie Harrell. Keep your eyes on Dickie.

'Be-Bop-A-Lula' is, shockingly, only the B-side of the Blue Caps' first single. The A-side is given to the non-Gene penned 'Woman Love'. When radio DJs realise they can't play the A-side due to Gene blurring the word 'hugging' so that it sounds like 'fucking', they flip the single and play the B-side instead: 'Be-Bop-A-Lula'. Gene Vincent was never one to not press the self-destruct button at every corner. However, this wanton act of self-vandalism paid off and the monster lurking on the B-side is unchained.

And so 'Be-Bop-A-Lula' enters world pop culture. Sure, 'Heartbreak Hotel' exists already, but the devil was in the detail and the devil was in all the grooves of 'Be-Bop-A-Lula'. Depending on how you see life, 'Heartbreak Hotel' was either an existential cry of pain or a self-pitying mope.[3] 'Be-Bop-A-Lula' was neither; a full-on wolverine prowl through the darkest recesses of mindlessness that the Stooges, Suicide and the Troggs, despite their finest efforts, never quite bettered. But it wasn't even Gene Vincent who invented modern rock 'n' roll as we now know it. It was drummer Dickie Harrell – all of fifteen years old – who at the end of verse two lets out a feral scream. Apparently so his mother would know it was him on the record. The studio engineer wanted the Blue Caps to cut another take of

---

[3] It took John Cale's 1974 re-imagining of 'Heartbreak Hotel' to wring out the full self-pity quota and alchemise it into psychosis.

'Be-Bop-A-Lula', sans the primal scream, but Gene liked it and insisted that the take with the scream was the one. And that is the moment the world was reborn.

Eugene Craddock had hitched a ride to Fuck-Up City long before he was Gene Vincent, but by the end of 1956 Gene was riding the rocket through the fuck-up cosmos on a one-way ticket. He'd pissed everyone off with bad song choices, heavy debts, got unhappy, threw down booze and pills to nullify the pain of his career and the pain of his leg. Then he started pulling loaded guns and knives on people. You see there was no big follow-up hit to The Massive Hit. Sure, incredibly, Gene was seen as a one-hit wonder.

Despite the dwindling chart action, the Blue Caps live act was all killer. Gene had expanded the sound, with piano and Jordanaires style do-wop harmonies from the fabulously named 'clapper boys', these motherfuckers were hipper than Elvis's Jordanaires. They had the moves and would crouch at Gene's feet clapping away as he stared upwards, looking for God while swinging his crushed leg over the mic stand. But then Gene went and got jealous of one of the clapper boys – the excellently named Tommy 'Bubba' Facenda. Bubba was better-looking than Gene and the girls dug him. And then there was the Cliff Gallup problem: The greatest guitar player of the age – get the Ouija board out and just ask Jeff Beck – had called time after the first album, *Bluejean Bop!*, feeling that he was too old for rock 'n' roll. Cliff left the Blue Caps, got a job as a janitor and never signed a single autograph. When he died, his wife did her best to make sure that there was as little mention as possible of his musical career in any obituaries. That's a fuck-off with style. There were many cool Blue Caps guitar hot shots: Johnny Meeks, Paul Peek, but no one could compete with Cliff Gallup.

By 1959, Gene Vincent was looking finished in the United States. Enter Jack Good. Good spent his latter years before his death in 2017 as a nomadic lay-Catholic seer, wearing robes and painting icons in New Mexico. A life in showbiz will do this for you. But hold on, Daddio, let's jump back to the 'before times'. The time before Good went mystical.

Jack Good was a British television music pioneer. A super-early adopter. Good saved Gene Vincent (for a while at least) and made him an enduring icon in the UK, when the US had dropped him like a cold, sad-sack of shit. Good had a vision, not of Catholic martyrs but of rock 'n' roll martyrs. When Gene and the Blue Caps first performed on US television, and crucially in *The Girl Can't Help It*,[4] they looked like skinny hillbilly farm-punks. Jack realised that Vincent wasn't capitalising on his latent feral menace and dressed him from head to toe in bad-boy black leather, including black leather gloves to go with his iron calliper that he wore on his fucked leg. 'Limp, you bugger, limp,' goaded Good from the sidelines. Amazingly, Gene didn't shoot him.

---

[4] *The Girl Can't Help It* is a 1956 Jayne Mansfield vehicle, with a teenage rock 'n' roll subplot. This is where John Lennon first clapped eyes on his idol, Gene Vincent.

FREAKS OUT!

Gene spent the hitless 1960s touring Europe and the UK. He's fucked his fucked leg in that fatal car crash with Eddie. He's hung out with the star-struck Beatles in Hamburg until he scared them with his gun play, and he even fired off a few gun shots at the hapless pre-Gary Glitter Paul Gadd, having decided, quite reasonably, that Gadd/Glitter was a person he didn't like.

And did those feet in ancient times, walk upon England's green and pleasant land? In this version of Blake's poem, Gene Vincent comes to England to create Heaven in Walton-on-Thames, in God's own county of Surrey. Vincent is Jesus and England makes him into a beautiful Freak.

It is now November 1969. I am two years old, Gene Vincent is staying in Dukes guest house, a few roads down from our house in Walton-on-Thames.

In 1969, thirty-four is not a great age to be a hitless rock legend. It's even debatable whether there are any rock 'legends' yet. It's just too early for such hindsight. In the half-light of the know-it-all twenty-first century, thirty-four is no age at all. But in 1969 this is uncharted waters, and the captain's leg is agony. Rock 'n' roll and thirty-four don't go. Rock 'n' roll and thirty-four, with Benzedrine, Dexedrine, heavy painkillers, more booze and more pills do go very well. Gene Vincent is on the oldies circuit, and in the UK for a short tour and a few TV appearances. On this tour every concrete hangover day is going to be caught on grainy celluloid for the Thames Television documentary, *The Rock and Roll Singer*.

'LIMP, YOU BUGGER, LIMP'

The Rock and Roll Singer begins as perhaps all rock docs should: with the Teddy Boys at the airport. English Teds. These would be the thugs who'd stab up young punks on the King's Road in a few years' time. They have come for Gene.

'If he don't play the old songs, he's a wanker...'

'He's trying to appeal to the skinheads now, he should wear 'is leathers.'

Don't worry, lads, Gene will be wearing 'is leathers. But right now, bloated Gene is signing autographs for the Teds at the airport. He almost feels like a star again. A few scenes later, we see him get out of a taxi and pull up to Dukes guest house. Gene does a radio interview with Radio Caroline DJ, Emperor Rosko. Gene is sitting on the bed of his sparse guest house room, and in that sad Virginia whisper he tells Rosko that he misses his wife and his dog. Gene smiles, a gentle sad smile.

In a Croydon basement, rehearsals with south London's finest, the Wild Angels, are taking place. The rock and roll singer sits beneath WEM speakers. The rock and roll singer always sits, he can no longer stand up very well. The Angels kick out a motherfuckin' dynamite version of 'Baby Blue' and Gene's weary eyes light up. The Teds are gonna dig this shit. Then a country song, 'I heard that Lonesome Whistle', dedicated to John Peel, who will put out Gene's country rock album, *I'm Back and I'm Proud*. The Teds won't be digging this. Neither will Peel. Rehearsals break and the Wild Angels ask Gene how he will be spending the evening. 'I'm going to the pub, to get drunk,' he announces. 'Mind

FREAKS OUT!

if we tag along?' asks a plucky Wild Angel. Gene looks crestfallen. There's no greater disappointment than when company seeks to ruin an evening of solitary drinking.

At the TV studio the nice middle-aged make-up lady is washing Gene Vincent's hair. That is the hair of Gene Vincent. The nice lady wants to put a hair net over that quiff. That is the quiff of Gene Vincent. You don't do that to Gene Vincent. He took pot shots at Gary Glitter for less. The TV presenter announces a few prices for shoppers at the weekend. 'Two shillings for beef brisket. Fish, three shillings, and sprouts, tuppence ha'penny. And now someone that you will recognise: Gene Vincent and the Wild Angels with "Be-Bop-A-Lula".' Utter transformative chimera. Black leather and chains. John Lydon fronting the Troggs. 'Limp, you bugger, limp.'

It becomes apparent in *The Rock and Roll Singer* that Gene Vincent is not going to get paid for this TV appearance and for the gigs. 'You see, the money is always locked in a room upstairs and it is the weekend now, so the room upstairs won't be unlocked until Monday,' announces a lickspittle lackey. Ah, the story about the room upstairs being locked until Monday. A story familiar to most musicians. I know this story as well. It's a story that is older than time. A story that is older and stupider than Gene Vincent feels right now. Gene announces that he's going to get drunk. Again. This time it will be alone on his terms.

An ominous caption flickers up on the film:

'Gene Vincent leaves Walton-on-Thames to play an overnight show on the Isle of Wight.'

'LIMP, YOU BUGGER, LIMP'

We catch one more glimpse of bloated Gene. He's in a Triumph Dolomite drinking from a Britvic orange bottle, with one hand clasping his rictus leg. He's babbling to the driver about the CIA being the Secret Police. 'Who runs the CIA? Nobody knows, it's a secret, that's why they are the Secret Police.' People tend to get conspiratorial when they lose their minds. The band and Gene Vincent trundle up the Portsmouth (Hampshire) ferry terminal bound for an overnighter on the Isle of Wight – where people go to live with the undead before they die.

Gene Vincent left Walton-on-Thames for Portsmouth, Virginia.

I left Walton-on-Thames for Portsmouth, Hampshire.

Gene Vincent died of a perforated ulcer outside his parents' mobile home in Saugus, California, in 1971. His last words were, 'Momma, you can call the ambulance now.' He was thirty-six years old.

CHAPTER 3

Crowded trousers

From Portsmouth in the '80s to New York in the '70s.

You grew up in a shithole in the UK. Am I right? All of my generation think they have land rights to growing up in the worst cess-dump in Britain. It's our prerogative to regard the vegetable patch where we sprouted our first shoots as a 1970s equivalent to Helmand Province. Truth and nuance are our own petit bourgeois inconveniences to ignore. I grew up mainly in Portsmouth, Hampshire. The wrong Portsmouth. Not Portsmouth, Virginia, the right Portsmouth. Portsmouth in the 1980s was big on truth. The truth meted out by a docker's fist usually. Nuance, on the other hand – or other fist – didn't come into it. Portsmouth, you will crop up again. Portsmouth – an island inhabited entirely by arseholes and surrounded by some sort of terrible stretch of water that they call the

FREAKS OUT!

Solent, you will never be righteous. I hate you as much as Hitler hated Vienna.

My mum and dad moved from Walton-on-Thames early doors. They then drove their wagon – or more accurately, a Humber Sceptre – around various sites in the south and south-east until my dad landed a good job in the civil service, working for the Ministry of Defence. It made sense – a sense that I could overrule at the drop of a bollock – for them to settle in Portsmouth; a polyp growing on a polyp within the colon of the south: Portsmouth.

How deadening a place was Portsmouth to grow up in? As stifling as Gene Vincent's leg iron, as soporific as the tube from the exhaust pipe in a locked-up garage, as deadening as Eamonn Holmes' Wikipedia entry. If there was ever anything to do in Portsmouth you would have needed John Dee's obsidian mirror to find it, unless of course you enjoyed Napoleonic Wars ephemera.

Just in case anyone ever got ahead of themselves in Portsmouth and tried to do something, anything really, they would instantly be reminded of the city's 'rich' naval heritage that sits there, unavoidable, immoveable, big, bold and ugly to behold as soon as one sets foot outside the front door: monstrous concrete monoliths dedicated to heroic or tragic maritime endeavours, massive concrete bollards along the seafront, ruined castles, horrific static fortresses in the sea that look like giant sea slugs about to engulf the city with a trail of sheer boredom and slug shit. A bombed cathedral and a ghastly model village. As a man in his fifties, I of course spend far too much time thinking about war and history, but as a teen, I really couldn't have given less of a shit.

Debbie's waiting tables in the backroom
Eric's pulling faces on his trip
Dee Dee's turning tricks
Johnny's looking for a kiss
Richard's in Beth Israel . . . smoking on a drip
New York Stars . . .

The above words are from a concept album I made about early-1980s Portsmouth from 2014. It was the third album in a row of concept albums. This one was ostensibly about one thing – a concept – but it had a whole under-story.[1]

The opposite of 'meta' is 'infra', and so *New York in the '70s* – the album in question – was an infra concept album. The uber concept being: Righteous New York rock 'n' roll from the mid- to late '70s. This was all straightforward enough: tribute songs to the New York Dolls, Alan Vega, Eric Emerson, Joey Ramone, Jim Carroll and Richard Lloyd.[2] All delivered as a kind of cartoon fantasy. The real album was not so much about 'New York in the '70s' but more about 'Portsmouth in the early '80s'.

---

[1] The three concept albums are *Nine and a Half Psychedelic Mediations on British Wrestling of the 1970s and Early '80s* (discussed in later chapters), *Rock and Roll Animals* (previous chapter) and *New York in the '70s*.

[2] The original front cover of *New York in the '70s* was to be the famous photograph of Television's Richard Lloyd smoking on a cigarette while recovering from hepatitis in Beth Israel hospital hooked up to a drip in front of a 'no smoking' sign.

FREAKS OUT!

Portsmouth in the '80s doesn't really work as an album title, so the real album, *New York in the '70s*, was not so much about Dee Dee and Johnny et al., but about fourteen-year-old me wandering around Portsmouth on my own, like a lonely southern England adolescent Jonathan Richman, looking for something or anything but finding nothing apart from the dreams in my head; dreams of Andy Warhol and the Factory, Lou, Nico, drugs, William S. Burroughs. For drugs I found my first packet of Rothmans, and as for the rest, I just found the monstrous sea defences.

To look back at the 'music scene' of the early '80s on the south coast is akin to looking at old photos of now-defunct budget supermarkets (Bejam for the south, fill in your own favourite retro emporium of frozen food) and trying to find the joy. There is none. The northern and Scottish outposts of outlier rock 'n' roll activity could lay claim to such all-time greats as Gang of Four, the Human League, Josef K, Orange Juice, Fire Engines, Cabaret Voltaire, Clock DVA. Manchester and Liverpool had all the known suspects (this is not *Mojo*, I don't have to name them).

Now take a look at any website dedicated to 'Portsmouth music in the '70s and '80s' – and there are a few – and you will find the likes of: 'Arms & Legs' (five very-pleased-with-themselves balding pub rock dudes);

'Backline' (white suits and bow ties and moustaches);

'The Chosen' (photographed performing on the roof of vile department store Alders in the city centre's imaginatively named Commercial Road in 1980); and 'Cruiser' (three bald guys in white vests looking very pleased with themselves). Portsmouth in the early '80s had been drinking some very strange Kool-Aid. As I wandered around the city in 1982, on my teenage 'derives', a year before getting in my first band, I would occasionally stop outside a pub and strain to hear the live band playing. It was always horrible. Behold this legend from a real gig poster:

Friday April 12th 1982 – Live Band:
75p Entry
Crowded Trousers

Crowded Trousers certainly weren't the Velvet Underground. It was almost as if some demented city councillor had passed a bylaw that all Portsmouth groups for at least two generations must sound like Sad Café. Or Smokie.

My dad, in his late forties in 1980, worked in an office with younger people. His twenty-something work colleagues all seemed to like him. Often they'd play in local bands. The bands all sounded like, you guessed it, Sad Café. Or Smokie. These dudes all wore flares and had moustaches, probably trying to look like Gerry Rafferty (or maybe even Cruiser). My dad would sometimes take me to watch them play in local pubs. It was a very Crowded Trousers kinda scene. One day my dad had a new young dude working with him: Chris. Chris, my dad informed me, simultaneously solemn and with a glint in his eye, was the drummer in a 'punk' band. The punk band were called 'Look Back in Anger'.

The punk band put me on the guest list. It was probably the first guest list I'd been on. They were kind people. Maybe they wanted to show me that the entire world hadn't been taken over by Sad Café (or Smokie). Sure, they weren't the Velvet Underground. They weren't even the Lurkers or 999, but most importantly, they weren't Sad Café. Or Smokie. There was a life beyond Crowded Trousers.

Within a year, I was in a band with a horrible name (see Chapter 1). Playing in Portsmouth was hardly in our remit, we saw Portsmouth as something to hide from, with its old ways and neanderthal townsfolk. We wanted to do our own thing away from the troglodytes. By now the curse of Sad Café had begun to lift and was being replaced by a new brand of retro horror . . .

The psychobilly sickness would soon be carried across the sick winds of the Solent. Portsmouth, as you may have gleaned, was not a forward-thinking settlement and had grasped the wrong end of the shitty stick tightly with both hands. Portsmouth had embraced the Quiff. Three decades too late.

The 'quiff', laddies, the quiff. The jet-black peacock astride the bonce of our great beloved free thinkers and violent intellectuals of the 1950s. Now in Margaret Thatcher's early '80s, and in the hands of the dull mass of psychobilly-bully 'straights' and Conservatives, the onetime badge of freakdom had now become the ultimate binding chain of stupidity. We need to go back. Back to the time of the quiff. The most righteous quiff. Here's . . . Johnnie!

CHAPTER 4

How Elvis's quiff knocked out Johnnie Ray

*Opera Bouffant, Bruce McLean and the Pose Group,
and the sad story of pop music's first real Freak.*

It is 2011. I am writing an 'Opera Bouffant' with the Scottish sculptor and performance artist, Bruce McLean, and with my friend, the film and documentary director Paul Tickell.[1] You've never heard of 'Opera Bouffant' before, have you? It is a form of opera concerned with hair. Specifically: the quiff. The quiff is the signifier of trouble. A man, or a woman, with a quiff is the type that will not have enough money to pay for their digs and may have to tap you up for a few sovs until payday. A man (or woman, or a dog or a cat) with a quiff will smoke 555 cigarettes, and carry a razor blade to slash up the seats in the Gaumont cinema in Southend, or carve you

---

[1] Director of the film adaptation of the B. S. Johnson novel, *Chrisie Malry's Own Double-Entry*, *Crush Proof* and the definitive BBC Arena documentary, *Punk and the Pistols*.

FREAKS OUT!

a wider smile. The quiff is the signifier in The Great Cosmological working of Rock. And. Roll. The quiff *is* Rock. And. Roll. Elvis had a quiff. So did Gene Vincent, Eddie Cochran, Francis Bacon, Stuart Sutcliffe,[2] James Dean and Vince Taylor. The quiff is both erect and droopy. Tumescent and post-orgasm flaccid. Johnnie Ray was antediluvian adept. His hair, as early as the '40s: quiffed up. His mind: fucked up. Johnnie was a Freak. Our first rock 'n' roll Freak.

Bruce McLean is one of the UK's greatest living artists. A man who lives and breathes 'Art'. Bona fide Art. The real signed-in-blood deal. Bruce's first job was as a roadie on a few gigs for Gene Vincent and Eddie Cochran, on the 1960 tour that ended with Eddie dead in a Ford Consul. *That* tour. The other passengers, Sharon Sheeley, Eddie's co-songwriter and girlfriend, and Gene Vincent, both survived. Although in Gene's case, post-accident he was pretty much a dead man walking (as reported in the last chapter).[3]

---

[2] Stu Sutcliffe was such an envelope pusher that he may as well have worked for the GPO. His super-early quiff adoption as early as 1960 turned into an over-the-right-eye fringe, making him look like a member of Suede *c.*1992.

[3] Eddie Cochran died in a cab en route to London on 17 April 1960. Travelling with Eddie were Gene Vincent and Eddie's fiancé and co-songwriter, Sharon Sheeley. The driver of the car lost control and crashed into a lamp-post on Rowdon Hill, Chipping Norbury. Sharon and Gene both survived the crash, though Gene suffered even more trauma to his already fucked leg. The driver of the cab was called George Martin. (Not that one.) Dave Dee, later of Dave Dee, Dozy, Beaky, Mick & Titch fame, was the police officer at the scene of the accident. The police officer (Dee) was later played by Sting in a re-enactment of the fatal crash in Chris Petit's 1979 movie, *Radio On*. Sting's character is called Just Like Eddie.

HOW ELVIS'S QUIFF KNOCKED OUT JOHNNIE RAY

Bruce, sixteen years old at the time, recalls being asked by Cochran if he could 'get him any whores'. Bruce, naively questioning the request, realised that he wasn't being asked to find a woman. He was being asked to score some 'horse'.

'Get me some heroin, boy,' roared Eddie Cochran.

If you are wondering what kind of performance artist and sculptor Bruce McLean is then we have to take a short detour into the roots of non-existent music. The heart of nothingness, if you like. The roots of non-existent music lie in John Cage's 1952 masterpiece of silence, *4' 33"*. However, I am discounting it as, a) it is written down as a score, and b) it is regularly performed in front of an audience. It therefore exists. The post-war *Goon Show* may be the direct precursor to avant-nothingness as the Goons were to all intents and purpose the pre-fab Fab Four. Without pop music. That is until they queered their pitch with the horrific 'Ying Tong Song' and Prince/King Charles patronage. So no Goons. Closer still would be the Alberts: the Alberts were the brainchild of another performance artist and inventor, Bruce Lacey.[4] The Alberts were funnier than the Goons and 'more' avant. They did, however,

---

[4] Bruce Lacey (1927–2016). Performance artist, comedian, painter, sculptor and robot inventor. Fairport Convention wrote the song 'Mr Lacey' in tribute to the great man. Bruce's homemade robots can be heard mechanically clunking around on the track. Mr Lacey appears in several Swinging Sixties' films: *The Knack ... and How To Get It* (1965) and *Smashing Time* (1967.) His most famous role was as George Harrison's flute-playing gardener in *Help!*. In later life Bruce became a New Age post-hippie shaman, bothering middle-class festival-goers by performing naked ritual magick rites in front of their family tents.

make a few records, often utilising mass coughing and spluttering (if you are a fan of coughing and spluttering, which I am, you should head towards the compilation *By Jingo It's . . . British Rubbish*). Regretfully, we must give the Alberts the sling test as well.

The heart of nothingness didn't really arrive until 1970 with the other performance art Bruce: Bruce McLean. In 1970 McLean put together the proto-irony pre-Roxy Music band: the Pose Band, originally called Nice Style #1. By 1971, Nice Style #1 had become the Pose Band and settled upon their classic line-up of Ron Carr (poses), Gary Chitty (poses), Robin Fletcher (poses), Paul Richards (poses) and Bruce (poses and plinth work). The genius of the Pose Band was that they played no music. Bruce McLean having maybe exhausted the possibilities of rock 'n' roll when he was 'tour managing' Eddie C., decided to concentrate on angles. The angles of the chin, the acute angles of the limbs, and of course the angle of the quiff, were far more important than songs to the Pose Band.

In 1971, Bruce McLean and the Pose Band 'played' their first gig supporting the Kinks at Maidstone College of Art: no soundcheck, a pose check instead, then a performance that consisted of standing on plinths, wearing sharp suits and assuming classic rock 'n' roll and movie poses. It is not known what Ray Davies thought of his silent but animated support act, but Bryan Ferry by his own admission was paying attention to the Iconic Ted/Glam stylings of Bruce McLean.

This is where 1970s art rock began: Bowie, Ferry, Big Brian Eno, Malcolm and Viv. They all had one eye on

HOW ELVIS'S QUIFF KNOCKED OUT JOHNNIE RAY

Woolworths and one eye on the Pose Band. The Pose Band disbanded in 1974 due to shape differences, having left behind a hugely influential body of poses.

The Opera Bouffant I am working on with Bruce and Paul is based on the story of deaf Nabob of Sob, Johnnie Ray. It's originally called 'Deaf Aid'. When I'm on board, I suggest 'Earache'. Eventually we settle for 'Hysteria – How Elvis's Quiff Knocked Out Johnnie Ray'. Bruce is getting late in years, he no longer 'poses', he mainly works in cardboard. Everything on the set of 'Hysteria' will be made of cardboard. Including Johnnie Ray. It is maybe worth noting that Bruce has been working on this Johnnie Ray masterpiece since 1968.

> *Earache*
> *Screaming banshees, screaming demons, screaming ab-dabs*
> *Social sickness, moral panic, burning witches, wailing women faint*
> *Hysteria just gives me earache*
> *Muscle spasms, fluid retention, pelvic massage*
> *Schitzophrenia, mass delusion, masturbation, shaking women quake*
> *Hysteria just makes my earache*
> *Detection of sound*
> *Good and bad vibrations*
> *Nerve impulses, perceived by the brain*
> *Air pressure valves, the auditory nerve*
> *A movement of molecules lead to . . . GBH of the ear'ole*

Johnnie Ray was the freak du jour even back in 1948. By the time he was cast in *There's No Business Like Show*

Business with Marilyn Monroe he was freak of the week, and by 1969 when he was staggering around like a rubber chicken – the washed-up, pissed-up only guest at fellow dipso Judy Garland's wedding to Mickey Deans – he was *le plus grand monstre du monde*.

'*Poor old Johnnie Ray, sounded sad upon the radio, moved a million hearts in mono,*' sang Kevin Roland, as a million '80s teenagers went 'Johnnie who?' Two years later, Stretford classicist Morrissey appeared on *Top of the Pops* wearing Ray's old deaf aid. Johnnie Ray hadn't been so present on the Hit Parade since the early to mid-1950s. And thereafter: nothing. Nothing except liver failure, death and conspiracy theories. Whispers in the shadows that eventually were the ruination of him: *Why did Johnnie's family change their original English surname from Gay to Ray? And why did Marvin Gaye add an E to his name when he first met Johnnie? And who was Dorothy Kilgallen, anyway?*[5]

Johnnie Ray was the real Captain America, the big hitter and teen dream of that peculiar white-bread pop impasse that began in 1952. The 'Before Time'. Before there was Rock. Before there was even Pop. In this time there was only Frank Sinatra, and it was his world, and everyone else just lived in it.

Little Johnnie Jewel was born a farm boy in 1927 in Dallas, Oregon. Deaf in one ear after an accident in a boy scout ritual called a 'blanket toss'. After unsuccessful primitive surgical intervention Johnnie was to all intents and purposes deaf as

---

[5] From Paul Tickell's original 'Hysteria' notes.

a fucking post. With just a couple of hearing aids to help him on his way, Johnnie entered showbiz and showbiz entered Johnnie, fucking him senseless, but Johnnie needed showbiz to make his lugholes feel better. Show business needed him for a short while, too. Johnnie was precocious, an instant hit in the African-American clubs of Detroit. By 1949, Johnnie had scored a recording deal with 'race' label Okeh Records; the plan was to get Johnnie on the radio, keep him off the TV and sell him as a black female R&B singer.

The plan didn't work. Once the kids copped an eyeful of Johnnie, falling on the floor, bursting into tears and tearing his hair out, the deal had been done. A whole pre-rock 'n' roll generation fell for their first Freak.

'Cry', the second Johnnie Ray single, sold 2 million copies on 78 rpm in 1952. 'Mr Emotion' was born. 'Mr Emotion' meet 'The Prince of Wails' and, best of all, 'The Nabob of Sob'. Johnnie was a teen idol, one of the first. And, like so many to come, his life was about to be ruined.

Things could only get better – before they got a lot worse – with an appearance on the *Toast of the Town* on network television; soon to become *The Ed Sullivan Show*. There was Johnnie, live in front of most of America, doing his bit, blubbing away and coming on like Frankie Laine having a nervous breakdown. It's quite a performance, it's up there with Piaf singing 'Je Ne Regrette Rien' (Johnnie would come to have a lot of regrets), or Jacques Brel at the Paris Olympia going full fugue during 'Amsterdam'. Or even Iggy walking on the crowd in Detroit in 1970, except Johnnie wasn't singing 'I Feel

FREAKS OUT!

Alright', he was seizuring his way through 'Little Wight Cloud', and it almost goes without saying that Johnnie never felt alright.

Johnnie Ray was openly bisexual. Early doors. What used to be called 'a Friend of Dorothy'. Let's make that two Dorothys. Dorothy Kilgallen, gossip columnist, *What's My Line?* TV panellist and household name in 1950s America; conspiracy theorist, UFO believer and possible victim of The Mob. Dorothy number two was 'Yellow Brick Road' Dorothy, Dipso Dorothy. The original Dorothy. The Dorothy's Dorothy: Judy Garland. With friends like these . . .

Johnnie met Dotty number #1, Dorothy Kilgallen, in 1954, when he was appearing as a guest on *What's My Line?* Johnnie at his peak. A year before Elvis's quiff appeared in silhouette looming at the window like a hillbilly *Nosferatu*, ready to knock jittery Johnnie off his piano stool. Johnnie and Dorothy were instant and intense bezzies. Some believed they were even 'at it'.

Elvis's hips burst through the sacred veil firstly with 'That's All Right', then 'Good Rockin' Tonight'. Neither songs were stratospheric sellers in the way that 'Cry' was. Not yet at least, but unlike 'Cry' they became enduring standards and Elvis Aaron Presley became Elvis. The id of rock. Elvis made Johnnie Ray and every other white artist who came before look cornball. By 1955, the hits were running out for Johnnie. Luckily the booze and the pills weren't.

Dorothy K and Johnnie were plastered in 1959. Johnnie also went to trial for soliciting an undercover cop in a showbiz bar in Detroit. Dorothy fiercely stood by her friend. A jury composed entirely of 'older' women found Johnnie Ray not guilty. In possibly the penultimate great public act of Johnnie Ray's career and upon hearing the verdict, the Prince of Wails fainted.

Dorothy was meanwhile getting into social justice, conspiracy theories and UFOs. The latter two interests making her less popular with the television network and the mainstream *Hollywood Reporter* magazine. Whether Dorothy was an early adept of Ufology or it was just the pills and liquor taking their toll will never be known, but in 1964 Kilgallen wrote a column entitled 'Memo To Lyndon Johnson'. The column continued: 'The Army has been perfecting a mind control technology called "cloudbusting".' Cloudbusting was a reference to maverick psychologist Wilhelm Reich, creator of the Orgone Accumulator.[6] Cloudbusting cannons firing off 'orgone' energy were apparently used by Reich in the Tucson desert to fight off UFOs. Dorothy was getting too far out.

In November 1965, in her Manhattan townhouse, Dorothy Kilgallen died. The cause of death was given as an OD of alcohol and barbiturates. At the time of her death she was doubling down on the conspiracy theorist's conspiracy: the death of JFK.[7]

---

[6] There will be plenty more about Orgone Accumulators later in this book. Worry not.
[7] The footnote for the Warren Commission is that there is no footnote. I assure the reader that I will not be positing any theories concerning JFK.

FREAKS OUT!

The conspiracy theorist should of course always have a conspiracy theory attached to their own death, and there were a few attached to Dorothy Kilgallen's expiry: Did she know too much about JFK (she was a pill buddy with Marilyn)? Did she rile Frank Sinatra in her gossip column one time too many and die at the hand of a Mob hitman? Or did she know too much about what she thought the CIA knew about UFOs? The only real certainty of Dorothy Kilgallen's death is that Johnnie Ray never really got over it.

By the mid-1960s the world had no need for Johnnie Ray. He didn't so much look like a product of a decade earlier but a product of another age. Like Gene Vincent, he could still draw an audience in Europe as a kind of novelty act, but what need was there for Johnnie Ray in 1969? He wasn't even the most obvious Freak in town any more. The counterculture had the real Freak show of Tiny Tim, delivering similar MOR fodder in a bizarre quavering falsetto voice and seemingly living in his own version of early 1950s mom and pop America. The main difference between Johnnie and Tiny Tim (voice notwithstanding) was that Tiny was ardently and somewhat creepily heterosexual and approved by the Beatles and super-hip Frank Zappa. No one talked about poor old Johnnie Ray any more.

Enter Dorothy number #2. Who's gonna call you when you're down and out, and the bookings have dried up, and you're absolutely soaking in booze? Why Judy Garland, of course. Judy Garland's fifth wedding to

HOW ELVIS'S QUIFF KNOCKED OUT JOHNNIE RAY

Mickey Deans was Johnnie's last great personal appearance. There he was staggering up the Yellow Brick Road, washed up and pilled up, the only wedding guest on the unhappy day of fellow dipso and friend of the pill box Judy Garland.

Elvis died in 1977. Ten years later Mojo Nixon sang the excellent 'Elvis Is Everywhere', contending that everyone had a little Elvis in them, even Michael J. Fox (it was the '80s). Everyone, that is except Debbie Gibson (it was the '80s), who, Mojo elaborated, 'had no Elvis in her at all'. Despite the '80s references the point is clear: even a decade after his death Elvis Presley was still the most beloved King of Rock 'n' Roll. Johnnie Ray died three years after that Mojo Nixon song, his body wiped out by chemical abuse and alcohol. His mind, finances and fame also long gone.

At the time of writing, Elvis's fame seems to have waned a little, but he is still most definitely the King. The King is dead but he's not forgotten. Johnnie Ray, however, still remains a footnote to Kevin Rowland's career. The queen is dead, boys, dead and forgotten.

Bruce McLean was taken by his mother to see Johnnie Ray at the Glasgow Apollo. He has never been the same since. At the time of writing this book, our Opera Bouffant, 'Hysteria', has yet to be staged.

CHAPTER 5

The psychedelic dawn of Hank B. Marvin and the Shadows

How my lower middle-class life was perverted by the discovery of the electric guitar, and how Hank Marvin and the Shadows invented psychedelia.

Nineteen seventy-seven. Elvis is dead and I am nine years old. I have an embarrassing secret. It's something for the adult world, the kids won't understand. My secret: I am a precocious student of the classical guitar. I started playing two long years ago, and while other children at school are strumming away on hopeless singalongs of 'Michael, Row the Boat Ashore', I am hurtling through the repertoire: Matteo Carcassi, Mauro Giuliani, Manuel de Falla, and my South American hero, the *Boy's Own* explorer/composer and black knight of the classical guitar, Heitor Villa-Lobos.[1] I have passed my Grade 4

---

[1] Villa Lobos (1887–1959) was a Brazilian composer, adventurer, multi-instrumentalist, folk artist and polymath of the highest order.

FREAKS OUT!

exam with ease. My guitar teacher – a stern and fastidious middle-aged gent, who has no idea how to deal with a precocious child – wants me to slow down, to stop tearing through each revered classical study as if it were a comic book. But I have no fear, and only the patience of a nine-year-old. I perform to audiences of grown-ups at the local 'guitar club'. I have made the audience wince by playing Isaac Albéniz' finger-breaking, tendon-popping 'Asturias'. One of the wincers is my guitar teacher, who at the following evening's guitar lesson tears me and my performance to wisps. He is of course right. 'Asturias' contains mental disciplines and physical techniques far beyond the grasp of a child. It was a terrible rendition – too fast, clumsy, and inaccurate. What on earth would possess a kid to try and take on one of the great pieces of the classical guitar repertoire?

After the lesson, by the time we park the Humber Sceptre in the drive of our bungalow I am distraught. My dad is pretty angry too, and after talking it over with my mum, he telephones the unforgiving guitar tutor. Dad is just bringing the phone conversation to a close, saying stuff about 'being too hard on me for my age' and how we will be looking for a more suitable guitar teacher, when I walk into the kitchen, still in tears. I get as near to the phone receiver as I can, then I let the genie out.

'You fucking cunt – I hate you.' Things are changing.

* * *

It is the early summer of 1977, there are only six weeks or so to go before the start of the long school holiday.

THE PSYCHEDELIC DAWN

I decide – even though I'm not being bullied and I don't mind the teachers so much – that school is really not for me. I fake a series of debilitating headaches and somehow, *somehow*, my parents (possibly still in shock from the 'cunt' calling incident) believe me. A day becomes a few more days, which then becomes weeks off school. The suspicious family GP sends me to a suspicious hospital specialist. Nothing is revealed. With little thought for my parents (who are terrified that I may have some kind of 'undetectable' brain tumour), I pull off this deception. I spend the days and weeks watching TV (this sets me up for a several-decades-long love affair with daytime TV). There's an advert on all the time – for a record, featuring a teenager miming in the mirror using a tennis racket as a guitar. It is the best music I've ever heard, it speaks to me of South American mystery (just like Villa-Lobos). But this time it is loud. Way, way loud. And it is electric. *Electric*. I need to hear more of this music. My parents, out of desperation, and perhaps hoping that musical happiness may help cure my mysterious doctor-confounding ailment, buy me the album in question. I carefully remove the disc from the plain white paper inner sleeve, and place it on the turntable of the enormous family gramophone that takes up a quarter of the living room. I watch the red and gold EMI label spin round for a moment, then gently place stylus upon vinyl.[2] *Drums: Dun dun dun*

---

[2] Because of *The Shadows 20 Golden Greats* I have a Pavlovian response to the gold and red EMI paper labels of the 1970s. I will buy almost anything that has this label.

dun – dun dun dun dun – dun dun dun dun – dun dun dun dun – and guitar. Electric. Guitar: *Draaang, naw naw nayyey ey, naw naw ne na nayyy. APACHE.*

The television news is full of punk rockers and the Queen's Silver Jubilee. The punk rockers want to put a stop to the Queen's Silver jubilee, for some reason. I don't care much about these punk rockers. I will do soon. I don't care much about the Queen either. For I have the *The Shadows 20 Golden Greats*. The record my parents bought for me to ease my 'pain'. The only 'punk' in the tiny village of Emsworth in Hampshire where we now live – en route to hated Portsmouth – is the 'backward' kid from the estate, the cat killer, who walks around wearing a sheet with the words 'White Riot' scrawled on it in felt tip. I have no idea what a 'White Riot' is, besides I'm too immersed in *The Shadows 20 Golden Greats*, which I play at least ten times a day (I'd play it more but ten times seems to be pushing the upper limits of my parents' patience). I stare at the front cover. *That* front cover: Three Fender guitar heads silhouetted against Aztec gold. The *20 Golden Greats* album sleeve is the only image I have of this most mysterious group – the Shadows – a group from a long, long time ago. For all I know this music could be played by a posse of Man-With-No-Name gunslinging motherfuckers. It certainly sounds like it. My only previous experience of pop music – apart from those Beatles' singles – has been my dad tunelessly singing along to Danny La Rue's 'Mother Kelly's Doorstep' in the car, and catching tantalising glimpses of Gary Glitter on *Top of the Pops*. Gary Glitter is fantastic. So are Suzi, Alvin and the

THE PSYCHEDELIC DAWN

Sweet. However, *The Shadows 20 Golden Greats* is the sound of God communicating via electric guitar. The needle skates across the run-out groove of side one and turns itself off automatically. I walk over to the gramophone and click the plastic switch into start position and listen to the first few seconds of vinyl snap crackle and whirr until the drums of 'Apache' begin again. I pick up the album cover and stare at it again. Because I am nine years old, and because *The Shadows 20 Golden Greats* is the first album I have owned.

* * *

Four and a half decades later, as I play the very same vinyl copy of *The Shadows 20 Golden Greats*, I am struck by two things. First, that for all the needless worry I put my parents through by feigning some sort of brain tumour – *a fucking brain tumour* – it was worth it. Many of my generation have Darts, Showaddywaddy (both cool) or ABBA (not cool) in their DNA; I, however, got lucky. For I have the Shadows in mine. Just as Townshend, Ray Davies, Syd and all those early '60s art-school rockers had been transported by the grooves of 'Apache', I too have the space-age twang of Hank B. Marvin careering through my Freak veins. Secondly, listening to this run of near-flawless, peerless, early- to mid-1960s singles, it hits me, like a four-way fucking acid tab, that these were not just vaguely enigmatic and catchy instrumentals that somehow invoke the optimism of the jet age. This sound is actually a pageant to the ancients. Just take in those titles alone: 'Apache', 'The Frightened

FREAKS OUT!

City' (*The. Frightened. Fucking. City.*), 'The Savage', 'F.B.I.', 'Atlantis', 'Wonderful Land', 'A Place in the Sun', 'Maroc Seven'. These are not mere tunes, they are sacrificial death dances for the immortals. Take heed, and this is no idle notion, the Shadows, in their imperial phase from 1960 to 1962, were psychedelic as all hell.

As early as 1959, the Shadows had already carved out a palpable place for themselves as Cliff Richard's backing group, with Hank tossing out louche and threatening licks over Cliff's one convincing stab at proper rock 'n' roll: 'Move It'. However, by the turn of the new decade, Cliff thought he had shrewdly weighed up his options and came to the wrong conclusion: that there would be few and far places in the firmament for an English rock. Cliff catastrophically threw in his lot on the side of 'wholesomeness'. Unrighteous, Cliff.

The Shadows were by now striking out alone as a mainly instrumental outfit and might have been remembered as mere light entertainment journey-fodder, had they not toured with an unsuccessful singer-songwriter called Jerry Lordan. One provincial night, pre-show, Lordan found himself hit upon by the Shads for any spare tuneage; he responded by plucking out an eight-note motif (E, A, E, A, F#, E, D, E) on a ukulele.[3] It was one helluva tune. Even on

---

[3] The ukulele, an instrument that should never have been popular, is mystifyingly popular again. The ukulele is an unrighteous blackspot. Approach with extreme prejudice. That most unrighteous Freak, Tiny Tim, was a wielder of the uke, and you really don't want to be like him.

THE PSYCHEDELIC DAWN

the dreaded uke. Within weeks the group had entered EMI Studios with producer Norrie Paramor at the controls and recorded the instrumental – previously unnamed – now brilliantly titled, 'Apache'. Woah, fucking *Apache*.[4]

You are a teenager in 1960, you are listening to *Saturday Club* on the radio. In between the BBC Light Orchestra renditions of American rock 'n' roll hits, and children's records like 'Nellie the Elephant', you will receive your first exposure to the Shadows' 'Apache'. This is what you will hear: four bars of ominous tom-toms, before a banshee shrieking fanfare played on a fiesta-red Fender Stratocaster from outer space.[5] It's the muezzin calling the demob masses of austerity Britain to prayer; the prayer that will lift the pea souper and banish post-war drabness for ever. Then Hank blinks away the last sleepy-dust of the 195, and as if it was the first thing that came into his head, effortlessly rips out a lead line, *that* lead line. The lead line[6] that any guitarist can play within six weeks of picking up the instrument – *downg ding, downg ding dawng, dow dow downg*. Show me a guitarist who hasn't played that riff and I'll show you a fucking liar.

---

[4] The Shadows have claimed many times that Lordan presented the tune to them untitled and they settled upon the title of 'Apache' after throwing around titles such as 'Thunder', 'Hawkeye', and 'Flame Rider'. Strange, as 'Apache' had already been recorded by old-guard twanger Bert Weedon one year earlier in 1959 . . .

[5] Famously, the first Fender Strat in the UK. As a guitar head I don't dig Strats too much. When Tony Blair arrived in Number 10, with 'his' guitar, the guitar was revealed to be a Fender Strat.

[6] There is a very distinct difference between a lead line and a riff: 'Apache' is a lead line. The guitar line in the Stones' 'Satisfaction' is a riff.

FREAKS OUT!

After two minutes and fifty-two seconds of rock 'n' roll perfection (lead guitar through tape delay, double-tracked rhythm guitar, bass and drums, all perfectly separated in the mono), you will want to hear it again. It is impossible to listen to 'Apache' just once.

There was a lot of instrumental fodder clogging up the British Hit Parade in the early '60s. But compare 'Apache' to its nearest counterpart – the Tornados more lauded 'Telstar' – and it is clear that it is the former that is truly not of this earth. Hank's Valhalla to Joe Meek's Val Singleton.

I offer no mealy mouthiness when I state that 'Apache' defined a kind of pagan futurism. That it achieved this without a single member of the Shadows – Hank, Bruce Welch (rhythm guitarist), Jet Harris (hooligan bass) and drummer Tony Meehan – all originally known as the Geordie Boys – imbibing anything more hallucinogenic than a pint of Newkie Brown, matters not one micro-dot. Within a month of its release in July 1960, 'Apache' was number one on the UK Singles Chart, staying there for six weeks. It went on to be a massive hit around the globe. The psych-vibes were strong, and as 'Apache' dominated the global airwaves, it was no coincidence that out in the real Apache tribe territory of New Mexico, the lysergic explorers of the '60s decade, were hanging out, and digging for, and *digging*, the holy sacrament: psilocybin – magic mushrooms. The Flesh of the Gods. On 9 August 1960, as the Shadows occupied the British top spot on the charts, errant Harvard psychology lecturer Dr Timothy Leary, staying in Mexico City approaching forty years old, and tiring of his middle-aged martini-academic lifestyle, took hallucinogenic mushrooms for the first time.

Maybe, as the trip comes on, it is time to cool out a little. Time to take stock, and while it is true that 'Apache' sounded as timeless as a Mayan death pageant, there were other Shadows' records. Oh yes. So for every lean mean brooder like 'Geronimo', 'Man of Mystery', 'The Savage' and 'Atlantis', there would be singles such as 'Guitar Tango', 'Shindig' and 'Foot-tapper'. Records that even Jimmy Young might have found to be a bit, well, 'square'.

Within less than three years of the release of 'Apache' and in strict accordance with the pop lifespan of the times, the Shadows were merely one of their former selves. In the pre-pre-irony world, where there was nowhere to hide and the Shads had revealed themselves. The dance moves were looking corny, and the instrumentals were sounding formulaic. Worst of all, they had not broken their bond with Cliff Richard (wince at them mugging away most un-psychedelically through Cliff's early '60s movies). The Shadows were light entertainment by association, and in post-war early '60s Britain the new species of 'Teenagers' could only take so much light entertainment. They wanted something else. Something that the Shadows had on their earlier records, the promise of freedom. The promise of the West. Just like Elvis and Chuck and Gene and Little Richard and Eddie had given them, before promptly scarpering (to the Army, to the jailbait, to the booze, to the religion, to the death). The people wanted Sun Gods.

FREAKS OUT!

The people didn't get sun gods, they got insect gods. Beatle gods. The Shadows' last massive single of the '60s was 'Wonderful Land'.[7] Once again written by Jerry Lordan and produced by Norrie Paramor, 'Wonderful Land' was an even bigger commercial success than 'Apache', taking up residence at the magic spot for eight formidable weeks. It's hardly surprising: every nanosecond of this transcendental record wordlessly signals a message to the people: 'It's 1962 and everything is going to be . . . Alright!' 'Wonderful Land' was the Shadows' most enduring recording and second great psychedelic single. By the following year the insects had taken over.

* * *

In 1963, LSD-25 was still legal (it would be made illegal in the US in 1966). Dr Timothy Leary, the highly vocal prophet of all hallucinogens, was drawing a lot of heat: from Harvard, from the press, from the cops, and from the CIA. Leary, along with fellow Harvard psychology lecturer Richard Alpert (soon to be known as Ram Dass), had established a psychedelic Camelot in a four-storey mansion on a 2,500-acre estate in Millbrook, New York

---

[7] The Shads did score two further number-one singles: the breezy 'Dance On' and 'Foot-tapper'. The other-worldly 'Atlantis' was also a number-two single just before Fab-mania took hold. But it was 'Wonderful Life' that was Hank's last great state of the pre-psychedelic nation address.

State, and was hell bent on a mission to destroy the straight world. Leary and Alpert's aim, in the pre-pre-irony age, was simple: to psychedelicise all society. The doctor, tripping for days at a time on strong acid straight out of the Swiss Sandoz laboratory, was preaching an all-out global psychedelic revolution. Humanity, if Leary had anything to do with it, would move on to a fifth dimension. Within this fifth dimension the mundane would be eradicated, time would be eradicated, space too. Hell, maybe even humanity could be eradicated and replaced with a pre-science cosmic rumble. *Ommmmmmmmmm.* Timothy Leary – in the face of unimaginable hostility from post-war mom and pop middle America, and before he revealed himself to be a whack quack charlatan – was playing hallucinogenic hardball.

Psychedelia found its way to London in 1965 via Millbrook emissary Michael Hollingshead. Hollingshead brought with him enough lysergic acid to produce 5,000 trips. He also brought with him thirteen boxes of literature, including Leary and Alpert's tome – *The Psychedelic Experience – A Manual Based Upon the Tibetan Book of the Dead.* Hollingshead (a dubious character even by the standards of acid evangelists) was becoming troublesome at Millbrook, and part of the reason for packing him off to London was to get rid of him.

After Hollingshead had been dispatched, Leary recalled saying to Alpert:

'Well that writes off the psychedelic revolution in England for ten years.'

FREAKS OUT!

John Lennon was spending a lot of time lying in bed in 1966. Rich, bored and stoned (presumably getting in some practice for his excellent bed-in three years later). Freak Brother John's après touring downtime was to be reflected in two songs that would feature on the Beatles' *Revolver* elpee. The somnambulist proto-Mandrax anthem, 'I'm Only Sleeping', and 'Tomorrow Never Knows', a homage to his favourite reading matter: Timothy Leary's *Psychedelic Experience*.

'Tomorrow Never Knows' is a rare example of outward-looking, future-seeking, free-falling, fifth-dimension Brit psychedelia, going to places few had dared to venture before. Only the Shadows, six years earlier.

By December 1966, the British psychedelic underground took up residence in the basement of 31 Tottenham Court Road. The UFO Club was where the Soft Machine killed jazz, and where house band Pink Floyd copped a riff or two from the Shadows on their free rock opus 'Interstellar Overdrive' (the Shads' 'Man of Mystery' played inside out). But the acid was turning the little Englander's gaze inward. While the American San Francisco groups like the Jefferson Airplane, Moby Grape, Quicksilver Messenger Service and the Grateful Dead had taken Leary's bid to 'psychedelise all society' as a statement of intent, the English had seized upon the acid trip as a chance to infantilise themselves and pootle around in a provincial version of the Mad Hatter's Tea Party. Soon, teeny-tiny lysergic vignettes about 'White Bicycles' ('My White Bicycle' by Tomorrow), 'Flowers in the Rain' (the Move)[8] and grocers ('Excerpt from a Teenage Opera' by Keith West), were clogging up the charts. Even Procol Harum's much-adored at the time 'A Whiter Shade of Pale' sounded more Blackpool Pleasure Gardens than 'Mind Gardens' by the Byrds. It would seem that while America rocked out to the moon, the English went back to the womb.

A real psychedelic masterpiece had been released back in the latter part of 1966 and nobody had noticed. It was of course by the already beaten and bedraggled Shadows. At this stage the poor Shads weren't even playing the chicken-in-the-basket circuit. They *were* the chicken in the basket. 'A Place in the Sun', written by Jerry Lordan's wife Petrina Lordan, limped to the not-so-magic number twenty-four spot in the UK Singles Chart. Then promptly fucked off. Unmissed and unlamented. 'A Place in the Sun' was the Shadows' last gasp for Utopia. For all the lyrical clunking around of Procol Harum et al., the Shadows managed to convey more of the acid experience wordlessly than any of their more lauded contemporaries. The unheralded last air grab of genius by these dream time psych-o-nauts, these riders on the psychedelic dawn – the Shadows.

But these were the End Days for the Shadows, who released just one single in 1967. An oddly strung-out and phased sci-fi meditation called 'Maroc Seven'. By now the Shads were entirely vibeless. If Hank had out guitar-duelled

---

[8] The Move were one of the great English groups, they deserved more than to be lobbed in with UK pop psych.

FREAKS OUT!

Jimi Hendrix (who in contemporaneous interviews of the time, he somewhat unwisely passed off as 'rubbish') live on the Lulu show, no fucker would have noticed. Our heroes – *my* heroes – were, rightly or wrongly, associated with the pre-Beatle age. Hank's chops were busted, man, so in 1968 the Shadows pushed the mission aborted button. By 1973 they had reconvened[9] just like every other hopeless lifeless rock 'n' roll corpse that pathetically churns it out on the remember-us-circuit of the early twenty-first century. The Shadows were always ahead of the game.

* * *

On a grim weekday evening in mid-1978, I stand outside the auditorium of Portsmouth Guildhall, tears falling into my lemonade as my dad tries to comfort me. His efforts cannot stop the pain in my head and the high frequency screeching in my ears. We have just abandoned my first rock 'n' roll 'gig', due to sonic assault with extreme prejudice. The perpetrators of this total GBH of my junior lugholes – the Shadows. So, yes, the Shadows are riding high in the UK Singles Chart again, with some dreck called 'The Theme from The Deer Hunter'. It's cack, no psychedelia here, nothing to look at, best move on. Even

---

[9] The Shads even scored a second place in the 1975 Eurovision Song Contest, with one of their rare, ill-advised vocal numbers – 'Let Me Be the One'. How cool would it have been if they'd stormed it with a Jerry, or Petrina, Lordan killer instrumental.

so, the Shads are playing the local Guildhall, and my dad has bought us tickets. I'm figuring that if they play the 'Deer Hunter' thing I'll just block it out. The band come on to a full house and big applause, Hank's wearing a red blazer. Oh no. Hank smiles too much. But then, *then*, they Crank. It. The. Fuck. Out. *The Frightened City*. '*The. Frightened. Fucking. City.*'

It's the loudest, most terrifying thing I have ever, *will ever*, hear. Why are you doing this, Shadows? Are you fucking insane? Are they fucking deaf? Holy Hearing Aids, Kevin. Yes, Kevin Shields, I am talking to you. This Shadows' noise-apocalypse shines the big bad searchlight on your entire My Bloody Valentine oeuvre. Revealing it to be, well, tiny.

I cower and huddle closer to my dad. The frightened city; the fucking frightened eleven-year-old more like. *Preeeoowww!* Fuck me, what fresh hell is this? It's the opening chord of 'Man of Mystery'. If there is Satan and if there is a God, then there is no longer. The Shadows have obliterated all. The earth is scorched. The 'song' ends and Hank walks to the microphone. What is he going to say, is he going to impart sacred knowledge from the Mahatmas? No, he is not. Hank plays a single (admittedly bone-rattlingly loud) note on his red Strat and makes an unattractive low bending sound using the guitar's whammy bar.

'That's what I feel like in the mornings,' says Hank Marvin in a jovial Geordie accent to a few ripples of polite laughter. Hank feels he is on to a winner and says it again, adding, 'That's what my stomach feels like in the morning.'

FREAKS OUT!

Less laughter this time, so Hank makes up for it by bending the note again and laughing. It's all getting very un-psychedelic, it will get even less psychedelic in a moment when Hank announces solemnly that they are going to be playing 'The Theme from The Deer Hunter'. They hit the first few bars and I erupt in tears. Tears of pain, tears of disappointment, tears of outrage, and tears of relief. My dad takes me out of the concert hall, and I tell him, through tears, that it is too loud for me and can we please go home. So, home we go. The tinnitus shrieking in my ears abates after about two weeks, but I am never the same. I have heard 'Rock and Roll'. Properly. And though I fear it, I now want an electric guitar more than I have ever wanted anything else. I don't play *The Shadows 20 Golden Greats* again for many years. There is no need, it has served its purpose. It has enabled my inner Freak.

CHAPTER 6

How the Beatles ruined everything for everyone ever

*In which we have to get granular about the Fabs . . .
. . . and the Male Genius Myth turns up early doors.*

The Shads infatuation lasted a little more than a year. I mean, obviously I am infatuated by them again now, as a mid-fifties dude. But by the end of 1978 I had outgrown Hank. I was even experiencing pangs of 'proto' embarrassment at my Shadows based un-coolness. This is good.

There is a certain kind of uncool that is to be celebrated. Liking the Shads is uncool in a groovy kind of way. Saying 'groovy' is uncool in a cool kind of way. Freaks gotta learn cool/uncool, dude ('dude' is cool/uncool in a groovy kind of way). Here are some examples: Smog/Bill Callahan are cool, but to the real Freak, Smog/Little Bill Callahan are totally uncool. My Bloody Valentine and Spiritualised are cool but also really uncool. The true Freak will scoff at the mention of MBV. 'They are for lightweights who haven't heard

FREAKS OUT!

of Les Rallizes Dénudés and they are not even as loud as the Shadows,' they will say. Don't say this aloud, though. If you do say it aloud that will just make you a rock snob, which has taken you back to Bill Callahan/Smog/MBV and Spiritualised. Woah, uncool.

Prince. No one cool has ever liked Prince; if you like Prince you are doomed. One day the people who don't love Prince will rise up, but for now we will bide our time safe in the knowledge that Prince made music for people who have solid careers and good finances (white ladies and gents who like Prince have not heard 'Chocolate City' by Parliament – and if they had heard 'Chocolate City', they would be appalled by it. Given that they have not heard 'Chocolate City' means that they are fairly clueless in all matters funkadelic. This is deeply uncool. Yet writing the sentence 'fairly clueness in all matters funkadelic' is kinda the holy grail of uncool. If you are a true Freak and uncool/cool, you will not have a 'solid' career, and you will be incapable of managing your finances.

Radiohead are totally uncool/uncool. If you know a Radiohead fan, just name any 'novelty' record from the early '70s and claim it is superior to the entire oeuvre of Thom and co. This will annoy them and confuse them.

The Clash: the Clash have gone from being uncool (for most of their existence) to being legendary, to being Marley, Bobby Sands and Lennon-ised (after Joe's death) to being, inevitably, uncool again. Whether it is uncool to like them is tricky. It may be best to keep your opinion to yourself, as Clash fans tend to be very sentimental and intransigent. They will cry, then they will hit you, then they may cry again. Bob Marley is cool. A wise man once said: 'There is only one question: Bob Marley or Big Youth? And the answer is always Big Youth.' The man who posed this question was a wise man, but not a cool man. He was too cool. So, although the answer – 'Big Youth' – is correct, because Big Youth was and still is a most righteous Freak,[1] Bob Marley is still, kind of, cooler. It is complex, I know, and to be honest, if you need all of this pointing out to you, then you are doubtless beyond help and you should just retire to your cave and enjoy your Steely Dan albums. Sadly, back in 1978 I hadn't worked out all of this important stuff and the Shadows, in my undeveloped view, were ditched as being irredeemably 'uncool'. Shit, man.

Christmas 1978 was goodbye to the Shadows, and hello the Beatles. Just like 1963 would have been, when the UK's teens and pre-teens quietly put their *Out of the Shadows* elpee to the back of the wardrobe and lost their minds to *With the Beatles* instead. On Christmas Day I was given a radio-cassette player. The year 1978 was a good time for radio-cassettes and taping records off the radio. 'Dreadlock Holiday' was on the radio all the time, a deeply uncool/cool record. A cassette, that my cousin Rob had recorded for me, of *A Collection of Beatles Oldies . . . But Goldies*, was receiving serious attention. In a year's time I will have moved on somewhat precociously into the weird. But right now, it is the Beatles.

---

[1] There will be more Big Youth, perhaps surprisingly in a chapter about Morrissey.

FREAKS OUT!

Achtung! Beatles! Achtung! Beatles! We have to tread very carefully here: Beatle lore has been fully examined by the masses ad nauseam. I sometimes worry that if anyone writes another book about the beloved four this could be enough to send humanity and the known universe hurtling into a black hole. I will not be the man who destroys all of humanity.

Throughout the 1990s, I had serious Fabs-fatigue. I could take no more of 'Anthology' singles and birds being set free by Jeff Lynne, and then Jeff Lynne being set free by the remaining Beatles. Threetles. Ukuleles. Britpop. Rutledom. But now I'm a more relaxed motherfucker. I fell back in love with the Fabs. Sometimes I even – *whisper it* – listen to them. The Beatles went beyond cool, uncool, too cool, uncool in a groovy way. They rose to the top of Holy Mountain and looked down and just . . . shrugged.

A Collection of Beatles Oldies . . . But Goldies is the greatest Fabs compilation. You don't need my guidance here. If you are reading this, you've doubtless reached the point in your life where you know as much as you need or want to regarding all things Fab. You don't need me to tell you the Beatles Story. The greatest story ever told. What you do need me to tell you is how the Beatles, through no fault of their own, ruined all rock 'n' roll for everyone. Ever.

The real outlier on *A Collection of Beatles Oldies . . . But Goldies*, among all the holy jewels – i.e. all their fabulous singles between 1963 and 1966 – is tucked away in the middle of side two: 'Bad Boy', an outtake that got originally shipped off to the American market but was made available here, in

Christmas 1966, for the first and only time. 'Bad Boy' is the Fabs at their most smokin' hot. We have no recording of their original leather rent boy residency in Hamburg,[2] when they were walloping out red-raw orthodox rock 'n' roll for eight-hour amphetamine sets. Indeed, the 1965 recording of 'Bad Boy' – recorded along with 'Dizzy Miss Lizzy' and 'Slow Down' – on what became known as 'Larry Williams Night', does give credibility to Billy Childish's not entirely outlandish claim that *The Beatles Live! at the Star-Club* is better than *Sgt. Pepper's*. Maybe, Billy, maybe.

'Bad Boy' is my favourite Beatles' recording. But who was Larry? Larry Williams. Larry certainly deserves some words here, although Larry was not a Freak. Larry was a very bad boy. One of the original rock 'n' rollers, incorrectly viewed as something of a minor songwriter. Minor! For Chrissakes, Larry Williams only wrote 'Bony Moronie', 'Dizzy Miss Lizzy', 'Long Tall Shorty', 'Slow Down' and 'Bad Boy' – the one that any kid discovering rock 'n' roll could relate to *'A bad little kid moved into the neighbourhood . . .'* the song that Fabs King Freak, John Lennon, dug so much. Larry – as were so many of the original rockers – was an early Freak enabler. 'Bad Boy' was nothing less than a two minute thirty aural manual for delinquency. Albeit, a cartoonish delinquency. In real life, Larry Williams' delinquency went a little further: serious drug addiction and dealing. Gunfights and pimping. After too much Larry Williams, even Little Richard – Larry's great

---

[2] The Beatles' *Live! at the Star Club* was recorded in December 1962 during their last Hamburg residency.

friend –turned to God. Williams was shot to death in 1980 in a drug deal gone bad.

The 1990s were a strange decade. It was the decade that I fell out of love with the Fabs. By the middle of the decade they were everywhere, whispering, 'Here we are, you forgot about us in the late '70s and you forsook us in the 1980s but now we are back, back, back to remind you that everything is a pale imitation . . . of us' or as Samuel Beckett wrote, 'The sun shone, having no alternative, on the nothing new.' Thankfully, the 1990s decade can now be viewed with a little more clarity and was not as important as some of those who were there seem to think it was. Let's apply a little clear-eyed black sky thinking and look at the Beatles through a freak-eyed lens. It's what Big 'Paulie' Mac would want.

The Beatles have to be viewed as an enemy. A hostile organism, even if they are not. This is a black-ops mission, against your own intuition: radical freakery. Y'see, Beatles are a threat to *your* freakery. They have made freakery acceptable. They have done this by their innate genius. They have solidified The Male Genius Myth. The Male Genius Myth is the enemy of the Freak. Sun Ra is not a genius, but he is 'better' than Paul McCartney. Paul is the embodiment of the Male Genius Myth. Sun Ra says he came from Saturn on a mission to peace. We believe Sun Ra even if we know that he didn't actually come from Saturn. Some (men, probably) will try and convince you that Sun Ra is a genius. The point is that the true Freak rejects the Genius Myth. Now if Paul McCartney said he came from Saturn, we would just laugh.

Sun Ra is a Freak, Paul is a genius. He is one of the keepers of the Arc. He is the Arc. He is Big Mac. Embrace this truth.

When David Bowie first tried on his early alien schtick it was kind of cute, but no one really believed him. It was just all showbiz. Oh, and Bowie was never truly a Freak. He may have been a talisman for the Freaks but Dave was too much of a pro to be one himself. If Marc Bolan had pulled the same 'alien' move we would have perhaps believed him. This is because it is entirely plausible that Marc came from space. Space is indeed the place, as Sun Ra so accurately said.

John, Paul, George, Stu Sutcliffe, Pete Best, Ringo, and their John the Baptists, their Brothers number two:[3] Brian Epstein, Neil Aspinall, Mal Evans, Derek Taylor. All were a northern heretic sect. They defied the orthodoxy. Just as the Cathars in twelfth-century southern France had defied the orthodoxy of the Catholic Church.

The Cathars, a heretic set, comprised of Listeners, Believers and Perfects. In the Cathar orthodoxy Listeners were sympathetic to the heresy, Believers adopted the Cathar's dualistic beliefs and strove to one day become Perfects. The Perfect had achieved spiritual tranquillity. Ringo was the Listener, John and Paul the Believers, and George the Perfect. John Lennon was the only real fully fledged Freak: bad John. Larry Williams loving John. Wounded John. Smart but couldn't give a flying cunt

---

[3] 'Brother number two theory': Brother number one (Jesus) creates the myth. Brother number two (John the Baptist) spreads the myth.

John. Rock 'n' roll evangelist John. John the Baptist. Unpretty John. Loved less in the twenty-first century John. Then there was Paul: the seeker. Richie: the primitive. The soul. The true Believer. And then, George: George the mystic. The Beatles were the first mystical group in rock 'n' roll. Mysticism didn't exist in popular culture before this four-headed Beatle beast. And that's what it was. It didn't matter if they weren't all Freaks. The sum of the parts was one big monster Freak. And that was their downfall, at least in 'Freak' terms.

The Sitar: In Robert Irwin's *Memoirs of a Dervish*, the author and Middle East scholar describes his very early adventures to Morocco and India when a student in Oxford. There were fellow travellers to the East and North Africa. Terry Taylor, a young pre-mod/beatnik and the inspiration for Colin MacInnes' *Absolute Beginners*, had done the whole jazz 'n' dope thing in Tangiers – described in his one novel, *Baron's Court All Change* – but this was marginal stuff. The exotic to most Brits in the early '60s was the soundtrack in an Indian restaurant. The curry house had arrived in the Victorian era to serve Asian seaman, then by the 1950s and '60s had multiplied. By the 1970s there were curry houses in every British city. Sure, the Kinks had dabbled with 'the drone' on their 1965, gender curious single 'See My Friends'. But the Beatles got there first, as George tentatively tickled his newly bought sitar with his 'mizran'[4] on 'Rubber Soul'.

---

[4] A plectrum for the sitar.

HOW THE BEATLES RUINED EVERYTHING

Consciousness expansion had been going on since the start of time. The ancients, perhaps disenchanted with their lives of hunting/gathering, brutality, ultra-violence, escaped via hallucinogenic natural substances. Opium became the actual opium of the masses as early as 2100 BC. *Nature Boy* written in 1948 by eden ahbez (the lower case was how ahbez liked his name to be written) was even a statement of proto eco hippie freakdom. Originally a hit for Nat King Cole, then sung by everyone from Ella Fitzgerald to Tiny Tim to Celine Dion to Alex Chilton to Lady Gaga. Sure, 'Nature Boy' was a standard, but it was the Beatles and their innate mystic psi-power that stoked the cultural fire, the cultural fire that Billy Joel so wisely said, 'Was always burning, since the world was turning.'

The hair, the quiff. Remember that when Gene Vincent gets his hair flattened down in *The Rock and Roll Singer* and says, 'I don't want to look like a girl', he knew what had happened. He knew that just as Johnnie Ray had been knocked out by Elvis's quiff, now Gene's quiff had been flattened by Ringo Starr's bangs.

Did the Beatles invent long hair? Of course they didn't, any more than Wild Bill Hickok invented the ponytail, or Thomas Chatterton invented the mullet. In the early 1960s, long hair was the preserve of the 'gentleman of the road', 'the street drinker', 'the salty sea-dog', 'the lunatic'. Those who had truly dropped out of society more by accident than free will. The real Freaks. The Beatles had stolen long hair from the real Freaks.

FREAKS OUT!

It was Michael Hollingshead, who claimed to have given LSD to the dentist, who first turned on John and George Beatle.[5] When Paul McCartney went on TV to admit (when pushed by the press) that he had taken LSD, a nation of old biddies, MPs and tabloid writers sighed and said, 'Oh my giddy aunt, what has become of our loveable all-purpose, all-singing and dancing mop topper little princes?' In the corrosive light of the twenty-first century, those of us in the know just sigh into our CBD-laced tea: 'Oh Paul, you even ruined drugs.'

If you are a wag of the alehouse of some sort, you might get a laugh out of the premise that anyone could 'ruin' Musique Concrète. But then, this book is probably not for you. There is a strong argument that 'Revolution 9' is the Beatles' Masterpiece. I'm not going to propose that here, but I would not say it's far wrong. Listen to it! Don't skip it. Don't be a Beatle bore (I am trying very hard not to be). 'Revolution 9' is the Fabs' track with the most hooks: 'Number nine, number nine, number nine . . .' You see, you know it. 'Awllriiiight, awllriiiight,' come on motherfucker, singalong: 'The twist, the Watusin . . .' In 'Revolution 9', the Beatles had made the previously thought-to-be-impossible challenge of making music concrete/avant sound collage popular by putting it on one of the biggest-selling records

---

[5] The story of the Beatles' 'dentist' has been told often. The most interesting part of the story is how provincial the Beatles still were in 1965. How gauche to be having dinner with your private dentist.

ever, but also achieving the superb bonus of getting millions of their, er, less enlightened fans to hate it.

As if all this wasn't enough, the Beatles even established the '60s myth that anyone from any social strata in the UK could break through class barriers and thrive anywhere they wanted. This notion was of course subconsciously thwarted by the middle classes, who established a middle-brow stranglehold of cultural mediocre thinking that by the late twentieth century was impossible for any fully fledged Freak to loosen.

The Beatles established freakery, but their own world-dominating success had also made it acceptable for at least a few fleeting moments in the late '60s. Long live the Freaks. The Freaks are dead.

CHAPTER 7

Weasel-faced dunces – how I might have killed Steve Peregrin Took (We have to talk about Steve, Part One)

Learning that pop music is a complex business of loyalties, social contract and a potential minefield of teenage embarrassment. The story of the many lives in the short life of Steve Peregrin Took. Part one of the early '70s Freak trilogy.

I'd had very little time to get out of my Beatles *A Collection of Oldies . . . But Goldies* stage and received little warning that there was a plague sweeping across England in 1980, emanating from Woking and the Midlands. A scourge you may not remember; it has been airbrushed out of history by the current lance corporal gatekeepers of culture and celebrated as a time of 'youth cultural revolution'. The reality was that a twin axis of evil had been born: the Jam and the Two-Tone movement. A brutal regime of fear and terror for the non-compliant: me.

As much as the Jam and the Specials made fantastic records, their audiences consisted of a high percentage of shaven-headed little cunts. The period is now seen through the rose-tinted contact lenses of today's ageing cultural commentators, who may or may not have been there at the time. The real 1980 ground-zero battleground was an un-pretty troglodyte mass of skinheads and weasel-faced Weller look-a-likey dunces, prowling the land, searching out non-Harrington, non Sta-Press wearing prey to mete out random violence and beatings upon. I was that prey.

The ultra-violence of Alex's Droogs from *A Clockwork Orange* only took place up on the screen in 1972. The 'for real' ultra-violence took place in the comprehensive school playgrounds of 1980, as an adolescent tsunami of green flying jackets, parkas, red and black Harringtons, tonic suits, horrific burgundy box jackets (for girls), wedges, tramlines and 500-hole oxblood Doc Martens went berserk on the doomy tolling of the break-time bell – kicking the shit out of each other and anything else that moved. As a long-haired ginger kid in a granddad coat and 'birthday' shoes,[1] I didn't stand a fucking chance.

I had two secrets. The first: that I really dug the Jam. I just couldn't and wouldn't get on board with Weller's 'I am thick' mod schtick. The second secret, and potentially most damaging, was that I was massively getting into Marc Bolan's pre-superstar weirdo Freak folk duo, Tyrannosaurus Rex.

---

[1] Southern slang for shoes that your parent bought for you, specifically to wear to school; Clarks Commandos. I have not heard the term 'birthday shoes' for decades, and certainly not north of Guildford.

WEASEL-FACED DUNCES

In 1980, pop worked in a very different dimension of time than our all-ages-all-welcome twenty-first-century definition of the pop timescape. Marc Bolan had died as recently as September 1977, just as he was on the verge – as all pop professors know – of a mini-Marc comeback, having lost his teen audience in 1974 and disappeared in a fog of brandy and cocaine.

Zinc Alloy and the Hidden Riders of Tomorrow was the album that fucked it for Marc. A sprawling puddle of bloated funk guh. To Marc's teeny fans, it sounded and looked like fatty Bolan was having a protracted blowout. To the heads, if there were any left still listening, it was manna from heaven.

Marc, influenced by his girlfriend Gloria Jones, had swallowed the whole American soul trip, hook, line and stinker, but *Zinc Alloy* is better, wilder and weirder than similar contemporary white English-Honky-Boys-go-soul experiments, such as Bowie's dry hump 'Young Americans' or Ian Hunter's 'All American Alien Boy'.

By 1977, Marc had lost the blubber, kicked the brandy and nose bag and was quite possibly *actually believing* that he was the Godfather of Punk. He even had a kids' TV show, on ITV – *Marc* – where he was allowed to put on the more poppy young punkas – Gen X, the Jam, and even, er, Bob Calvert with Hawkwind, performing 'Quark Strangeness And Charm'. Calvert, true to form, appeared with a stuffed hawk (do you see? Do you see?) perched upon his shoulder.

Marc was at the very least 'back . . .' Whether he was ever going to be 'back, back, back' is down to conjecture.

FREAKS OUT!

Marc Bolan died on 16 September 1977, at the age of twenty-nine, in a car crash, like his hero Eddie Cochran. Just like Eddie.

> Old 1970s school playground joke:
> Q. What was Marc Bolan's last hit?
> A. A tree.[2]

One Saturday afternoon in 1980, I wandered into WH Smith with three pound fifty burning a hole in my pocket. I was eager to buy a record. I had a vague memory of T. Rex and a foggy memory of the *Marc* TV show. I have no recollection as to why I needed to buy a T. Rex album, but I knew that I did. Remember, Marc Bolan was from space and he had that kind of otherworldly effect on people. I flicked through the album sleeves in the 'T' rack. There wasn't much. By 1980, despite it only being three years since his death, Marc was largely forgotten. A dead teen star, who hadn't had a top-ten single since 1973. Music was perceived to have come on a lot since Marc's death. Punk and New Wave had been and gone and Raymond Baxter was leering into the camera on *Tomorrow's World* (every Thursday night before *Top of the Pops*), telling the country that 'real' musicians would soon be replaced by 'synthesisers' that could 'imitate the sound of orchestras'. Bummer.

---

[2] It's tasteless, but it has always stuck in my memory since I first heard it in the playground shortly after Marc's death.

WEASEL-FACED DUNCES

There were only two Bolan albums in the rack. The cheapo *Solid Gold T. Rex* album,[3] the one with Marc wearing a leopard-skin catsuit on the cover. The safe option, with all the EMI hits, from 'Telegram Sam' to 'Dreamy Lady'. The other option was a 'twofer': *Unicorn* and *Beard of Stars*. It was about to become the habit of a lifetime, but I went with the 'other' option.

We really need to talk about Steve. Steve is the whispy-looking hippie bum fluff Freak sitting next to Marc Bolan on the front cover of Ty Rex's 1969 masterpiece, *Unicorn*. He is Steven Ross Porter, born in Lewisham, south London, in 1949. At the age of seventeen, Steven Porter, taking his new name from Tolkien's horrific *Lord of the Rings*, became Steve 'Peregrin Took', and for two years, between 1967 and 1969, 50 per cent of Tyrannosaurus Rex.

The year 1969 ushered in a new age of Freak. The pre rock 'n' roll Freaks: Gene and Johnnie, who would have given anything not to be Freaks, were replaced by a bunch of willing, dropout longhairs on speed, Mandrax and heroin. The Freaks of Ladbroke Grove. Steve Took was the Freaks' Freak, unlike his partner, Marc Bolan, who despite living on Blenheim Crescent (and coming from space) always had one eye on Middle Earth and the other on Woolworths, naturally.

If Marc Bolan was dead and somewhat forgotten in 1980, then at least Steve Took was alive. Just about. Alive but

---

[3] The excellent *Solid Gold T. Rex* is another of those talismanic offerings to the gods with the EMI red and gold label. As mentioned in the Shadows' chapter.

completely forgotten. A victim of his own hard-to-classify talent and a casualty of his own excess and the 'bad' company he kept.

In 1969, just prior to the Tyrannosaurus Rex American tour, Steve Peregrin Took was incarcerated in Feltham young offenders institution for possession of cannabis. This was not the image Bolan or his management wanted. Marc had long taken exception to Took's 'Heavy Frendz' in Ladbroke Grove. Bolan had also been spiked with DMT at a London launch party for *Rolling Stone* magazine. Bolan's management put out the rumour that Steve Took was the spiker. It turned out to be untrue, but as Took did rather revel in his nom de plume of 'The Phantom Spiker', the charge stuck.

The first Tyrannosaurus Rex tour in 1969 of the US was a disaster. Took, who had taken to flagellating himself with a mic lead Iggy Stooge style, was not what Marc and his management had in mind in their bid for Bolan to be the great new twentieth-century superstar. Took was also pushing his own excellent material on the non-receptive Marc. 'Tookie', as he was known to the Ladbroke Grove Freak community, was T. Rex Toast, and at the age of twenty, was unceremoniously dumped by Marc and replaced by the photogenic, less musical, and most importantly, far more compliant Mickey Finn.

Not much was written about Steve Took until the Internet Age, when true heads started gathering and sharing information about this very much lost Freak of the Freak Age. Throughout the early '70s Bolan's new-found star of T. Rex-tacy shone so brightly that it all but eclipsed his past lives in John's Children, and Tyrannosaurus Rex, and Steve Peregrin Took was seen very much as part of a necessary purge – get rid of the useless bongo-tapping hippie – and get the teenyboppers wet between the legs. The truth was that Took couldn't give a bandy-legged mandy about being sacked.

Steve Took's contribution to the first three Ty Rex albums cannot be overstated. He is all over them, doing a virtuoso turn of ten-fingered percussion, arranging and providing exceedingly freaky harmonies and genuinely disturbing feral animal noises. In producer Tony Visconti's words, 'Steve and Marc were very much equal partners.'

By 1972, Marc Bolan was such a huge star that he was fronting a 'Keep Britain Tidy' campaign on billboards over the country's city centres. Over in Ladbroke Grove, Steve Took was helping to keep Britain untidy.[4] He had already been kicked out of the utterly deviant Pink Fairies – who he had been a co-founder of – for a drunken, prolonged harangue of the audience at a 'show' in Manchester and for being entirely, er, 'un-together, man', which by Pink Fairies' standards must have been quite an achievement. He was now fronting the terrifying hard rock group Shagrat, with soon-to-be Pink Fairy, Larry Wallis.

Shagrat – Steve Took, Tim Taylor on bass and psychedelic Lazza Wallis on guitar – appropriately took their name from a minor Middle Earth antagonist in the ever-present 'Lord of

---

[4] Took appeared in a spoof advert in *Frendz* magazine. 'Keep Britain Tidy – Eat shit' written underneath Took's photo.

the Sodding Rings'. There have been many blink-and-you-miss-them-cos-they-barely-existed mythical bands in rock – Larry Wallis's magnificently named Entire Sioux Nation, Cleveland's Electric Eels and Rocket from the Tombs, London's Flies and New York's Flies, Brighton's Dodgems[5] – but perhaps the greatest blink-and-you-miss-them-'cos-they-barely-existed mythical band in rock were Shagrat. The only documentation of Shagrat's brief non-career is a small collection of seven demos, with titles like 'Still Yawning, Still Born', 'Boo! I Said Freeze' and the demonic 'Steel Abortion'.

Shagrat were all about drugs. In all probability Shagrat were made entirely of drugs, making such modern lightweights as the dreary, sweaty Fat White Family sound like a Nancy Reagan tribute act. It goes without saying that as brilliant and disturbing as Shagrat were, they were utterly doomed. Larry and Steve trudged back to Ladbroke Grove; Lazza joined the Pink Fairies, and Steve Took continued on his one-man mission to rid London of drugs by taking them all for himself.

For someone who had effectively been written out of rock history for three decades Steve Took 'did' a lot in the '70s. By 1972 he was living in ex-Move and T. Rex manager, Tony Secunda's Mayfair flat, and was seemingly one of the few old friends that the dissolute and dislocated Syd Barrett – who Bolan idolised – was still seeing. Secunda having recently been fired by Bolan installed Took, perhaps as some kind

---

[5] My own band, Black Box Recorder, covered the Dodgems' 'best-known' song, the marvellous 'Lord Lucan is Missing'.

of revenge against Marc, in a basement studio to work on that elusive masterpiece. Much was recorded, some of it brilliant ('Flophouse Blues'), much of it a Mandrax, heroin fug of missed opportunity. Syd turns up, trying to make sense of a guitar on a few tracks, unless it's not him, and it's someone else trying to make sense of a guitar. It's that kind of scene.

It was around about this time – 1972 – that Bolan was asked by the *Melody Maker* what had happened to his one-time partner, Steve Took. Marc replied that he was 'probably in a gutter somewhere in Ladbroke Grove'. A rare appearance in the mainstream music press, and very much the perception of Steve Peregrin Took for the next three decades.

More short-lived bands were formed. More opportunities were, perhaps, squandered. Good time 'Tookie' turned up at benefits and CND festivals doing a rambling shambling head/comedy turn. Charles Shaar Murray wrote of this period: 'Most people know who Steve Peregrin Took is, but few people know what he does. A few more know him as a somewhat bizarre figure who materialises at concerts, armed only with an Epiphone guitar, performing a freeform set of songs, raps, jokes and anything else that flashes through his mind.'

In 1974, Steve Took was due to support Hawkwind's resident Space Poet Robert Calvert on his Captain Lockheed and the Starfighters album tour. The tour proved to be financially unviable and didn't happen. Of course.

At the end of the 1970s decade Took had managed to get a genuinely great band together with a couple of future members of Nik Turner's Inner City Unit: Steve Took's

Horns – named after a horned pendant that Took habitually wore. As ever, Steve Took's Horns couldn't keep Took's attention and they were over before they had a chance. But would an 'old' Freak like Steve Took stand a chance in the decade that Super Dave Bowie predicted would become known as 'The dreadful 1980s'?

'What the fuck is this bullshit?' I thought to myself as I put *Unicorn* on my mum and dad's old gramophone that by 1980 had now found its way into my bedroom. This wasn't what T. Rex sounded like in my misremembered mind. But then, back in the days when I would really *obsess* over records, eventually it all started to make a really weird kind of sense. Within a few weeks I loved Tyrannosaurus Rex. Sure, in years to come I would come to love *Electric Warrior*, *The Slider*, *Tanx* and all things Marc. But right now, as the kids in my class were dancing to 'Baggy Trousers' at the school disco, I was at home, brooding on *Unicorn*.

Steve Peregrin Took died on Monday, 27 October 1980, aged thirty-one. He was living in Notting Hill Gate in west London with his girlfriend Valerie Billiet and her daughter. Steve had recently received a royalty cheque for the three Tyrannosaurus Rex albums that he featured on. The couple decided to have a blowout. They took magic mushrooms and injected themselves with morphine. Took's cause of death is often given as 'drugs misadventure' but his death certificate states the cause as 'asphyxiation of a cocktail cherry'. A death as murky as his life. With my adolescent purchase of 'Unicorn/A Beard of Stars' I sometimes wonder if I contributed to that last blowout royalty cheque.

CHAPTER 8

Mick Farren ruined my marriage

Part two of the early '70s Freak trilogy.

30 July 2013. I am playing the Borderline Club in Goslett Yard[1] in London's West End. I am performing my new elpee: *Rock 'n' Roll Animals* – you know it, the psychedelic children's story about Gene Vincent, the Cat, Jimmy

---

[1] Goslett Yard is the location where Freddie Mills' dead body was found. 'Freddie Mills is Dead' is a song on my *Off My Rocker at the Art School Bop* solo elpee of 2006. Mills was perhaps the first real post-war British 'celebrity'. A boxer and the World Light-Heavyweight champ from 1948 to 1950. Post-boxing career, Freddie became a beloved entertainer, and a restaurant owner (Freddie Mills' Chinese Restaurant opened in 1946 was the UK's first Chinese restaurant). Mills appeared in 1961 as the subject on *This Is Your Life*. If Freddie is known today, it is perhaps due to the manner of his death: on 15 July 1965 Mills' dead body was found in his car outside Goslett Yard, W1, a fairground rifle by his side and a bullet through his eye. A verdict of suicide was given. There are, of course, many rumours surrounding the life and death of Freddie Mills...

FREAKS OUT!

Pursey, a Fox, and Nick (Lowe), the Badger. When I say I am 'playing my new elpee', I mean I am 'acting it out'.

It's an insanely hot night in a bastard London heatwave. Two hundred and fifty people, mainly middle-aged, mainly male (okay, entirely male), are sweating it out in the cramped basement, waiting for me to impart the ancient knowledge of the battle against the Angel of the North that took place in the Surrey Delta and was passed down to me by home counties' elders. The album's reviews have been great. If I were younger, I'd be 'back, back, back'. Nowadays, I'm just 'back'. I'm no longer twenty-five years old. I am forty-five years old. Running around town with a puffed-up head is no longer an option. I just do what I want. There is, and there never really was, anyone to answer to. Only God. And apparently Mick Farren.

Mick Farren: ex-Deviant, almost Pink Fairy, UFO doorman, David Frost botherer, Germaine Greer beau and botherer, partner in crime to previous chapter anti-hero Steve Peregrin Took. White Panther, poet, solo act. *International Times* editor. *NME* punk flagpole hoister. Author.

Mick Farren had done a turn on the Borderline stage two nights before my own turn. Mick ended his 'turn' by pulling out the big one: dying. Not metaphorical dying. Nope, literal toes-up bucket hoofing dying. Old skool. Dead like Dimebag Darrell. Dead like Tommy Cooper. Sid James dead. Eric Morecambe dead. On-stage dead. There is an old 'showbiz' tradition/warning/superstition: Never be the next person on stage after a turn has gone stiff. I am that person. Bugger.

MICK FARREN RUINED MY MARRIAGE

Back to 1957, ex-Shepherds Bush estate agent and now notorious slum landlord Peter Rachman had annexed large parts of west London, minimised statutory rent controls and filled up properties with recently migrated West Indians. On 24 August 1958, English Teddy Boys committed a serious of racial assaults on six West Indian men. Later that night, up to 400 white people attacked the houses of West Indians in the Notting Hill area. Violent disturbances – that became known as the Notting Hill Riots – lasted until 10 September. A hundred and eight people – seventy-two white, thirty-six black – were charged with violent crimes. The area of west London was blacklisted for property development as a consequence of the Notting Hill Race Riots. Portobello, Notting Hill Gate, Westbourne Park and Ladbroke Grove fell into a state of dereliction. Enter the Freaks.

If Steve Peregrin Took was the Freaks' Freak, then Mick Farren was the Freak El Presidente, running around Ladbroke Grove agitating, facilitating, 'freaktaiting', man. Mick wasn't really a Freak. He had the look, the honky afro, the studded belt, the aviators, the White Panther bullshit, the harangue, the serious motherfucker *aaaatttttituuude*. But the one thing Farren couldn't be was a real Freak. He was the editor of *International Times*, fer Chrissake, and then, he wrote for the *NME*. No one who has ever worked for the *NME* in any way could be described as a Freak. Mick was too together, man. Organising benefits, organising festivals, trying to start a revolution, trying to start *the* revolution, Mick was just too busy doing stuff. Just about the only thing Mick Farren couldn't do was the one thing he really wanted to do, and that was to be able to sing.²

The Deviants – Mick Farren's group – were a whole bag of smash-it-up, burn-it-down, kick-it-till-it-breaks good agitating fun. The band's history is long, entwined and meandering, with a revolving Deviant door of membership. Much like any fiscally challenged band, the Deviants found it hard to hold a line-up together, and if there's no audience, then there is no dough,³ so it follows that there is no drummer, and where there is no drummer, there is no bass player. That said, the Deviants did manage to knock out a trio of frayed-shoestring-budget decent albums that may or may not have been much improved with a 'better' vocalist.

And then there was Twink: John Adler, drummer with Tomorrow and the Pretty Things. Underground Scenemaker and general bad egg . . . or good egg, depending on how you like your eggs done (keep eggs in the forefront of your mind, they will feature later). Twink had been a prime mover in 'The Pink Fairies Drinking Club and Motorcycle Gang', a boozing and drug-taking Freak gang, whose main purpose was to do what was said on the tin: get drunk, take

---

[2] I remark on Mick Farren's singing ability, or lack of, as this is often pointed out as evidence of the Deviants' failure. Perhaps. In general regard to 'singing', I firmly believe that you sing with the voice that you have, and that is good enough.

[3] Mark E. Smith's legendary hire 'em and fire 'em schtick is, I suspect, more to do with the Fall's seemingly permanent wobbly fiscal state than Smith's concept of constantly changing the band line-up to keep it 'fresh'. A line swallowed by many.

drugs, and disrupt each other's, or anyone else's gig. A noble cause, of course. Members included Farren, Steve Took, Twink, Phil May and Jon Povey from the Pretty Things, and – according to Mick Farren – 'a bemused Syd Barrett' (there is no evidence of anyone in the Pink Fairies Drinking Club and Motorcycle Gang actually owning a motorbike). As perhaps an afterthought to all this utterly worthwhile nonsense, Twink was also about to become an actual Pink Fairy, and was about to give the universe one of the great insurrectionary punk-as-fuck anthems of all time, in the bovver-boot, heavy flower-power, freethinking classic: 'Do It'.[4] But first there was *Think Pink*.

Released on April Fool's Day 1970 as a kind of 'warm-up' to the Pink Fairies' debut album, *Never, Never Land*. *Think Pink* is one badass, bummed-out trip, stink-up-the-muthafuckin-room, nasty-drug attitude, heavy-as-fuck, motherfucker of a disc. Recorded in December '69, it's the aural equal to Danny the drug dealer's speech about the end of the '60s in *Withnail & I*. It's the real soundtrack to *Performance* beamed in with a 3 a.m. 1969 comedown from Turner's Powis Square basement, but with no money and, even worse, drugs. What hope is there for an album that starts with Twink intoning from the Book of Revelations on opener 'The Coming of The Other One', against a backdrop of Steve Peregrin Took's reliably horrifying animal screams? Took and Mick Farren – who did an oddly brilliant production job – are

---

[4] Sample lyric: 'Don't write about it . . . just do it. Don't think about it . . . do it. It's rock 'n' roll man . . . just do it'.

FREAKS OUT!

all over *Think Pink* and Took contributes his only two compositions released during his lifetime: 'Three Little Piggies' and the weirdly diseased 'The Sparrow is a Sign'. One can only tip one's crushed velvet fedora and salute whichever deluded poor record label bastard sanctioned Twink to go forth with this enterprise, and imagine what the suits at Polydor thought when this most excellent stinking pile of fuck-U dung got dumped upon the desk.

By 1970, the Deviants had given up after more sackings and disastrous tours. Mick Farren found himself deserted and sacked by his fellow Deviants, in America, and free to have his own drug meltdown and make his one masterpiece.

If you were to destroy your entire record collection – and why not? – just leaving one artefact to remind yourself of the utter wonton, unholy, righteous, free-thinking, dumb-as-fuck, balls-on-the-goddamn-sacrificial-slab genius that is the great folk-art experiment known as, uh-huh, 'rock 'n' roll', then you could do worse than make that one artefact Mick Farren's *Mona – The Carnivorous Circus*.

Mona – The Carnivorous Circus might be politely described as a montage of audio-vérité and, er, 'rock 'n' roll standards'. But then no one would want to 'politely' describe something as deviant as *Mona – The Carnivorous Circus*. That would be to attribute some kind of commercial worth to this mudslide of blurgh. This whole nervous breakdown of a record starts off with a freakbeat version of Bo Diddley's version of Ellas McDaniel's 'Mona'. Mick doesn't bother singing any more (a good move). He just snarls with teeth bared, like the devil on David Frost's shoulder.[5] The band are all killer-diller: Twink on drums, Steve Hammond on guitar, Johnny Gustafson on bass (Gustafson was a member of Liverpool's Big 3, whose drummer, Johnny Hutchinson, was headhunted to be a Beatle. Hutchinson hated the Beatles and turned them down. He never once regretted his decision!). And future Grammy Award winner Paul Buckmaster provided early use of cello as pure rock instrument.

Much as literary bores will claim that 'everything you need is in the pages of *Ulysses*', the same could be said of *Mona – The Carnivorous Circus*, except rock bores tend not to have heard *Mona – The Carnivorous Circus*, an album that is unlikely to be joining the serious canon of serious rock anytime soon.

There are three (ish) songs on *Mona*. The title track twice; in short and evil form and again in longer and more evil form. And then there is an extremely low-slung and heavy version of 'Summertime Blues' and, yes, read it here: it is better than Eddie Cochran's original. Between the attempts at the orthodox there are two sound collages. This is the meat and gristle of *Mona*. We get to hear Farren interviewing British Hells Angels boasting about 'beating the shit out of the Irishman', and Steve Took talking about his experience in the nick – 'unscrewing radios and putting them back

---

[5] Mick Farren's best TV appearance is on the *David Frost Show*, 5 October 1970. Known as the 'Frost Freakout'. The self-serving one really came unstuck when he invited a bunch of long hairs on to debate the state of the nation. Farren stands up and does a lot of finger-jabbing at Frost. Jerry Rubin smokes a joint, and Felix Dennis tries hard. Freaks invade the set. Excellent fun. Seek it out.

together' and eating raw potatoes. Some kind of reckoning for the whole horror show that is *Mona – The Carnivorous Circus* is suggested at the end of side one, as Farren, Took and Twink begin a five-minute chant of 'Who Needs the Egg?' that rises to such levels of intensity that the listener feels like crying, 'I don't know – please just leave me the fuck alone.'

Mona – The Carnivorous Circus (released late 1970) was Mick Farren's last album for eight years. There were a few forays into lyric writing with Lemmy and for the Pink Fairies,[6] but after the apocalyptic nastiness of *Mona – The Carnivorous Circus* what more was there to say? As if to prove this point, Mick Farren went on to write for the *NME* in the 1970s.

When I made the *Rock 'n' Roll Animals* album, I hadn't realised that Mick Farren, now two days dead, had been such a Gene Vincent fanatic. As Gene appeared on my album in the form of a ship's cat (Vincent was in the US Navy, lest we forget), I figured that the best way to make peace with the gods of karma would be to read out on stage Mick Farren's John the Baptist soliloquy to the time that Gene Vincent played in Brighton. The audience were rapt as I solemnly intoned Farren's most righteous words to his hero. A prayer from the recently dead to the long dead. The whole show had been a success.

One week later, after the Borderline show, my wife left me. So much for the gods of karma and rock 'n' roll. Never follow a dead man on to the stage.

---

[6] 'Lost Johnny' with Lemmy on Hawkwind's *Hall of the Mountain Grill*, and 'When's the Fun Begin' on the Fairies' *Kings of Oblivion*.

CHAPTER 9

Mad Bob from Margate

Part three of the early '70s Freak trilogy.
Bob Calvert and how to build your own orgone accumulator.

I am sitting in a wardrobe. A wardrobe I have modified. If I sit here long enough, maybe I'll end up in Narnia. That or I'll get so horny that my motherfucking balls will explode. Woah! You see I am sitting in an orgone accumulator, my own homemade orgone accumulator. And the foremost function of the orgone accumulator is to give the orgone recipient the horn. When Wilhelm Reich, the discoverer of the orgone, built his first orgone accumulator in 1940 he was interested in harnessing magnetic rays and turning them into 'orgone' energy. What he actually did was send the world's finest Freaks off to the moon with a massive boner.

First we need to do the science bit. I'll make this easy: Wilhelm Reich was a second-generation Freudian shrink practising in Vienna. We don't need to worry too much about this. Reich, like his mentor Sigmund Freud, was obsessed with horniness and getting horny. Reich reckoned that the 'libidinal energy' that Freud was interested in was the energy of life itself. This is unarguable really. Reich decided that 'orgones were everywhere' (much like Mojo Nixon had decided that 'Elvis is Everywhere'). All Reich had to do was find a way of harnessing this elusive orgone energy and this would lead to a huge improvement in all walks of human life, and humans would be hornier. So, in 1940, Reich constructed his first orgone accumulator.

All the real gone heads loved orgone accumulating. Wild Bill Burroughs built his first orgone accumulator – or 'orgone box', as he liked to call them – in 1949 on a friend's farm in Texas. Dorothy Kilgallen, Johnnie Ray's columnist confidante, published a memo addressed to Lyndon B. Johnson about 'orgone energy'. J. D. Salinger, Saul Bellow and even Norman Mailer all dug the potential of orgones. And then there was Bob: Mad Bob from Margate, completing the holy Freak trinity of Brother Mick Farren and Brother Steve Took.

By 1973, buoyed by the success of their surprise hit single 'Silver Machine', Hawkwind were at their imperial peak. The royalties from this deathless space-biker standard, written by Bob Calvert – not about motorbikes but about riding his pushbike around Margate – would be ploughed into Hawkwind's most highly righteous manifesto: *The Space Ritual*, a live double album.

MAD BOB FROM MARGATE

The Space Ritual was an attempt to represent ideas of metaphysics, dimensional metamorphosis, suspended animation and music of the spheres. Sure. Of course what *The Space Ritual* really was: a hard rock prolapse of the mind on a fuck tonne of drugs. The advertising poster for the original release read '90 minutes of brain damage'. Doubtless the most honest advertising campaign ever.

As a know-it-all teenager, and art student, I had dismissed Hawkwind as simple-minded, undisciplined free-festival space cadets. The provincial early '80s were the hinterland of one of the truly forgotten subcultures: the acid punks, or perhaps more accurately: the misnomer-ed punks, as all the acid punks I came across were inevitably off their blocks on sulphate and worse – amyl nitrate. The acid punks traded in a lethal toxicity of pure nihilism and really bad cheap concrete-comedown drugs. The acid punks were randomly violent and not often super bright, in some way bridging the gap between third generation punk bands (Chron Gen, Anti-Pasti, the Exploited, English Dogs, the anarcho-punk of Crass and Poison Girls), to the burgeoning travelling scene. Hawkwind straddled the whole fucking mess. While there's no doubt that Hawkwind were certainly a Ladbroke Grove Freak band, they weren't all Freaks. Sure, Lemmy was a speed freak, and topless-dancing petrol pump attendant Stasia was a Freak for real (and a first glimpse of Freak crumpet for the adolescent Freaks). But Hawkwind were too of the people and for the people to be Freaks, and weird as it is, under Captain Dave Brock's ultra-authoritarian regime,

Hawkwind were just too much of a well-ordered warrior fighting unit.

Bob Calvert was of course the real Freak genius of Hawkwind's imperial period (1969–79). He's not on all the albums – when he wasn't scrawling out visionary space poetry or writing plays he was often convalescing in the psychiatric unit – but even when he's not there, he's there, on the deep six dive into nowhere that was second elpee, *In Search of Space*, based on a Calvert concept of the three-dimensional Hawkwind trying to escape their spaceship only to find themselves trapped within the two-dimensional design of Barney Bubbles' gatefold sleeve. There are no Calvert songs on *In Search of Space* and he doesn't appear on the album, but much as Syd Barrett is not on Floyd's *Wish You Were Here*, he is all over it. There is no Calvert on the next album, *Doremi Fasol Latido*, as he was in the psych unit again. But then came the hit singles; both co-writes with Commander Brock: the Lemmy-sung 'Silver Machine', followed up, ludicrously and brilliantly, by Bob's homage to terrorism du jour, 'Urban Guerrilla'. And then, the power and the glory of *The Space Ritual* with Bob as 'Space Poet' and MC leading the whole demented cacophony in his signature song, 'Orgone Accumulator'. An anthem for the horniest of the heads.

As Hawkwind were grooving around in space, Calvert was crashing back down to earth. His 1974 solo concept album, *Captain Lockhead and the Starfighters*, is surely number one for ever in the greatest albums about the Luftwaffe purchasing schonky aircraft from the US military. Here is

MAD BOB FROM MARGATE

the military history bit: after the Second World War, the German Air Ministry, with its hands tied behind its back due to allied post-Second World War munitions restrictions, purchased 916 Lockheed F-104 Starfighters from the US government. Whether the US government knew that the aircraft were faulty remains in the realm of conspiracy even today. Nevertheless, almost 300 of the starfighters were lost in accidents. The Lockheed F104 was grimly nicknamed 'The Widow Maker'. Oh. Bad vibes.

Captain Lockheed and the Starfighters was essentially a Hawkwind album, with a score of primo early '70s industrially heavy space-rock numbers interspersed by spoken-word satirical skits performed by Calvert and Viv Stanshall.[1] The rest of *The Space Ritual* period Hawkwind line-up are all over this no-half-measures classic, with walk-ons from every Ladbroke Grove Freak: Paul Rudolph, ex of the Pink Fairies soon to be in Hawkwind, Twink, Steve Peregrin Took (of course), Arthur Brown – on the quite astonishing 'Song of the Gremlin' – and just to make sure that people don't have too much fun, Big Brian Eno.[2]

As with any true unpredictable head, Bob's follow-up album to *Captain Lockheed*, 1975's *Lucky Leif and the Longships*,

---

[1] The reader may be wondering why there is no Viv Stanshall in this book. I'm afraid, from *Sir Henry at Rawlinson End* to *Teddy Boys Don't Knit*, I have always been rather immune to the charms of Viv.

[2] A friend describes Eno as: 'a private dentist from Suffolk.' It's not that I really dislike Eno's earlier albums, it's that I view him with extreme suspicion! A Freak does not shy away from adopting unreasonable attitudes and striking a pose on top of a plinth.

was something of miss-shot. The brilliant concept: the possibility that American culture would have been vastly different if the Vikings had managed to invade the land of the free, felt too heavy for Eno's (sigh) weedy balsawood production. It's fair to say that Bob Calvert didn't scrimp when it came to committing to an idea though. None more so than with his return to Hawkwind. This time as full-on frontman.

After Lemmy's famous sacking – 'for taking the wrong kind of drugs' (speed) – during an American tour, Hawkwind were floundering. Their next album, *Astounding Sounds, Amazing Music*, is the first of the returning Calvert offerings. And it's great when Calvert is fully there as on, 'Steppenwolf', 'Reefer Madness', 'Kerb Crawler'. Less so when ex-Pink Fairy Paul Rudolph offers up his disastrous 'funk' instrumental, 'The Aubergine that Ate Rangoon', which one can only hope was an act of deliberate sabotage by the Canadian guitar warrior for being demoted (in true logic-defying Hawkwind tradition) to playing bass.

Bob Calvert's perhaps most memorable Hawk moment in the sun came with 1979's *Quark, Strangeness and Charm*, sometimes attributed to being 'New Wave Hawkwind'. It sounds more like Calvert and Brock dosed up on a whole load of Dave's so-called Berlin trilogy for this one, as Calvert skewers our current obsession with the dark mythos of AI on the defining anthem 'Spirit Of the Age'. Indeed, Mad Bob splurged out many of his greatest songs on *Quark*: 'Damnation Ally', 'Days of the Underground' and 'Hassan I Sabbah'. Of course, it all went predictably nuts again with an increasingly paranoid and terrorist-obsessed Calvert being dumped by the band on

MAD BOB FROM MARGATE

a European tour. Mad Bob was last seen chasing the group tour bus through Paris while brandishing a samurai sword.

Robert Newton Calvert died too young, of a heart attack aged forty-three, in Ramsgate. One of his four children, Darren, is buried next to him. Much like his father, Darren was a seeker. He joined the Foreign Legion and died after contracting a fatal illness. The word 'Adventurer' is engraved on his tombstone.

With all the knowledge you have accrued within this chapter you too are now ready to build your very own orgone accumulator. This is another science bit. First, you will need a wardrobe large enough for one person to sit in. You will need tin foil (naturally) and cotton wool. Insulate the walls, floor and ceiling of your wardrobe with a layer of tin foil. Next, add a layer of cotton wool. Keep on adding layers of organic material and metallic material. You are now ready to begin accumulating orgones.

Do not sit inside your wardrobe/orgone accumulator for longer than thirty minutes.

And remember: misuse of the orgone accumulator/wardrobe may lead to symptoms of orgone overdose. Headaches, anxiety, loss of libido. If you experience any of these symptoms, leave the vicinity of the accumulator/wardrobe and call a doctor immediately.

CHAPTER 10

Psychedelic Morris Men

Cometh the hour cometh the men.
The Morris Men. Enter Morris.

It had never been my intention to dabble in Morris. But as every traveller knows, there comes a time when the Freak will cross paths with the bowler-hatted, braces-wearing, stick-wielding, bell-jingling, hanky-panky dancing bastards of the English countryside.

In 2011, I was rewriting the history of the world in a theatrical show. For theatrical read: a slide projector — called *The North Sea Scrolls*. 'I' was actually 'we'. 'We' being myself, writer and radio presenter Andrew Mueller and the legendary late Irish singer-songwriter Cathal Coughlan. The narrative of *The North Sea Scrolls* went something like this: some time in a far-off future or unwritten past (time is of no importance in the Scrolls) a manuscript is found in a

FREAKS OUT!

bin in a derelict supermarket car park. The supermarket is thought to be Lidl. This found manuscript comes to be known as *The North Sea Scrolls*, and purports to be the fevered ramblings of a bit-part actor called Tony Allen.[1] Allen, who once had a small role in '70s hard-nut TV plod show *The Sweeney*, claimed to be the artist Francis Bacon and also the man who spiked Fleetwood Mac's Peter Green. Tony Allen had a wild and visionary take on history. His writings tell of a world where Irish gangland boss Martin Cahill is Prime Minister (with Tim Hardin serving as Minister for Health), the radio DJ Chris Evans was a fast-tracked saint and Enoch Powell a team leader on the popular '70s and '80s game show *It's a Knockout* (Powell's team featured members of Gong, the Groundhogs and the Edgar Broughton Band). Perhaps the most disturbing part of Allen's demented document was the involvement of the Morris Men. Rural Herberts[2] protecting their own orthodox 'border' vision of England, clubbing heretics to death with their sticks and bells. It should be noted here that *The North Sea Scrolls* was written some five years before the UK's Brexit vote. It should also be noted that *The North Sea Scrolls* received somewhat 'mixed' reviews.

---

[1] Not to be confused with the legendary Nigerian percussionist.
[2] The popular '60s and '70s term 'Herbert' meaning a low-level hooligan. 'I'll give that long-'aired 'erbert a clip 'round the lugholes' derives from the French term 'Herbertistes', an insurrectionary group in the French Revolution. Possibly.

The Morris Man Cometh

You hear the bells
You heed the warning
You know the Morris Men are coming
No rabbit's foot
or four-leaf clover
protects you from the rambling Herberts
When you stray from the city
an act of Morris may be committed
The Morris Man cometh
The Morris Man cometh
Slapping thighs
and kicking arses
The Morris Man cometh
The Morris Man cometh
Up from Kent
Across Devizes
Now Mr Fox, he walks among us
The ides of spring
Our country masters
We took our leave in the Star and Garter
From prancing aled-up-clogg-dance bastards
Click, click, click
go the sticks
Kick, kick kick
up the arses
Fuck, fuck, fuck
Says the ram

FREAKS OUT!

We have hanky but no panky!
Keep your distance from rural mincers
they'll gouge your eyes out with butchers' fingers
The Morris Man Cometh!

The Morris Men of *The North Sea Scrolls* were deeply un-psychedelic; as un-psychedelic as Noel Gallagher's sock drawer. The Morrises of the Scrolls, or indeed of 'reality', would have been no friend of the Freak. At least that is what I thought.

If you were a head, Freak or a student in late 1972, chances are you were tripping out and bonging off to an un-cosmic but strangely righteous stew: *Morris On*, one of the oddest albums ever recorded. Ostensibly an updated version of – get this – traditional Morris dance music with, ugh, bells on. That is: electric guitar, bass and drums.

Morris On was the brainchild of ex-Fairport Convention man, Ashley Hutchings. Hutchings and the 'Fairports' were occasional Freak enablers, certainly not Freaks. After the horrific Fairport Convention 'breakout' album, *Liege & Lief* (1969), Hutchings went black-ops and deep cover, up the Mekong river into Colonel Kurtz's lair, Cecil Sharp House, where he emerged, bloodied and hallucinating, clutching a pile of ancient Morris dance music in his mad hands. Hutchings was on a mission: to repopularise Morris dancing throughout early-1970s Britain. Recruiting fellow Fairporters Richard Thompson and Dave Mattacks and with the addition of authentic Morris musician John Kirkpatrick,

PSYCHEDELIC MORRIS MEN

Morris On was born. Boasting one of the most ur-Freak front covers ever conceived: Hutchings in full Morris regalia standing on a vacuum hoover wielding a Gibson Flying V. *Morris On* was a huge hit, both commercially and critically. These were strange times.

Perhaps it was only a matter of time before the dreaded spectre of Morris rose up to spread fear across the land. In 1969, there had been reports of a frightening new Morris-Dancing troupe: the Blackheath Foot 'n' Death Men, self-styled 'Psychedelic Morris Men'.

The Blackheath Foot 'n' Death Men's most notorious appearance came at Mick Farren's disastrous 1970 Phun City free festival in Worthing (witness statement: 'it wasn't fun'). Where the Pink Fairies, Shagrat, the MC5, Kevin Ayers, and, erm, Mungo Jerry were among the somewhat bewildered acts who turned up. In between the bad acid and dazed bands, the Foot 'n' Death Men spent their time chasing frightened, tripping hippies up trees, wielding their sticks at them like heavy coshes of oppression. There's a school of thought that says the '60s dream ended either with the Manson murders or with the death of Meredith Hunter at the Stones' free concert at the Altamont Speedway, but I reckon if you were in at the festival in Worthing on bad acid and being chased up a tree by a Morris Man, you might disagree.

The Blackheath Foot 'n' Death Men were a new brand of Morris: brave visionaries willing to take Morris out of its fifteenth-century, Maypole, country-dancing rural bastard past. Dragging it kicking and screaming into the 1970s; a

FREAKS OUT!

brand new agitprop amphetamine-crazed version of Morris. What the Foot 'n' Death Men had not counted on was Ashley Hutchings arming himself with his own orthodox folk-dancing scrolls direct from the fountain of evil: Cecil Sharp House. How did this happen?

By the end of the '60s, the British counterculture was bedraggled and disillusioned, dragged down by in-fighting, bad drugs and interminable theorising from its gurus of the New Left. By late 1969, top New Left guru Herbert Marcuse had abandoned the idea that student leaders such as Rudi Dutschke and the ludicrous Daniel 'La Rouge' Cohn-Bendit would lead a student revolution. Bring on the Angry Brigade.

The 'Angries' had already announced to the prominent leftist activist Tariq Ali that they were intending to bomb the American Embassy at the Grosvenor Square demonstration against the Vietnam War in 1968. Ali begged them not to. Nevertheless, by the end of 1970 the Angry Brigade had claimed responsibility for twenty-five bombings; amazingly, no one was hurt. Space doesn't permit a detailed retelling of the Angry Brigade story here, but according to Jonathon Green's excellent *Days in the Life* history of the English Underground, the counterculture didn't much like the Angry Brigade. Much of the counterculture found even Mick Farren to be 'a bit much', so it's hardly a surprise that they were none too keen on the Angry Brigade. They were too real, too, 'actually trying to kill people', too heavy, just too angry, man. But not in a

PSYCHEDELIC MORRIS MEN

cool pop music way – in an uncool guns and bomb squad kind of way.

The Angry Brigade trial (one of the longest in British legal history) ran from May to December 1970. The revolution, it would seem, was over and there was a new conservatism in the air. Exit the Angry Brigade, enter Ashley Hutchings, Thompson et al. and their ultra-traditional Morris Men.

In December 1972, ex-'60s folkies (and Sandy Denny's old band before Fairport Convention) the Strawbs were rising up the singles chart just about to have a huge hit with their satirical trade-union smashing 'Part of the Union'. Meanwhile, sitting high up in the album charts was *Morris On*. Folk music had taken a strange detour since the days of Pentangle's witchy feminist 'Let No Man Steal Your Thyme' of just four years before.

Morris On went on to spawn several sequels: *Son of Morris On* (1976), *Grandson of Morris On* (2002), *Great Grandson of Morris On* (2004), *Morris On the Road* (2005) and the excellently titled *Mother of all Morris* (2007).

Importantly, it should be stated that *Morris On* is not in any way a bad album – it is in fact a wonderful record, full of rustic weirdness and occasional Morris menace, with in-studio stick dancing by the Chingford Morris Men, no less! But if Ashley Hutchings' writing on the 2002 CD reissue sleeve notes are true – that after *Morris On*, 'Morris dancing and Morris Men enjoyed a massive revival . . .' – then maybe the angry seeds of resentment

FREAKS OUT!

that bloomed into British punk weren't just sewn by the usual suspects – the Eagles, Rod Stewart, Pink Floyd, Yes, Genesis et al. – but also by Ashley Hutchings and his demented visions of a New England in thrall to the *Way of the Morris*. Perhaps in some way UK punk was partly a protest against the Morris Men.

* * *

It is 2015. I have just recorded an album called *Smash the System*. The album is a kind of rural occult protest album. We are now a few years on from *The North Sea Scrolls* and the Brexit Project is coming sharply into view, as Tory Prime Minister David Cameron, upon winning a small majority at the 2015 general election, promises the public a referendum on leaving Europe. The Morris Men of *The North Sea Scrolls* seem to be back and this time they don't need clay pipes and handkerchiefs to terrorise the country. This time they can just make the mark of an X in a polling booth to preserve the 'old ways'.

I stumble upon a 1969 photograph of Morris Dancers on the prowl in Devizes, Wiltshire. Running amok through the town, their be-belled kneecaps aloft and their sticks held high, ready to act out Morris heavy manners. This picture will become the cover to my *Smash the System* elpee. Next, I need a video for the album's title track. Film-makers Tim Plester and Rob Curry step up. Rob and Tim have form – they have made the aforementioned excellent documentary, *Way of the Morris*. Better still, Tim is a member of a Morris troupe.

PSYCHEDELIC MORRIS MEN

Come video shoot day and we have procured a troupe of Morris Men,[3] who Tim and Rob will follow with a camera as they dance through the pubs of London's East End. Some of the Morris dancers are brandishing signs that I have made: 'Heavy Morris', 'I Like the Monkees' and 'Do You Like the Monkees?'[4] I follow them around wearing Morris bells and waistcoat, lip-syncing in a Second World War gas mask.

A few days after filming, and I am trying to find out who this urban Morris troupe are. It seems they come from Blackheath, a handful of them are getting on in years. A few hours' detective work provides the answer: I have made a video with the original Blackheath Foot 'n' Death Men. Woah.

Postscript

As we approach the quarter of the twenty-first century, it transpires that Morris continues to make cultural ripples. Boss Morris are a female Morris group who call themselves 'creatives'. They are apparently a prog rock Morris troupe, they perform at music festivals and give 'workshops' in Morris dancing. Once again, post-Brexit, Morris is on the rise.

---

[3] Up until the 1950s Morris dancing had been decreed a strictly male practice. However, there were troupes of female Morris dancers in the early seventeenth century. The Women's Morris Federation was founded in 1975.

[4] For the ever-confused reader, the song 'Smash the System' features the chorus, 'I like the Monkees, do ya like the Monkees?'

CHAPTER 11

Something entirely fucked up

An obituary for my friend, Cathal Coughlan.

The real star of the last chapter deserves a chapter of his own: Cathal Coughlan. My dear friend Cathal Coughlan died on 18 May 2022. There were fulsome obituaries in the national press and music magazines, and outpourings of shock and grief on social media. The love and loss was real. I was sad and angry at many things: the loss of my friend, who I had been unable to see due to the Covid lockdowns, the indifference of disease and, as ever, those that can only wake up after the death of a Cathal, that wouldn't or couldn't sing what should have been considerable praise, and who were asleep for much of Cathal's visionary and uncompromising artistic life.

I was introduced to Cathal Coughlan at the turn of the twenty-first century by Andrew Mueller. I was aware of Cathal's previous: The feted and much-adored by John

FREAKS OUT!

Peel, Microdisney, and the cage-rattlingly confrontational Fatima Mansions. I knew about the riot at the Fatima Mansions U2 support show in Rome; there was an incident involving a crucifix inserted into a part of Cathal's anatomy (in telling this story, CC was always somewhat coy, so I am being uncharacteristically coy in my retelling!). I may have been aware of the existence of Cathal's music, but I had heard none of it. Friends had enthused but I'd somehow missed it. What I really knew of Cathal was his fearsome reputation and there it was drawn out on his stern countenance several feet in front of me on a late December evening.

Cathal had long forsworn off the easy social lubricant of alcohol. I had not. Our first encounter was, perhaps unpromising, as I babbled a one-way monologue at a stone-cold sober Cathal about the 'genius' of David Crosby. Cathal politely accepted my inane Crosby, Stills, Nash & Young blatherings with wit and bemusement. Like Roy Keane, Cathal was a Cork man. We became firm and easy friends.

At this point, in the early 2000s, Cathal's career was adrift and solo, and skewered by an unholy semi-legitimate record label that he had got himself signed to. These kind of contractual spider webs are everywhere, unseen and spun, like landmines. It's not a matter of 'if' you step on one, it's a matter of when. This enforced wilderness was playing out heavily on Cathal's mind.

Andrew Mueller, our friend, had for some time convinced himself that what the world really needed was a collaboration between myself and Cathal Coughlan. I was in quite a jolly place at the time. I'd discovered the sweet spot between appearing to not give a flying fuck, not giving a flying fuck born out of expedience and not

SOMETHING ENTIRELY FUCKED UP

actually giving a flying fuck because when you cease to give a flying fuck, God tends to step in with His own ideas anyway. It was working out rather well. Cathal also didn't give a flying fuck, because, alas, he was more fucked than I. So in the spirit of we are fucked anyway, we decided to produce something entirely fucked up.

Writing, recording and performing *The North Sea Scrolls* was a rare joy. Cathal was a fierce and intense live performer. He played it straight at all times. One of my fondest memories of *The North Sea Scrolls* live was catching Cathal trying not to corpse while singing the falsetto chorus of 'The Morris Man Cometh'. I gave the Scrolls some of my wildest shots but Cathal bested me. Cathal has written many songs beloved by his growing number of fans. 'The Australian IRA Show' is perhaps not one of his better known, but it should be:

> *All tomorrow's parties*
> *Our agent says it's called*
> *As we pull up in the seaside rain*
> *To the Butlin's bingo hall*

We met, the three of us, Andrew, myself and Cathal, for a *North Sea Scrolls* dinner three or four times a year, in an unpromising Vietnamese diner in east London's Dalston. As the service and menace from the staff increased in intensity, the more determined we became to meet at this dump.

Cathal told us about his diagnosis a few months before the Covid lockdown of 2020. As ever, life, and what it can dish out and serve up cold, was proving to be unfair to Cathal Coughlan. He had just left his job at the BBC to grab the tiger by the tail. That is, pursue his songwriting with a seriousness that he had maybe put to the back of the drawer in the preceding years. His timing was awful and immaculate.

Then Covid hit. Cathal was deep into the writing and recording of what became his last solo album, *The Song of Co-Aklan*. His treatment was seemingly going well and he was cautiously optimistic. I played some bass and guitar on a few tracks before lockdown claimed us all. And that was the last time I saw him.

In the next eighteen months, Cathal released three brilliant albums – for me his best work, *Song of Co-Aklan* and *a Dó* and *a hAon*, two collaborations with producer Jacknife Lee under the name of Telefís. I kept in contact with Cathal only by email and phone calls. He was having to strictly shield from Covid due to the nature of his illness, so even when lockdown was lifted he couldn't be visited.

In late April 2022, Andrew and I received news that Cathal was able to meet up outside. It would have been our first face-to-face meeting for two years. It didn't happen. Cathal died a few weeks later.

I'm not sure if Cathal was a Freak. I think he would have balked and dismissed it as something only protestants could do (as he memorably did in the instance of Irish cricket). He would have enjoyed being in this book. I just wish he was here to read it. And like all the best, he enabled me. But that's to miss the point. I wrote this section for a friend I miss every day. Life's shortcomings are underexposed since my friend went AWOL. Cathal Coughlan was too much of a force of nature to be dust. He's somewhere, and wherever that is, I hope he is okay. For now, take this small offering. One day the library will be full of books about Cathal Coughlan. Until then.

CHAPTER 12

Male Genius Myth Buster – (Thomas Chatterton teenage rampage)

In which romantic fatalism and bohemia go on the bonfire.

Previously, in Chapter 6, a chapter concerning Beatle 'things', the dreaded 'Male Genius Myth', priapic as ever, rose up. Much as we would all like to think about Psychedelic Morris Men for ever, we have to address the Male Genius Myth factor. It will come up again, but for now, while we have it in our crosshairs, let's fire.

Thomas Chatterton, the Boy Poet, was a teenage tearaway. Maybe not quite as much of a hoodlum as Joan of Arc, who went on her own teenage rampage through fifteenth-century France, leading a brutal army in the Hundred Years' War. The Maid of Orleans, under divine guidance, even deployed Gilles de Rais[1] – the proto-Jimmy

---

[1] Gilles de Rais (*c.* 1405–40), French aristocrat, Military commander and occultist. De Rais was found guilty of the murder, sexual abuse and disembowelment of between 100 and 600 children. He was executed on 26 October 1440, in Nantes, France.

FREAKS OUT!

Savile/Gary Glitter, if you will – as one of her leading knights in her bid to coronate some old king or other. Nonetheless, Chatterton was a problem child, whose strange short life would cast an unsung black hand over art, bohemia and rock 'n' roll for centuries to come. Chatterton's pervasive influence is still not done and looks like it will be hanging around like the stale odour of wet dog fur for a good few years to come.

Chatterton, the Boy Poet, was born in 1752 in Bristol, England. Fatherless, poor and extremely precocious and studious. Chatterton's gift to the world was to pass off his own poetry as the work of Thomas Rowley, an entirely fictitious fifteenth-century poet, the product of Chatterton's feverish imagination. All this at the age of eleven. The hoax paid off for a while and Chatterton was lauded as a sort of gatekeeper of the 'classics'. Until downer historian, Horace Walpole, bummed out Chatterton's trip and denounced the kid as a fake! *Quel dommage!*

Whether being rumbled was part of Thomas Chatterton's plan we will never know, but the boy cashed in, went to London and made some influential friends. The radical insurgent John Wilkes was particularly impressed by the Boy Poet, and for a season or two Chatterton was the toast of the chattering classes. Until inevitably, like all teen idols, he wasn't. The hits dried up, the girls and boys were no longer going moist and Chatterton, not even out of his teens himself, was cast, so we are told, into penury.

And so, tragedy struck. At seventeen, Thomas Chatterton, Boy Poet, depressed and despairing, ended his life with an overdose of arsenic. The first 'great artistic suicide'. The original romantic death trip to be followed by van Gogh, Mark Rothko, Kenneth Halliwell, Jim Morrison, Chris Cornell, Elliott Smith, Nick Drake, Ian Curtis and Kurt Cobain.

Except it probably didn't go down that way. Recent research from Bristol University[2] reveals that the two suicide notes found at the Chatterton death scene were likely fakes. That Chatterton was in fact reasonably financially solvent and was successfully publishing his poetry in various journals. Chatterton was also a heavy opium user. The smart money is on Chatterton accidentally taking an overdose of arsenic (laced with his daily intake of the poppy) as an attempted cure for syphilis.

If it is so, that the Boy Poet did not take his own life, it follows that the romantic myth of the struggling yet misunderstood artist must also be debunked by one large chaser of arsenic and pure smack. Oh dear.

Samuel Coleridge, Williams Blake and Wordsworth. Percy Bysshe Shelley and Big Bad Lord Byron. Feisty teenagers Arthur Rimbaud and Paul Verlaine, join the queue, and while you're at it, bring 'outlaw' Keith Richards with you, and every tuppence ha'penny mediocre mind who has fallen for the fatalistic romantic Male Genius Myth over the decades. Gather round, laddies, let me tell you where it all went wrong.

'Oh woe is me,' you poor suffering artists! If, and it is not a big *if*, the Boy Poet did not take his own life, but

---

[2] Dr Nick Broom, Department of English, Bristol University.

just accidentally over-medicated his sore cock, then where does that leave all post eighteenth-century popular culture? And, pray tell, what of the common or garden bohemian?

When my second group – the Auteurs – started out at the end of the last century, the scribes of the day (who incidentally three decades on are still the scribes of the day) wasted no time in branding us as foppish bohemians. Nothing could have been further from the truth. I had rejected all notions of bohemia at an early age, correctly assessing it to be the stuff of soppy bollocks nitwits. What we actually were was premium Art rock. That's Art with a capital A. Art as in Art, not as in 'arty'. There is a universe of difference.[3] At this point the reader may be fretting that this paragraph is perhaps wallowing in pomposity. Especially if you have read the footnote. Quite possibly. But it does illustrate the great problem the Brits have with Art: that Art is a thing to be feared, and when not understood – remember Art does not need to be understood – casually cast aside and dismissed as simple-minded bohemianism.

---

[3] Art has wisely and deliberately covered its arse with a byzantine unseen and unwritten rulebook. Art is quite rightly feared. The bourgeois Art-loving class are the ones who fear Art the most. Art is best understood using the following 'rule': the question is not 'But is it Art?' as everything that calls itself Art is indeed Art. The real question is: 'But is it any good?' The answer, yes or no, is relatively unimportant. It is worth pointing out that every artist I know has no idea what the Art is that they are creating and are as baffled by 'the critic's response' as the average Art baffled man on the Clapham omnibus. The difference between Art and arty is best demonstrated by the following equation: Franz Ferdinand are arty but not Art. Luke Haines is Art.

MALE GENIUS MYTH BUSTER

Of course one cannot be a Byronic bohemian fatalistic romantic without being a male genius. Women tend to get in the way of the Male Genius Myth and are best left as 'footnotes'.[4] After all, Byron, Joyce, Rimbaud and Verlaine were all lads, weren't they? The Male Genius must be mad or be going mad (Brian Wilson, Syd Barrett). Or better still, a kind of exalted genius but 'failed' human (Lennon or Sly Stone). From the late nineteenth century onwards, it has been impossible to accept any kind of artistic 'accomplishment' without invoking 'the myth'. We fear Art, and we fear visionary magic, and mostly we fear the not entirely unreasonable assertion that some people just see the world differently.

Where does the Freak fit in to all of this? The Fatalistic Romantic Myth, the Bohemian Myth and the Male Genius Myth are a full-on declaration of war against the true Freak. The real Freaks do not have to have waded through Thomas De Quincey's stodgy yet acrid prose of *Confessions of an Opium Eater*. Yer actual Freak does not sit in squalor

---

[4] Rather than have a man explain why women are a footnote in the Male Genius Myth, I asked my wife, Rebecca, to give her view. The irony that this is a footnote is not lost. Rebecca: 'Historically there is less tolerance of women displaying "genius" (mythically or otherwise). Women are viewed with suspicion – locked away in attics/loony bins rather than respected as artists. Women still are in some places of the world second-class citizens. Also, there has often been no network of support for female genius, and no benefactors, particularly for those of the lower classes. The male genius is indulged, and the female genius is vilified.'

FREAKS OUT!

with Pete Doherty in a pseudo-bohemian smack den in east London, shooting gunk. The bona-fide Freak needs none of these accoutrements of the chattering classes. The Freak only needs the metaphor of their Freak flag, and the true aim of their Freak bow and arrow.

CHAPTER 13

The Fall can no longer be Freaks

More teenage embarrassment via the Fall group, and why the Fall can no longer be considered as Freaks. More weasel-faced Weller dunces, and an idea borrowed from a Mitford sister.

Make no mistake, genuine Freakdom is a precious 'commodity'. Like a faraway stay in an uninhabitable universe, or a creature on the precipice of extinction. But, alas, no zoo can contain us.

It is early 1982, I am a fourteen-year-old Freakchild. I am sprouting wings. Our school music teacher tells all us scraggy-arsed comprehensive kids that we have to do a presentation on our favourite pop group. 'Yip, yip hoorah,' we all whoop. But for some of us, it won't be 'yip, yip hoorah'. Remember, we are still in the age of the skinhead. The weasel-faced Weller dunces are still running rampant. The fanciable girls and wedge haircut ferret-faced boy-bastards go wild-eyed at the prospect of showing off their knowledge of various Jams, Specials, Adams and (the not very) Nutty Boys. I shrink into my shell, for I know what I have to do.

A year earlier I had discovered the Fall – it was to last for life. I suspected it even then, when Cousin Rob's best friend's punky older brother (it's always punky older brothers) rather helpfully made me a cassette of his Crass singles. All good. (Crass are best listened to and viewed as a singles' band.) But it was the other side of the Dindy C90 – that for some reason he had recorded the Fall's 1980 compilation album, *Early Fall 77–79*, on – that really split my adolescent mind in two. From the manifesto of the first track, 'Repetition', this fourteen-year-old weirdo was smitten.

Within a year I had as many Fall records as I could find and afford – *Live at the Witch Trials*, *Hex Enduction Hour*, *Totale's Turns* – which utterly blew my tiny mind, and the masterpieces, *Grotesque* and *Slates*. It took me a few more years to track down *Dragnet*, which was hard to score in provincial 1982 Portsmouth.

Come music 'presentation' day, I am a dead kid walking, headlong into a blur of humiliation, blushing and ridicule from the keepy-uppy boys and the box-jacket-wearing casual girls. The true Freak is strong though, like a soldier going over the top into certain death, for Freak and country. I press play on the radio cassette recorder.

After the onslaught of 'Baggy Trousers', Modern Romance and Tight Fit, the Fall sound spectacularly crap. It is probably a mistake to start proceedings by playing 'In My Area' from *Totale's Turns*. The footy boys guffaw, the girls point out my shaking hands and reddening face. Even

THE FALL CAN NO LONGER BE FREAKS

the teacher is laughing at me. I wished I'd pretended to like Echo & the Bunnymen instead. But I push on, my face on fire, my hands shaking – a fourteen-year-old with early onset Parkinson's disease. Fifteen lifetime minutes later, I finish with the live 'No Xmas for John Quays', which at least wipes the smirk off the music teacher's face, with Mark E. Smith's exhortation for the group to 'Fuckin' get it together and stop showing off'. On the long walk home, I imagine I am in for a lifetime of being pointed at, ignored and howling into the wilderness. I'm half right. I imagine that Mark E. Smith would have been proud of me.[1]

* * *

Christmas 2013. A signal goes up in the sky to answer the Freak phone. I leap off the sofa and turn *Bargain Hunt* off. The message (okay, it's a text message) reads thus: 'Idea for micro-opera, about Ian Stuart, lead singer of Skrewdriver, crashing into Mark E. Smith's caravan. Forever.' The message is from the artist Scott King. I don't need to hesitate. I've never met Scott before. 'I'm in,' I reply, and press send.

Scott King is an artist of renown. He has been the art director of both *Sleazenation* and *i-D* magazine. He has exhibited a cigarette lighter on a plinth in a Paris gallery. The cigarette lighter belonged to Kurt Cobain.[2] Scott was

---

[1] He wouldn't.
[2] The lighter may not be Kurt's. It could just be a common or garden disposable lighter bought from a common or garden corner shop . . . we may never know.

fortuitously at a Tad show with the nascent Nirvana supporting when Kurt threw the lighter out onto the crowd and Scott miraculously caught it. 'Kurt's' lighter now resides under glass in the French capital, where Japanese tourists gaze at it, absorbing its grail-like secrets and mysteries. Scott has also drawn up plans, applied for planning permission and launched a petition to erect a 300-foot statue of the late singer of Dr Feelgood, Lee Brilleaux, in Southend-on-Sea. This has yet to happen.

The micro-opera that Scott King is proposing has been commissioned by the Berlin Kulture Festival – well, not the exact idea that Scott is proposing, the one about Ian Stuart, Skrewdriver and Mark E. Smith, but *an* idea. Free rein. And so it goes that we will write a micro-opera with actors that will come to be called: *Adventures in Dementia*. The plot – such as it is – concerns a Mark E. Smith impersonator going on holiday with a caravan and crashing into Ian Stuart's car (Stuart being the deceased fascist singer of white power nit-wit band Skrewdriver). First, we take Canvey Island, then we take Berlin.

* * *

The Fall helped make a Freak of me, helped me reach my true Freak potential. It was all there anyway. But then, the unthinkable started to happen.

Did it begin with 1985's *This Nation's Saving Grace*? The album beloved of all rock critics. It's easy to see the reason why. *This Nation's Saving Grace* is an organised rock album,

THE FALL CAN NO LONGER BE FREAKS

by an almost unrecognisably organised Fall group. The soon-to-follow ballet, *I Am Kurious Oranj*, with avant-garde Billy Elliot, Michael Clark, was a step off the right track into the wrong direction (i.e. it was great) but then the late '80s saw further steps in the Fall's journey towards being a 'normal' rock band. Major record labels. Pointless cover versions of the Kinks' 'Victoria', and R. Dean Taylor's 'There's a Ghost in My House'. Sadly, both inferior releases and predictably the only time the Fall scored 'hits'. And then there were the awards! Freaks don't win awards. If the *NME* bestow something called 'Godlike Genius' upon you, then you may have made a wrong turning. Thankfully, Smith always received these plaudits as ungracefully as humanly possible.

And then they came. First, Frank Skinner, then a newsreader guy, Krishnan Guru-Murthy. Proclaiming their love of the Fall. Doubtless both were sincere in their newfound Fall Joy, but to the Freak (well, me) there was the feeling that, guys, *the Fall are not for you, you didn't fight the Freak wars*. Then there was the time that Mark read the football results, and the comedy, car crash, drunken interviews. A strange mid-level of actual fame was achieved, which translated as: known by the wankers in bars as that 'drunk bloke who can't sing but who's a total "legend"'. The Fall, or to be more accurate, Mark E. Smith, became bona-fide famous. The records got admirably stranger and interesting and sold less and less. And then . . . death. The inevitable fast-tracking to canonisation followed. You cannot be a national treasure and a Freak.

FREAKS OUT!

Summer 2014. Scott King and I are in Berlin for a two-night stand to perform our micro-opera, *Adventures in Dementia*.[3] The micro-opera is part of a wider installation called The Festival of Stuff, which features an Ian Curtis dance competition (free for anyone to enter, with a good uptake and high-quality dead fly dancing from the Germans) and Turkish drag artists dancing to 'East' by Earl Brutus. For our micro-opera I have written seven songs, all to be performed live by our actor, who is playing our Mark Smith impersonator. Confused? You will be if you are German and are in the audience over the next two hot nights in Berlin.

Our actor, a twenty-something called Jessie – who is also a male model – has been giving Scott and me the heebie-jeebies during rehearsals. However much he rehearses and researches he just seems to get further and further away from the postcode that even the worst Mark E. Smith impersonator may live in. Obviously, as 'Mark E. Smith impersonator' is not at the time of writing this chapter a recognisable career choice (like, say, being an Elvis impersonator), then we don't really have a barometer to measure the efficaciousness of Mark Smith mimicry. However, we are in too deep now to worry or care.

---

[3] Some months after the performance of *Adventures in Dementia* in Berlin, the soundtrack gets a record release as a 10-inch vinyl EP. One day, Cherry Red (who put out my records and at this time the Fall's records) gets a call in the office. Mark E. Smith is on the end of the line, he has got wind of *Adventures in Dementia*. Let's just say he is not happy and park the caravan there.

THE FALL CAN NO LONGER BE FREAKS

Our stage set consists of a few bits of caravan wreckage, an amplifier for me to plug my Fender Telecaster into and a large screen video backdrop with footage of caravans crashing endlessly into hedges and falling into ditches. Our artist friend Jon Ellery has manfully stepped up to play the part of the dead Ian Stuart, his role mainly to lie motionless on stage for fifteen minutes or so. He looks fucking terrifying in his blood-stained Union Jack flag T-shirt; his shaved bonce bouncing the light onto his thirty-hole yellow-laced Doc Martens.

The lights go up, and something has happened. Jessie has had some kind of supernatural transformative episode. Oh Christ, this is called acting. The thing is, Jessie is very good. He has somehow changed from summer festival-loving weed-head hippie kid into Mark E. Smith. He's become more Mark E. Smith than Mark E. Smith. I start playing the guitar solo to 'Caravan Man', (a psychobilly homage to the Fall's 'Container Drivers' about the pros and cons of taking caravan holidays with ex-spouses), and I notice that the guitar is absent from the cacophony. I glance behind me and see that Jessie is fiddling with my amp while simultaneously rummaging in a carrier bag. The cheeky fucker has gone full Smith. I go over to enthuse and get a push in the chest from Jessie for my trouble, who seems to have taken the Fall's infamous turn at Brownies in New York as his source material. Ten minutes later and Jessie has become fully shamanic. Images of David Baddiel flash up on the screens behind us; somewhere within the byzantine 'plot' of *Adventures in Dementia* the comedian Baddiel has effectively been 'blamed' for 'everything'.

FREAKS OUT!

'Ian Stuart' (not the real one) rises from the dead and lines up with me (the real one, I think) and 'Mark E. Smith' (not the real one, but acting up even worse than the real one), at the front of the stage in a chant of 'David Baddiel' over a finale of feedback and white noise for five inexplicable minutes.

The lights go down. And then go up. The 'cast' take a bow – myself, 'Ian Stuart' and 'Mark E. Smith' – and 200 Berlin Kultur lovers sit in baffled, fearful silence.

CHAPTER 14

Australians in Europe

In which Brisbane comes to London and shows the kids how to do it.

London in 1984 was bleak. I had moved to 'The Smoke' in September of that year. Battle-hardened. Just before term had finished in the summer of 1984, I had been asked to leave Portsmouth College of Art (I was 'surprisingly' an obnoxious little know-it-all). This arrangement suited me fine. In the nick of time, I had managed to secure myself a place at music college in central London studying composition (remember: I was a precocious and obnoxious little know-it-all). On a Friday afternoon my dad drove me up to London. He helped me carry my favourite fifty or so LPs – Iggy, the Velvets, the Modern Lovers – into the room of a shared rented house in Brixton. I was on my own and I was ready for London. Or so I thought. Within a couple of hours and a few tower blocks from where I now lived, the Brixton sky was on fire. I wandered down Railton Road – known to others as 'the frontline' – and watched from the sidelines. Petrified by fear and rocking with adrenalin, as hundreds of advancing dreads hurled petrol bombs at terrified lines of shielded riot police. The second Brixton riots raged for three nights. One of the worst inner-city insurrections Britain had ever seen. My generation had reached the dreaded marker of time: 1984, and London felt like the apocalypse.

The Go-Betweens were the greatest rock 'n' roll band of the '80s – second only to (for me) the beloved Fall – and Robert Forster, the band's 'sonic rhythm guitar' player and co-lead singer, along with the late Grant McLennan, was the first proper Freak I'd ever met; that is a Freak who was really doing it, in a kinda successful rock 'n' roll band.[1] The Go-Betweens land in London from Australia four years into Thatcher's mad, despotic era, and two years into her second term as Prime Minister. Violence was everywhere: at the gigs (from 1981 to early '85, I rarely attended a gig without the ever-present threat of aggro), in the pubs, on the street, in the drugs, in the ever-brooding London weather and in the suspicious British psyche (we will explore London in the '80s further in the next chapter). Into this, the Go-Betweens

---

[1] There was/is a music press mythology about the Go-Betweens, which claims they were commercially unsuccessful. Within the context of the times – the dreadful '80s – when R.E.M. were the only 'guitar rock band' to sell significant amounts of records, the Go-Betweens were relatively successful; they toured the world, they made albums on 'proper' record labels, and they did in fact sell 'enough' records to keep going. Anything more, in the '80s, would have been an anomaly. And it was never going to happen.

had arrived. A band as far away geographically as well as psychically from spiteful London as could be possible, and they were about to give rock 'n' roll their three most memorable albums.

By late 1986, I'd ended up playing lead guitar in a west London band called the Servants. The Servants were great. They'd made a couple of classic singles then broken up. Enter me. Well, better to join a great band on the point of dissolution than not be in a great band at all, I reasoned to myself. Singer-songwriter David Westlake, blessed with songwriting chops to burn, was going to start a new line-up of the Servants (he drolly referred to this line-up of the band as the 'Cut the Crap' Servants). As well as a seemingly endless supply of demon songs, David had a few other tricks up his corduroy sleeves. Not least a deep love for a band that had passed me by: the Go-Betweens. The Servants (pre my tenure) had recently supported the Go-Betweens on tour. So, on a bright October morning, David sat me down in the living room of his parents' council house in Hayes, Middlesex, and played me a VHS recording of the Go-Bs performing on the BBC's *The Old Grey Whistle Test*.

Great rock 'n' roll should be like a Peter Cook joke: sharp and devastatingly funny. The Modern Lovers, late-period Velvets, Iggy, even Big Jim Morrison (okay, often unintentionally) — all funny as hell. The Go-Betweens on the *Whistle Test* was one of those. Grant's 'Apology Accepted' was the first Go-Bs song I ever heard. It was actually a 'song', and upon hearing it, the idea of 'actually' writing songs — something that I'd kind of forgotten I could do — burnt deep into my internal wiring. In the early- to mid-1980s, songs were a rare commodity. Sure, Roddy Frame and Edwyn Collins had been writing them, but elsewhere what later became known as post-punk had rendered the scorched English earth grey; it was all angles, scratches and dust. Dabbling in songs meant you were 'rock' or 'rockist'. Morrissey didn't really write songs – he wrote Morrissey manifestos.

It was the Go-Betweens' second number on *Whistle Test* that really got me. For life. During Grant's 'Apology Accepted' (a kind of Velvets' circa 1970 New Age drone-age confessional), the rhythm guitar player could be seen lurking twitchily with a certain amount of intent. Intent to monopolise the camera, which he did when it was his turn to take the mic. Suddenly the Go-Betweens were led by a towering presence of a man. A man who looked like a rock 'n' roll version of Russ Abbot and a stretched Prince. Quizzical, hammy and earnest simultaneously. Like Jonathan Richman caught in a Motown reverie. Here was a man – Robert Forster – entirely lost in his Freakdom. The song – 'Head Full of Steam' – is of course not only a Go-Betweens' 24-carat classic but an *all-time* classic. When Robert sang the questioning line, 'Can I wash your hair?', I was cracked and floored. Like every all-time 24-carat rock 'n' roll classic 'Head Full of Steam' should have been number one for 600 years. It probably made it to number 600 for one second. Who cares? Only fools and record company drones get into rock 'n' roll to crunch numbers. For a small but significant amount of people in the London music scene of the mid- to late '80s, Robert Forster and Grant McLennan were nothing less than rock 'n' roll gods.

AUSTRALIANS IN EUROPE

Liberty Belle and the Black Diamond Express landed in early 1986. The British music scene was changing. A sketch had been created by Postcard Records at the start of the decade, and now clambering out of the wreckage over a million discarded copies of (the excellent) *Dare*, *Lexicon of Love* and the Bunnymen's attempts to become the scally U2, came a brave generation of fey young men. All of whom wanted to escape the hollow '80s and sound like the Byrds and Love. This, and the *NME*'s inability to sell themselves to the rap and hip-hop kids — the rap kids who already dug rap and cared not a flying Run-DMC what the *NME* was — helped to create the C86 'scene'. The Go-Betweens were viewed as wise elder statesmen by this new micro underground, though *Liberty Belle*... had very little in common with the Byrds or Love, or C86. (It sounded and still does sound contemporary and of its own.) It did have something in common with the Beatles — whether they liked it or not, Robert, Grant, Lindy Morrison and Robert Vickers were the Fab Four of the C86 generation. With Grant as Paul and Robert as John. John the Freak.

Through '86 and '87, via David Westlake, I devoured everything Go-Betweens. Every album sounded different and seemed to come with a soap opera of travails. Here was a band that inhabited a world of the well-travelled and exotic. One of their friends, Peter Milton Walsh, was in, and still is, in a fantastic band called the Apartments. The Apartments' album, *The Evening Visits... and Stays For Years* (which sounded like it was recorded in a busted motel out in the desert), stayed on my record player for years. Best of all, the Go-Betweens were from Brisbane. David and I loved everything Australian: *Neighbours*, *Home and Away*, *The Sullivans*, *Young Doctors*, *Prisoner Cell Block H*, *The Triffids*, *Ed Kuepper* . . . all the best music came from Australia. Just as the Fall had made Prestwich and the Arndale Centre in Manchester seem like the most mysterious places in the world to my teenage self, the Go-Betweens had now done the same with Brisbane.

I didn't meet the Go-Betweens until early 1987. David Westlake and I ended up supporting them at Wolverhampton Polytechnic. Grant and new member Amanda Brown were super friendly, Robert Vickers seemed oddly suspicious, while Lindy . . . well, Lindy was too much for my just-out-of-teenage head to cope with. And Robert? Robert Forster was a star. Polite, otherworldly, palpably a rock 'n' roll star and most importantly: a Freak.

Tallulah from 1987 is my favourite Go-Betweens album. It may not be their best album but it's my favourite. It's their London album. With great songs from Robert – 'The House that Jack Kerouac Built', 'I Just Get Caught Out' and my absolute fave, 'The Clarke Sisters'. Other things I love about *Tallulah*? Grant's stagey tough-guy black eye on the front cover. The way that 'You Tell Me' is really the title track. The should-a-been hit singles, 'Right Here' and 'Bye Bye Pride'. The magnificent B-side, 'When People Are Dead', that should-a-been on the album. Robert's silver hair that wasn't actually silver (the dye job didn't take and his hair is actually blond, but everyone went along with it). And Robert's sleeve credit for 'Sonic Rhythm Guitar'.

AUSTRALIANS IN EUROPE

Tallulah also contains 'Cut it Out', the Go-Betweens' worst song. All great albums have to have a worst song. It's one of the things that makes them great and 'Cut it Out' is heroically bad. David Westlake and I used to listen to it and wince . . . until we convinced ourselves that it sounded like Prince[2] and must therefore be an act of subversive genius.

I got to see the Go-Betweens half a dozen times between 1987 and '88. I got to know Grant a bit. Grant seemed to be the most outgoing and the most out-and-about Go-Between. I have a fond memory of him trying to hustle songs to Tracey Thorn and Ben Watt at the Cricketers pub in Kennington at a sparsely attended Apartments show. In the later post-Go-Between years, whenever I would catch up with Grant, he would always refer to me as 'family'. That meant a lot. Grant even came down to watch David and myself play a gig supporting Felt at Dingwalls in late '87. It was Grant's last night in London before heading back to live in Australia. The London scene was feeling mean again. It was a bitchy night. David and I had made a record on Creation.[3] Alan McGee, who seemed to be spinning a lot of plates at the time, had perhaps understandably lost interest. Grant was encouraging though and said what we

---

[2] The reader should not misinterpret any comments on Prince. My stance on Prince remains consistent. I consider his output to be worthless. I will die on the right side of history.

[3] The album, that would have been the Servants' first album, came out as *Westlake*. It was the first proper album – albeit a 'mini' album, that I had played on. Alsy MacDonald and Martyn Casey from the Triffids played drums and bass. More omnipresent Australians.

were doing was so much better than all the 'Byrds and Velvet imitators'. He said we were young and our time would come. He was wrong about that. Then off he went, back to Oz. The Go-Betweens' next album would be their crowning glory: *16 Lovers Lane*. But for now they were gone.

London was bleak again.

CHAPTER 15

Never work

How the war against work was won.

Perhaps it was down to the faked brain tumour when I was a nine-year-old and the ease in which I carried off two months of school skiving. The secret world of 'daytime TV' – long before daytime TV became a flagellation parade of cooking, bad debt and laughing at poor people – was the making of me. In the 1970s, daytime television was populated by Peter Wyngarde as Jason King: uber heterosex playboy private eye. *The Persuaders*: Roger Moore as uber heterosex playboy 'crime solver' Brett Sinclair; *The Sullivans*: middle-class wartime Australians; *Crown Court*:[1] provincial legal

---

[1] *Crown Court* was set in the fictional town of Fulchester. *Viz* comic, in tribute to *Crown Court*, was also set in Fulchester. Chris Donald started *Viz* while on the Enterprise Allowance Scheme.

people; *House-Party*: 1970s housewives on the verge – but never getting there – of swinging; and *Crossroads*: Brummies. All of these things conspired to mean that one day I would attain my one true achievement in life: black belt third dan in avoiding work.

The 1980s, as noted previously and numerously, were not much fun. It is said by historians that one doesn't really have a 'sense' of the decade when you're actually living in it. The 1950s were not seen as 'the '50s' without hindsight. Ditto the '60s – especially in the UK. The Swinging Sixties was the stuff of a few movies and really wouldn't have touched you if you were not living in a handful of London boroughs. The '80s, I suspect, were different. They felt bad. You could feel the *heavy* in the weather. You could feel the dread in the trees, in the lousy clothes, and throbbing from the 1960s brutalist concrete that was now covered in dirt and mould and towered over the outskirts of cities like huge, petrified lumps of dung. I felt that, having been born in 1967, and becoming a teenager in 1980, I had very much drawn the short straw, generationally speaking.

My 1980s consisted of desperately wanting to get out of the place that I grew up in (you know it – and the thought of the place even now gets me reaching for an extra dose of antidepressants) and then finding out that London was maybe even a 20 mg antidepressant dose worse.

In terms of taking your life in your hands, south London in the mid-1980s was the Wild East. Camberwell and Peckham were no-go areas, unless you were unlucky enough to live in them. My memory of south-east London, Streatham and

NEVER WORK

South Norwood is just of black night darkness. Pubs seemed to be inhabited only by the insane and dangerous; south London had cheap suicide sulphate vibes and the feeling that one was tramping over murdered bodies buried on common ground. Willesden Junction, Harlesden – places I haplessly found myself living – and God praise my luck, Stonebridge Park, were even worse. Forgotten outposts where barely alive old Irish fellas and desiccated toothless West Indians found themselves face to face in a game of chicken, to see who would dare to live the longest. Nobody had any money in London in the 1980s, apart from the wankers in Barnes and Putney.

The leafier parts of north London, Highgate and Hampstead, were alien to me. I had no reason to be in them and more to the point, they had no reason for me to be in them. And then there were the bomb threats. The real sign of the times was when the IRA stepped up their campaign of bomb warnings, and how little notice the ground-level Londoners took of it: 'It's just a bomb threat on the Northern Line, needs must.' That was London in the 1980s.

There was one light, shining as brightly as the split atom of Cold War paranoia: Unemployment.

The 1980s were the golden age of unemployment. I was born with an exceptional conviction that I must never work, and I have successfully avoided work since the day I left school. There should be a blue plaque outside the dole office in Neasden marking the day that I gave my first of many signatures to the DHSS (as it was known then). I never looked forward and I never looked back.

FREAKS OUT!

The true Freak should never be employed in any way. As a Freak, society is not your concern. As it is not your concern, you should feel no guilt in being (what others will describe) a 'burden' upon it. I feel the opposite: that society is very much a burden on me. If you do feel any guilt about any of this then you are probably not a Freak.

My particular 'genre' of unemployment was 'income support'. Income support was a sort of inferior type of unemployment benefit.[2] To receive 'unemployment benefit', the claimant had to have paid enough income tax into the system to be allowed to get a little back, gratis, from the system (not from you, the tax payer, I'm afraid) until you were 'rehabilitated' back into the wonderful world of work and the dignity of labour was once again restored to all and sundry. I had never worked and therefore had paid no income tax into the system, so I was only granted income support. Income support in 1987 was paid at £52 per fortnight. That meant I had £26 to live on per week. A perfect amount. I didn't need anything anyway.

In the Servants, unemployment was a mandatory requirement; *de rigueur*. A lifestyle choice, like mod or becoming a Hells Angel but with less overheads. David Westlake and I would have a routine of meeting once a week, working out a song or two watching *Neighbours*[3] – and later *Home and Away*

---

[2] Although philosophically I would say that income support is superior to unemployment benefit as it demonstrates that the claimant has put in precisely zero working hours.

[3] The comedian Peter Cook's daily routine in the 1980s would consist of watching *Neighbours* at lunchtime, then taking a couple of Es waiting for the tea-time repeat. Time well spent.

– then going to the pub – which though populated by psychopaths was inexplicably in the mid-1980s affordable. Occasionally we would audition a new bass player or a drummer (it was impossible to hold on to drummers and bass players for long). We would never take our potential recruits seriously if they had a job. Unemployment was crucial, a way of life and an attitude. That's all we did for five years: cups of tea, *Neighbours*, pub. An idyllic existence. But, in true '80s style there was always the carrion of doom on the horizon, getting nearer and circling us.

The Restart Interview. David arrives at my flat one day, clearly worried.

'I've been sent on a restart interview,' he announces, brow furrowed. We had heard the whispers in the shadows of the signing-on queue of the 'Restart Interview' before, but we hadn't been bothered. We were premium unemployed people. It couldn't happen to us. Except it could and now it had.

The restart interview was one of Thatcher's innovations in massaging those toppermost of the poppermost 1980s unemployment figures. The concept being that if you'd been unemployed for six months and had been busily applying for jobs in the job centre and failing to get them, then you were in need of being 'restarted'. This meant that you would be sent to sit in a room with a benefits officer, who would then 'interrogate' you about what efforts you had been making in seeking work. Most importantly, had you been 'actively seeking work' (a strong rule of claiming unemployment benefit). If you hadn't been 'actively seeking work', then fuck off out of the Costa del Dole, Pedro. Go and live in a cardboard box on the Southbank. The alternative was to prove that you had been 'actively seeking work'[4] but it just hadn't worked out well and you were still . . . unemployed. At this point in the 'interview', your benefits officer would fill in some slips of paper that would require you to go to something hilariously called 'Job Club', which took place in somewhere I had never visited this place called the 'Job Centre', where you would be sent off to attend 'job interviews'. *Quelle horreur!* There was no option to fail your allocated job interview, as the kind of job you would be offered would be shifting boxes, snorting asbestos or, most likely . . . benefits officer, so that one day you would be on the other side of the chair, sending yourself off to go over the top into the futile no-man's land of gainful employment.

David bluffed his way through his first restart and was back in the unemployment saddle for three months, unbothered by restart interviews. Dole bliss. It was my turn next. I bluffed it, too. The benefits officer was a kind woman, hardly the Rosa Klebb I had expected, who clearly couldn't care less about whether her charges were successfully rehabilitated or not. She smiled wryly at my bullshit and off I went into the balmy unemployed afternoon. David and I got pretty good at restarts. If we knew

---

[4] To be 'actively seeking work' one would have had to visit the 'job centre'. I had no idea where the job centre was.

of anyone who had 'failed' at their 'restart' we would scoff loudly, like witch-finders of dole-dodging, branding them 'lightweights' to their face.

Unemployment was great, but the constant threat of being rumbled as a complete time-waster was becoming a massive drag, and the grind of leaving the house and having to sign on every two weeks was a downer. If these two draggy things could be eliminated, then life could be vastly improved.

We had heard rumours, David and I, from our rock 'n' dole compadres in a faraway land: Australia. The word on the (easy) street was that if you could manage to evade and avoid employment for a mere ten years – in Australia – you would become entitled to a kind of 'pension', as you were deemed to be utterly unemployable.[5] To us, Australia seemed like the land of milk and honey. Such were our ambitions back in the '80s.

The restart interviews got tougher and on the third and final attempt to rehabilitate me back into 'gainful' work, I was greeted by the benefits officer of my gestapo nightmares. The visit to the mythical job centre was getting harder to avoid. Thankfully, there was a light at the end of the DHSS tunnel: the Enterprise Allowance Scheme. The three-word poem, enough to conjure a story or existential meaning. Here's mine:

---

[5] I have no idea whether this was true or some kind of urban myth for the dedicated unemployed. In this case it seems a shame to destroy the myth.

Enterprise Allowance Scheme. The Anchored Tercet – or a three-word poem:

Jim's not dead.
We were friends.
Drink your whisky.
Leave me alone.

The Enterprise Allowance Scheme: an attempt by the mendacious – the Thatcher government – to be devious. The main aim of the Enterprise Allowance Scheme (established: 1983) was to rub down the high 1980s unemployment figures by getting the long-term unemployed to sign off benefits and become self-employed. All the thrusting, hip, young, gunslinging terminally unemployed jobseeker had to do was trot down to the bank, get their Enterprise Allowance Form stamped by the DHSS and sign up for a £1,000 overdraft that was guaranteed by Mrs Thatcher herself. These future titans of business (me) were then guaranteed £40 per week to live on for a year, without the hassle of signing on. What the nefarious government hadn't factored in to their grubby dole-massaging free-trade baloney scheme was that they were dealing with a truly inspired and subversive jobless generation, who really had no fucking intention of working.

Before the aspiring Businessman or Woman of the Year dove headlong into that year-long government-sponsored sabbatical, there was one hurdle: an Enterprise Allowance Scheme open day had to be attended. This was a fantastic afternoon out, that had the feel of a detention class.

NEVER WORK

A chance to exchange ideas with some of Britain's most unambitious and exotically unemployed people. The idea was that you would present some ridiculous business plan scribbled out on a fag packet to a disinterested hapless government emissary, who couldn't wait to get shot of this room full of losers and get into the pub.

The Enterprise Allowance open day was very much a Freak symposium. Some of these dudes weren't just Freaks, they were imperial Freaks. Operating on another *higher* level of freakery. *I am really going somewhere* . . . I thought, as I glanced over at the guy on the table beside me, his head resting on the desk in a deep solvent and cider slumber.

Doubtless, the Enterprise Allowance Scheme did help get a few double-glazing entrepreneurs off the ground. And that guy on my open day, the one who was going to weave bags, probably did make a fortune. But what the government hadn't counted on was the number of musicians and artists who were quite rightly using the dole as an arts grant. All of whom would make the great leap forward on board the Enterprise Allowance Scheme. A whole generation of Freaks freaking out on a government grant.

The end of the dole age maybe subconsciously ended the Servants. David and I both did Enterprise Allowance Schemes at around the same time. Free of having to sign on every two weeks, David went on holiday to Australia to hang out with the breaking-up Go-Betweens and I wrote most of what became the Auteurs' first album. The Enterprise Allowance Scheme faded quietly away in the 1990s as the great Freak cull began in earnest.

CHAPTER 16

The children with Xs carved into their heads

*The case against being a cult artist and
the case for being a cult leader.*

November 1993. I am a safe enough distance from restart interviews, job clubs and Enterprise Allowance Schemes, but the dollar has dropped. I am never going to be a 'pop star'. The Auteurs' current single, 'Lenny Valentino', has politely knocked on the door of the top forty and after a grilling from the bouncers has been allowed to come in and have a look at the number thirty-four: two bedrooms, small outside area, sun trap in the early afternoon. Unfortunately, the guardians of the pop chart – that is the singles-buying public – have had a butcher's at the group and decided that, after a few days, we are not wanted in the starter-home of pop. So we have been unceremoniously kicked out to reside at number forty-one, in the council house down the road, the one with the smashed window, and a shopping trolley and broken pram in the garden.

I'd gone along gamely with the whole notion of being a pop star in late 1992 and 1993. It wasn't something I'd really, *really* taken seriously. Even in the '80s the idea of being a pop star seemed fucking dumb (I wasn't Bobby Gillespie and had no intention of being Bobby Gillespie). A pop star is something to be in your dreams as a twelve-year-old, right? Wrong. We are in the '90s, my friend. We are ironic and we are post-ironic. We have reduced everything down to the 'football you-win-you-lose mentality'. Besides, when you have enough people telling you that you should become a 'pop star' and they are giving you (some of) the money that pop stars have, and they are saying, 'If you need anything, dear boy, just ask,' then invidious ideas and idle contemplations start to creep upon you and mess with one's mind. So if I didn't want to be a pop star, what did I want? Come on, 'fess up. Okay, I wanted to be . . . 'A Serious Artist'. Hahahahaha.

While the Greek chorus pick themselves up from the floor, loosen their laughter girdles and dust themselves down (and who can blame them, in 1993, even Damon Albarn in his pre-Serious-Artist I'm-just-a-drama-student-wearing-bovver-boots phase would have found the notion of being a 'serious artist' absurd), the harsh truth was that by 1993 standards, and these standards must have been pretty damn high, I was not pretty enough to be a proper pop star. I was also too clever (most pop stars are 90 IQ guys). I was too, well, anti-everything in the age where it was seen to be much better to be a joiner-in than an opter-out. So what do you do if you can't become a pop star — and bear in mind that in the 1990s the option of becoming a Freak is very much off the table? You become a cunt. I mean a cult.

The transition to cult star from failed pop star should be easy, but there is a problem, y'see: cults ain't what they used to be. In the 1960s, according to Jenny Fabian's terrifyingly bleak but quite possibly horribly accurate memoir *Groupie*, bands were either 'on the scene' or 'big'. The logic of this in terms of *Groupie* being that a band such as Family, were 'on the scene', kind of on their way up but never really to 'be', and the Fugs — presumably due to being American and carrying counterculture 'heavy-ness' — were 'big'. The 1970s could be divided into three categories: Early '70s: Freaks 'n' heavy versus teeny bop (Man versus T. Rex). Mid-'70s: Early Professional Rock versus teen and pop (ELP, 10cc versus Sailor). Late '70s: in which Punk and New Wave become the ultimate manifestation of everything that has come before, although the commentariat of the time mistook this for being 'post punk'; of which there will be more to follow, blessed reader.

By the 1980s, if you were not in the pop charts, then you were a cult band. In the 1980s it would be nice to say that I was in a cult band, but the Servants just didn't really have an audience, certainly not one who seemed to turn up to the sporadic gigs we played, or who seemed to flock to the record shops to buy the sporadic singles that we managed to release. Sure, by the twenty-first century the

Servants had some cool retrospective words written about them; *Mojo* magazine even claimed that our one album from 1990, *Disinterest*, was one of the top ten 'most influential independent records ever' released. Quite how *Mojo* came to this rather grand conclusion given that the album in question on the month of its release had sold nine (nine!) copies, does question either: the magazine's credibility a little, or the power of those nine individuals (did David Geffen buy a copy?). The Servants were a band with a tiny-to-none metrically measurable audience, as were many of the independent bands of the era. For every Jesus and Mary Chain or Sonic Youth there were Fire Engines, TV21s, Close Lobsters, Mighty Mightys, Cherry Boys, Mystery Girls – and Servants. All kind of cool. All seeking an audience of three figures. By the early 1990s, the notion of the cult was running thin. It was either pop or drop.

Where did the notion of the cult star come from? As rock 'n' roll outlasted expectations, i.e. after it had been ruined by the Beatles (as discussed previously) and had become some kind of career and heroic economic trick, it became 'necessary' to venerate 'long' departed bands for cash (the money-for-old-rope equation) and to give the burgeoning 'serious' music press something to get their teeth into. This is where the great bands of the 1960s start to re-emerge. As the 1970s withdrew and the nuclear sun came up on the 1980s, Rock's Second Act began. By 1980, the Doors and the Velvet Underground were retrospectively seen as cult acts, forever talked up by the 'post punk bands' (see also Scott Walker, Love, 13th Floor

THE CHILDREN WITH XS

Elevators, any number of garage bands), but they weren't really cult acts; the Doors were massive in their heyday. The Velvets weren't, but Lou sure tore the arse out of those old songs when he became a top-selling glam Frankenstein after *Transformer*, making the riff of 'Sweet Jane' as inevitable as 'Smoke on the Water' or 'Paranoid' in guitar shops the whole world over.

The real cult acts of the very early 1980s bore more resemblance to actual cults: Psychic TV, Death in June, Current 93. Unfortunately, cultish philosophy, interest in paganism, chaos magick, the writings of Peter Carroll, inevitable interest in little Charlie M and Kali Yuga, and accelerationism tended to end up going one way: when you reach the end of the road, take a hard right.

There is only one true cult band, a band so mythical and fanatically obsessed over by their devoted and possibly sub-intellectual dribbling super-fans. Their name may be translated as the Empty Suitcases, the Naked Suitcases, the Fucked Up Nobodies From Nowhere, or more 'popularly', Les Rallizes Dénudés (popular being relative here, in that the Les Rallizes' 'story' makes the likes of the Sun City Girls seem like Racey).

When sitting around the rock 'n' roll fire, and imparting the knowledge of Les Rallizes Dénudés, it is worth pointing out to the uninitiated reader that facts are very hard to come by. It's entirely possible that Les Rallizes were/are the first 'post truth' rock 'n' roll band. Obfuscation and obscurity are very much the currency of their myth and the obfuscation and obscurity are played masterfully, making other Zen masters of misdirection – the Residents – seem like mere amateurs. Forthwith, much of the information concerning Les Rallizes Dénudés may be entirely mythical.

This much we know: Les Rallizes Dénudés were formed in Kyoto by Moriaki Wakabayashi and Takashi Mizutani. These are the two to watch. (There will be innumerable Les Rallizes droids over the years, they are of less importance.) There are maybe only two truths that you need to know at this point in the story: 1). That a Rallizes gig was the live equivalent of psychedelic assault and battery. Think: half-hour 'songs' of jet combustion-engine blitzkrieg, howitzer trails of phased guitar trampling to death the most moronic troglodyte three-note girl-group bass lines, with occasional yelps or phonetic mumblings from Mizutani (when he can be bothered), and you may be partially there, there being: a prolapse in a black hole inside Ozzy Osbourne's last working brain cell. 2) That Les Rallizes couldn't get their idiotic but entirely righteous cack-ophonic stew down on tape – ever – in the studio. This incompetence, which would cause lesser groups to perhaps take stock and maybe think, 'Fuck it, man, we totally suck at this going into the studio and recording our songs caper, maybe we should just jack it the fuck in', is integral to this whole sorry story.

And then there is the hijacking. Many rock 'n' roll bands toy with political militancy: Primal Scream (as ever), the Clash, Me![1] Safe in the knowledge that if they

---

[1] I made my own moronic terrorism 'concept' album in 1996. The self-explanatory *Baader Meinhof*. I stand by every note and word.

THE CHILDREN WITH XS

ever had to get their delicate mitts grubby in an Isis kidnapping video, they could hand that machete and black hood to the nearest roadie and run away to the hotel bar. This was not how things worked for Rallizes.

In 1970, Les Rallizes bass player Moriaki Wakabayashi, a member of the radical left Yodo-go Group of the Japanese Red Army Faction, invited Takashi Mizutani to hijack a plane. Mizutani, perhaps too busy sulking about his botched studio recordings, turned down the offer. Undeterred, Wakabayashi made good on his terror-Freak promise, and on 31 March 1970, along with nine other hijackers brandishing samurai swords and guns, hijacked passenger jet Japan Airlines Flight 351.

Originally the militant heads demanded to be flown to Cuba, where they would hopefully receive communist guerrilla training. Unfortunately, or fortunately for the guerrilla cause – who maybe didn't really need spindly legged leather-trousered rock 'n' roll bozos fighting for them – the plane did not have enough fuel for Cuba, and a diversion to North Korea was agreed upon.

Seoul Airport was disguised to look like North Korea, but upon landing, the hijackers sussed out the ruse. Eventually it was agreed that the hijackers would be granted political asylum, and the plane finally landed in North Korea, and it is in North Korea that Moriaki Wakabayashi lives today. Les Rallizes Dénudés very much the anti-Primal Scream.

The hijacking laid the foundation of the Les Rallizes myth. Takashi Mizutani, paranoid that the authorities had his number and deep in hiding, plotted a new Rallizes in

FREAKS OUT!

his own image. Lo it was that for three decades Takashi Mizutani put his entirely monomaniacal fucked-up vision of rock 'n' roll into practice, like some demented psychedelic monk. The credo went like this:

Thou shalt only have nine songs over a thirty-year 'career'.

Thou shalt never, ever release an official album over a thirty-year 'career'.

Thou shalt only ever play a dozen 'gigs' over your thirty-year 'career'.

Thou shalt always dress like a rock 'n' roll moron, wearing a Ramones wig, red lippy, and leather jacket and trews (over a thirty-year 'career').

Thou shalt only allow bootleg albums to be released with scary but marvellous titles such as *Blind Baby Has Its Mother's Eyes*.

Thou shalt have more 'group' members than the Fall. All barely competent, all in the image of The Master.

Thou shalt never, ever utter a word. Over a thirty-year 'career'.

All of the above may be true. Or untrue. It doesn't really matter. If you're reading this book, and you haven't heard of Les Rallizes Dénudés, you will doubtless fancy dipping your toes in. Resist temptation. No good of it will come. One album leads to another and another, and soon you will have a mountain of Les Rallizes' bootlegs and twenty-six versions of brain-death classics such as 'Strung Out Deeper Than the Night'. You will lose the few friends that you have left and think of nothing else but Les Rallizes

THE CHILDREN WITH XS

Dénudés while you stare into the void that is Mizutani's terrible vision. Well done, fucker, you've joined a cult.

In the early twentieth century Les Rallizes appeared to have an official website. Ah well, I thought to myself, even the true greats succumb to the most mediocre demands of our age. The website didn't impart much information, until 2018 when it announced that Takashi Mizutani, a true sun king of Freaks, had passed away.

* * *

The true bona-fide, scary-ass Freak should never settle for anything as underwhelming as being a cult hero. The true bona-fide, spiders-in-the-eyes Freak should really have their sights set on being a cult leader. The best cults are all run by wannabe creepoid rock stars. David Koresh, a shithead thickie, knocked out soft rock originals on a pointy '80s guitar, hoping to score with teenage runaways. Mel Lyman went from being a purist folkie harmonica player in the early 1960s to being a kind of anti-hippie megalomaniacal cult leader. Lyman was not unambitious, and in between proclaiming himself to be Jesus Christ, hanging around waiting to be transported to Venus, and pulling the odd bank job, he managed to cut a few albums of what would now be called 'Americana'. Most of Lyman's recorded output is fairly standard country fodder, if you squint hard enough it can give you the heebie-jeebies though. Lyman's best musical endeavour was to perform a 25-minute unaccompanied harmonica solo at the 1962

Newport Festival. This is surely enough to win the admiration of any true Freak.

Trees Community were an Episcopal Christian Bible group who held meetings in a Manhattan loft space in 1970. A year or so later they started getting culty, embarking on 'a pilgrimage with no destination' in their converted school bus, and becoming an itinerant singing group. The Trees made a couple of super-duper freaky-deaky albums: 1973's *A Portrait of Jesus Christ in Music*, and *The Christ Tree*, two years later. Admittedly, the Trees Community's recorded output is a lot more eerie than the group, who were more interested in a fairly wholesome form of 'all things bright and beautiful' Christianity. Ah well.

Father Yod, or Ya Ho Wha, one James Baker, was a slightly different prospect compared to some of the other doomsday death-cult merchants of the 1970s. Jim Baker got in on the 1960s mystic trail early doors and created his own brand of health food vegan utopian ideals, becoming the patriarch to the Source Family in Los Feliz, California. Father Yod wasn't that interested in too much mind control or bullying – he was happy enough with his fourteen wives. Yod's thing was health food restaurants. When they weren't plucking radishes out of the ground, the Source Family, operating under the name of Yo Ho Wha 13, recorded some pretty wild apocalypto-sounding free rock that they inflicted upon (presumably) unsuspecting high school audiences in the early '70s. By 1975, Yod was living in Hawaii.

One day in the summer of 1975, and on a whim, Father Yod decided to give hang gliding a shot. Something he

THE CHILDREN WITH XS

had no experience or previous training in. On 25 August, Jim Baker/Father Yod leapt off a 1,300-foot cliff in Oahu, Hawaii, and died. Whether Yod was a Freak or a hippie business guy is difficult to figure out. I can guarantee that if you do choose to research Yod and the Source Family further, then you will at least feel less grubby than reading up on Aum Shinrikyo,[2] the Ant Hill Kids or . . .

The Manson Family! Woah. Let's just say it. Balls out on the goddamn dune buggy trail: The Manson Family were super-cool. Bear with me on this, laddies. Many words have been written about Charlie, and we can safely surmise what Charles Manson really was: a life-sapping, bottom-of-the-well, fuck-up-fuck-you-up stain on the drained swamp, and if-you-meet-this-scrawny-little-motherfucker-you'd-better-have-your-wits about-you kind of guy. Charlie's murderous lapdogs, Tex Watson, Bruce Davis and Bobby Beausoleil, were even worse, or no better, depending on which books you've read. So, when I'm putting out this Freak truth that the Manson Family were, like, kinda cool, what I'm saying is that the Manson Girls were kinda cool. Now if we apply a little nuance, we can separate the Tate–LaBianca, Cielo Drive slaughtering Manson Girls – that is, Susan Atkins, Linda Kasabian, Patricia Krenwinkel and Leslie Van Houten – from the high-watermark Freak

---

[2] Shoko Asahara, Aum Shinrikyo's leader, predictably did record a couple of songs released as a limited-edition single in 2007. The A-side, 'Lord Death's Counting Song', bears a strong resemblance to 'One Step Beyond' by Madness.

other Manson Girls, the ones who weren't on trial, but were, for better or worse, true believers.

I'm talking about the girls who shaved their heads and carved Xs into their foreheads, and sung spooked-out ditties sitting on the pavement of the Los Angeles Hall of Justice in July 1970.

In late 1969, as the main protagonists in the Tate–LaBianca murders awaited trial, the remaining members of the Family retreated back to Spahn Ranch, Death Valley, to record a soundtrack for Robert Hendrickson's *Manson* documentary. What transpired on tape over the upcoming months ended up being some of the eeriest jump-scare-in-the-dark-junk ever recorded by humans. Manson is not on any of these recordings, as he was incarcerated, and it's all the better for it. You see, Charlie, although he dressed like a Freak and passed around the LSD like Satan's evil hippie uncle, was really a crooner, and for all his demented blatherings about the messages and hidden meanings in the Fabs' *White Album*, he was really a '50s guy at heart. Not an Elvis guy, more a corny balladeer.

Listen to Charlie's *Lie – the Love And Terror Cult* album. This is the material that Manson was pinning his rock star dreams upon, but armed with the knowledge of Charlie's '50s guy roots, it becomes apparent that his most famous song, 'Look At Your Game, Girl' – the one covered by Guns N' Roses – is pure 'Champion the Wonder Horse' Frankie Laine candy floss.

The music that the Family recorded in late '69 and early 1970 became known as *The Family Jams* album. The Family

THE CHILDREN WITH XS

had got real good at harmonies and call-and-response vocals after all those campfire acid sing-songs at Spahn. The lead vocals are sung by Paul Watkins and Clem 'Scramblehead' Grogan, but it's the harmony vocals by the Manson Girls (Sandra Good, Gypsy, Squeaky, Catherine 'Cappy' Gillies, Nancy 'Brenda' Pitman and Ouisch) trilling, 'When you see the children with Xs on their head, if you dare to look at them, soon you will be dead' that really, er, kill.

If only those Manson Girls had never got on the bus. *The Family Jams* album is a bad vibes classic that pushes any of the neofolk pretenders headfirst into the garbage dumpster. Sandy, Squeaky, Gypsy, Cappy, Brenda, Ouisch, you were all bad, bad ladies, but I salute you for being the Freakiest of the Freakiest.

CHAPTER 17

Gary Glitter was my Big Bang

How the Glitter Band took on the Atheists and lost.

There are a couple of other cults that need to make the cut, the first being the Glitter cult: those that still fly their Bacofoil flag for Big Bad Gazza Glitter, despite what WE ALL KNOW now. This has become a kind of extreme stress test for the old 'separating the Art from the artist' argument. The second cult is the Atheists. In the early 2000s I wrote a song about the former, and five years later played it to the latter. My half decade beats your full century.

Christmas 1973. I am six years old. I got lucky, I grew up with the imperial age of *Top of the Pops* in the 1970s. One generation. Mine. Got this gift: Pre-cynicism, pre-adolescence, pre-teenage rebellion. When you are six you can watch *'the Pops* and not think about whether Marc Bolan had sold out or was on the slide or had got fat, and you didn't have to think about whether Steve Priest or Dave Hill were 'just hod-carriers in lippie'. Pop singles were a national event that took place every Thursday evening after Raymond Baxter had threatened some kind of robot apocalypse on *Tomorrow's World*, and these pop singles were the most important topic of conversation on Friday morning, from the typing pool to the school playground.

'Why was that fella from the Sweet dressed like a German stormtrooper on *Top of the Pops* last night?'

My dad liked watching *Top of the Pops*, probably for the usual Dad reasons. He didn't really give a shit about any of the groups. He enjoyed pronouncing on the various fellas in dresses and the girls not in dresses. It was very 1970s, with no impure thoughts redacted. Indeed, my dad was such a regulation 1970s father that come that feted date: Thursday, 9 May 1974 – he would let out the communal national Dad reaction to Sparks and Ron Mael's debut *'Pops* appearance.

'Joy, come in here,' shouted Dad through the kitchen door to my mum. 'It's bloody Adolf Hitler on *Top of the Pops*.'

I was there. This happened in my front room, as it happened in multiple millions of living rooms across the United Kingdom. Don't let anyone tell you otherwise.

I have no memory of David Bowie from the early '70s. I don't remember 'Starman' on *Top of the Pops*. In 1972 I guess I was just too young. Pop music got me pretty young though; 1973 was the year when it all started to come together in a haphazard way. I liked Suzi Quatro. 'Devil Gate Drive': a

GARY GLITTER WAS MY BIG BANG

fierce 45 that gave me the screaming abdabs. I liked Alvin. Why was he pointing at me (wearing Gene Vincent's leather glove)? And I loved Gary Glitter. He did a lot of pointing as well, and his records sounded like gangs of futuristic street hooligans out on manoeuvres. 'D'ya wanna be in my gang?' Obviously I don't now! But, back then if I *did* wanna be in a gang, or if I had a gang, it would be like Gary Glitter's gang. Yes, I am aware that I have just written that sentence. Years later, when I got around to watching *A Clockwork Orange*, I was kind of disappointed. Kubrick's Droog mess possessed none of the threat of those Glitter singles. There he was: Gary Glitter, dementedly staring down the gun of the camera lens – giving it the famous Kubrick gaze – with eyebrows arching impossibly. Questioning, always questioning; 'Do ya wanna touch? Do ya wanna touch? Do ya wanna touch me there? Where? There? Yeah!' A kinetic hot dense mass bursting out of his shiny girdle. Gary Glitter was very much my rock 'n' roll Big Bang moment.

We all now know what an utter cunt Gary Glitter is.[1] Irredeemable. There will be no comeback tour. Or reappraisal. Many of us know that the records were fantastic.

---

[1] In the early 2000s, my then manager, 'Harry', told me the story of how he was Gary Glitter's tour manager in the '80s for the gang show comebacks. Glitter was so disliked by the road crew that he was ceremonially beaten up at the end of the tour. The administers of this beating also included a very close relative of the singer. There was no knowledge among the crew of the crimes that Glitter was later found guilty of and imprisoned for being committed on these tours. Glitter was just vile, as Gene Vincent realised.

FREAKS OUT!

But we don't play them. When we do, we feel a bit transgressive. We comfort ourselves in the knowledge that producer and songwriter Mike Leander was the brains of the operation (Leander died before the true horror of Glitter had been exposed) and that the Glitter Band, who were entirely blameless, were the force behind that run of classic 45s. There will be no rebalancing of the books. Remember, Gene Vincent tried to shoot Gary Glitter.[2] And it's another reason to praise Gene. It's only too bad that he was drunk and missed. Gene knew. What did he know? Well, not what we all know now. He knew that Paul Raven, as Glitter was known in the mid-1960s, was an imposter; a rock 'n' roll imposter and a Freak imposter. And if there were two things that Gene Vincent really knew about, it was Freaks and rock 'n' roll.

In 2006 I wrote a song about Gary Glitter, and in 1968, Bob Dylan said, 'Don't go mistaking paradise for that home across the road.' I would counter Bob by saying, 'Don't play your new song about Gary Glitter and the Glitter Band to 3,000 drunken Ricky Gervais Fans,' and then I would add, 'and if you are going to play your new song about Gary Glitter and the Glitter Band to 3,000 drunken Ricky Gervais fans, then make sure that you are drunker than them all combined.'

---

[2] Okay, so it's probably a little fanciful to think that Gene Vincent was totally discerning when he took aim at people. Pulling a gun or a blade on people was one of Gene's 'quirks'. The victims were seemingly quite random.

GARY GLITTER WAS MY BIG BANG

It started with the Atheists. As I'm sure they would point out, most things do. I would tend to disagree. This is how my song about Gary Glitter and the Glitter Band goes:

Goodbye My Love
It's a Helluva record
They did it by themselves
the Leader was not present
And Gary Glitter
He's a bad, bad man.
Ruining the reputation of the
. . . Glitter Band.
It's guilt by association
for the Glitter Band.

So the perceptive reader will glean that the song, while stating the obvious (that Gary Glitter was and remains a bad, bad man), makes a case for the Glitter Band suffering from 'guilt by association' and that 'Goodbye My Love', as indeed is much of the Glitter Band's output, is excellent. I wrote the song in 2006, I was kind of nowhere in the accepted version of the music landscape in 2006. This is a fairly usual occurrence for the dedicated Freak, one often finds oneself out in the desert. Giving it a bit of the old metaphorical forty days and forty nights. It maybe didn't help – help being subjective and in this case related to commercial value pertaining to fiscal solvency – that I had recently written some other songs about: The Yorkshire Ripper, Jonathan King, Aum Shinrikyo. The only slightly radio viable song I had written – 'Off My Rocker at the Art School Bop' – contained references to Viennese Actionists, De Stijl and László Moholy-Nagy. I didn't set out to write these kinds of songs. When something rushes my brain I have to grasp it quickly and capture it. In 2006 my brain was being rushed by these kinds of songs. What can I do? I'm a fucking Freak. A Freak who had an art house concept album about sex offenders. A Freak with a family who is fucking broke.

This is where the atheists come in. The atheist leader (they have leaders) asks me to perform a song at the Big Atheist Anti-Christmas Christmas Show. The Atheist Show is more of a conference, but unlike a party political conference, where everyone disagrees with each other, at the Atheist conference everyone agrees with each other. If you're an Atheist, you kind of have to be fully in. That's it. I am neither in nor out. And I'm no other kind of 'ist', to boot. I look for God every day. I haven't found the motherfucker, but I've seen traces of where God has been: in the paintings of Richard Dadd, in the cruel card hand that was dealt to Pauline Boty, in Gene Vincent's version of 'Over the Rainbow', hiding in among the choral harmonies of John Tavener's 'The Lamb'. I've even turned around suddenly, half expecting to see God standing there. Only to find that it's my own damned good luck tapping me on the shoulder. If you're a Freak then you don't want to be too sure of dismissing God. So I really shouldn't be appearing with the Atheists, but I need the dough, I can hardly afford to turn down anything. And I really should. Anyway, the chief Atheist is a good dude. Well, he's not really a dude in a 'hey dude' way, but he is a front-of-the-cloth stand-up kind of guy, though.

And so over a couple of miserable nights just before Christmas 2008, I find myself baffling several hundred polite but occasionally enthused science students. And several thousand leering, drunken fans of the comedian Ricky Gervais with my excellent song about Gary Glitter and the Glitter Band. A lesser writer may at this point add, What could possibly go wrong?

It is the second night of the Atheist Anti-Christmas Christmas conference at the Hammersmith Apollo. Rotten venue. Not rock 'n' roll. Too stand-uppy. A wasteland where fleetingly popular comedians come to serve themselves up. It's a way-too-early soundcheck, which means a way-too-early adjournment to the alehouse. Always, always a rookie error. Jarvis is on the bill tonight. So we meet in the pub for drinks. My first book, *Bad Vibes*, is about to be published. While Jarv and I sit drinking amiably, I wonder whether he'll appreciate the fantasy sequence I have written about him in the book. He comes out of it quite well, probably, maybe? But it's kind of disrespectful to the Queen Mum of Pop. I figure that Jarv won't mind it being a bit, er, irreverent. I get the impression that he doesn't really enjoy being the Queen Mum of Pop. But then again, it's only really me calling him the Queen Mum of Pop. Ah well.

I'm fucked. I've just been sitting in the dressing room with Jarvis. On the monitor screens we can see and hear Ricky Gervais doing his turn. It's the usual routine, designed to make estate agents howl with laughter. The dressing room is full of Atheists. I am surrounded by Atheists: atheisting. The atheists atheation manifests itself in being gently offended by King Atheist Gervais (all atheists are gentle by definition – and oddly Christian). They have nothing to be offended about really, as Gervais – doing one of his now customary 'rape bits' – is entirely meaningless. He doesn't seem to understand the Lenny Bruce rule of comedy, i.e. suppression of the word; the more you say the offending word, the less power it has. Ten minutes into Gervais's routine he has done so many rape 'gags' that under normal circumstances even the most low-level junior estate agent would tire. But these are not normal circumstance, we are at the Atheist Anti-Christmas Christmas conference and the junior estate agents just can't get enough of it. Rape rape rape. Ho fucking ho.

I am now waiting in the wings to do my turn. Jarvis is on before me. This being ostensibly a comedy variety type show, the billing is all over the place. Jarv is doing a great version of that Greg Lake Christmas song. Even the estate agents are digging it. Right now, I'm not feeling so smart about laughing at Jarvis's cuddly national treasure status. I could do with a bit of Queen Mother status myself. Gervais is bouncing around in the wings, an excitable man-puppy-child. He wants to run on during Jarvis's performance. He is gently but firmly told not to by a large security man.

And so, I step up to the gallows. Death by execution would be less excruciating than the next four minutes. The audience have no idea who I am. I am so drunk now that

I also have no idea who I am. I get to the chorus: 'Gary Glitter he's a bad bad man, Ruining the reputation of the Glitter band.'

'Boooooooooooooo!' go several thousand junior estate agents.

The estate agents will have forgotten me within seconds. There's not a single person in the audience who would have paid for a ticket just to see me. I'm just an obscurity among several other obscurities in an Atheist variety show. It's not really a bad position to occupy.

At the 'after-show' Richard Dawkins, the Pope of Atheism, seems quite impressed by the celebs. He has no God, but he's keen to meet the false idols of light ents. He spies Gervais and pushes past me, pausing briefly to gaze benignly at Jarv. He likes the wealthy people. Anyone in the Western world can make money, but not everyone can be a Freak.

CHAPTER 18

Freaks don't wear shorts, they wear leotards

*Eccentricity versus freakery versus elec-trickery.
The war against short trousers, and the story
of the psychedelic wrestlers.*

One cannot learn to be a Freak any more than one can learn to be a great artist or an athlete. You've either got it or you ain't. You is or you isn't. At this juncture I'd like to address another misapprehension: the eccentric is not a Freak.

My dad, Mick, was an eccentric. A mortifyingly embarrassing eccentric. Never a Freak. He wouldn't have known what a Freak was. He was a big man, with an enormous personality that could be draining and claustrophobic. He wore drainpipe demob trousers, a jacket and tie, had a long wispy comb-over across his large head, and a fucking wild, bushy mad sea-dog beard, and sometimes he liked to wear a fez. He had artistic ambitions that were, perhaps, foiled by the times he lived in. He missed out on the Royal College of Art after he was ambushed by national service (he felt, probably quite rightly, that after the two world wars, national service was the greatest collective waste of British male youth of the twentieth century). He married young and perhaps got trapped by the world of reality and nine-to-five work. He spent most of his life being a graphic designer for the Ministry of Defence, providing detailed hand-drawn charts and exciting graphs of Polaris missiles and other weapons of mass destruction. From the ages of eight to eleven he took me to work with him in the summer holidays. I was even given a tour of a nuclear submarine when it was in for maintenance at HMS *Vernon*. Mick was largely a peaceful, good-natured man with only the occasional flash of 1970s staggering ultra-violence towards bullies when extremely provoked or protecting his family. He seemingly had no need for friends, though he was adored by his work colleagues. He was emotional and sentimental and expressed a benign amusement at the absurdities of the everyday. From somewhere, he had adopted a very strong sense of self and a belief that 'you should be your own man'. I took this and ran with it.

* * *

In his superb book, *A Licence to Pop and Rock – An Inventory of Attitude*, Jim Fry – of legendary Art Glam Situationist Wreckers of Any Venue Unlucky (or Lucky) Enough To Put Them On – Earl Brutus makes the clear-eyed assertion that within the world of pop and rock, 'sport, is for cunts'. It hasn't been said enough, so I will repeat it here: sport is for cunts. One more time: sport really is for fucking cunts.

One of the most dispiriting aspects of the 1990s decade was the grim sports revival cheer led by *Loaded* magazine and its editor James 'Loaded' Brown. Throughout the '80s, we, that is, the fey guitar strummers, had felt that short-trouser sports – football, rugby, running, throwing objects – were the ephemera of a different time. That different time being 'school'. Once school was done and dusted, then surely the shorts and the rest of the motherfucking PE kit should have been thrown into the nearest bush and set fire to.

Come the 1990s, there had been a meeting, and it would seem that I had not been invited. I could partially buy into the rumour that 'rock 'n' roll and football were the great working-class escapes', but that was really all about Rod the Mod and the Clash. And as I always felt that the Clash were the Action Man dolls of music I didn't take too much heed. Us thin, young, noble men in Chelsea boots with haircuts like Brian Jones were above football studs and mud. Besides, we had records by the Chills to listen to. The football pitch was as alien to me as the job centre. I had, however, clearly underestimated the emasculation effect of the dreaded Thatcher years.

I felt betrayed and defiled by my own generation. In 1992, if you were in the business of being in a 'pop group', eccentricity was still a noble affliction. By the mid-1990s the Stasi minds of the media guys (it was mainly 'guys') had clamped down on the interesting and strange. So God help you if you were an actual Freak. We had entered a new unwelcome age. Hopefully, and quaintly, this weak epoch became known as the age of Cool Britannia or Britpop. Grandiose indeed. I would call it: the age of Short-Trouser Thinking.

Malcolm Ross, the trail-burning guitarist from Josef K and later Orange Juice, once told me how dismayed he was when Edwyn Collins informed him that, no, the group Orange Juice would not be wearing suits. They would be wearing 'short trousers' for their debut *Top of the Pops* performance. Malcolm was right in his disapproval. No great group has ever worn short trousers. Look:

A roll call (not a list) of non-short trouser wearers (Non-S), short trouser enablers (SE) and short trouser wearers (S):

Non-S

Gene Vincent
Eddie Cochran
Buddy Holly
The Shadows
Johnny Kidd and the Pirates
The Beatles
The Merseys
The Incredible String Band
T. Rex
The Jimi Hendrix Experience
X-Ray Spex
Bob Calvert

FREAKS DON'T WEAR SHORTS, THEY WEAR LEOTARDS

Sun City Girls
Daphne and Celeste (probably have worn shorts but
    would be against male short-trouser wearers)
The Edgar Broughton Band
Sham 69
Ivor Cutler
Dr. Alimantado (Trench Town dispensation)
Big Youth (Trench Town dispensation)
Vince Taylor
The Raincoats
Silver Jews
Swell Maps
Kevin Coyne
Crass
Siouxsie and the Banshees
Roxy Music
The Aquarian Age
Ash Ra Tempel
The Three Johns
The Velvet Underground

SE

Tony Wilson

S

Rage Against the Machine
A Certain Ratio
Michael Eavis

FREAKS OUT!

New Order
Red Hot Chilli Peppers
AC/DC – (entire output rendered useless due to
   misplaced trouser beliefs)
Pavement
The guy from Limp Bizkit
The guy from Pearl Jam
Bob Weir from the Grateful Dead
Helmet
Britpop bands in five-aside football tournaments against
   teams of A&R men and *Melody Maker* music journalists.
Kraftwerk when out cycling.

Fer Chrissakes, you bottom-list motherfuckers! You can form a band for many reasons: to change the world with your unique world view, to score drugs and sex. To avoid work. Whatever. But surely one of the main reasons to form a band is to never, ever partake in sport or the wearing of short trousers again. Take a look at the last line but one of the three above (incomplete) roll calls – Britpop bands playing five-aside against teams of A&R men and music journalists – versus the Velvet Underground. The unrighteous versus the most righteous. The Velvets perhaps being the pinnacle of non-short trouser wearing freethinkers.

The Freaks, at least the Ladbroke Grove variety, strangely did take an interest in one sport, as they intuitively aligned themselves to test cricket; a game of rippling Swedenborgian mysticism, esotericism, and more importantly, a celebration of full-length trouser wearing. Steve Peregrin Took and the

FREAKS DON'T WEAR SHORTS, THEY WEAR LEOTARDS

Deviants[1] had even formed a cricket team in 1969 called . . . The Freaks XI. The Freaks XI even played a few matches against the unfortunately named 'Straights', who included members of Peter Frampton's – 'the face of 1968' – the Herd. Took even collaborated on a novelty reggae song with Bob Calvert and Adrian Wagner,[2] 'Cricket Star', credited to The First Eleven.

I wouldn't have given Roy Harper the space/time continuum in this book, although I do dig a few of his elpees; however, my approval has to remain distanced as I find his Led Zeppelin, Floydian[3] hobnobbing highly distasteful and most unrighteous. But Big Roy did write the finest sport-as-lifecycle-as-death metaphor ever, 'When an Old Cricketer Leaves the Crease', that even managed to successfully name-drop the uber non-Freak's non-Freak: Geoff Boycott.

There was one sports endeavour that the true Freak could get aboard with. The real high-tension drama was not played out at Wembley, Old Trafford, Edgbaston or Twickenham. This was happening on mid-week evenings

---

[1] Russell Hunter, Deviants drummer, became a fully qualified cricket umpire. He officiated in the Surrey Cricket League for fifteen years.
[2] Adrian Wagner (1952–2018) co-created the Wasp synthesiser (with Chris Huggett). Adrian was the great-great grandson of Richard Wagner. The Wasp synthesiser that Adrian Wagner presented to Robert Calvert can be heard all over Calvert's electro miners' strike concept album, *Freq* (1985).
[3] Proof of the Floyd's post-Syd uncoolness can be seen on the inner gatefold of the *A Nice Pair* compilation, with a photograph of Roger, Dave and the roadies, arms folded in full football team formation. Wearing shorts.

FREAKS OUT!

in the guildhalls of provincial Britain, in the Mecca and Gaumont, the Hackney Empire, Wolverhampton Civic Hall and the Derby Assembly Rooms. There were no cricket whites or shorts. Just brave men and women. In leotards. As me and my dad were to witness.

My dad didn't really like the football that much. He took me to Fratton Park, Portsmouth's ground, a few times in the 1970s. Perhaps out of misplaced fatherly duty. I showed no interest in whoever the two teams were. I just wondered why they were spending an interminable ninety minutes hoofing around a sack of shit in the gloomy Portsmouth mud. My dad wasn't that interested either. He did enjoy the fighting on the terraces though. Pointing out scuffles on adjacent stands and roaring his approval. From watching '70s hooligan tear-ups my dad and I progressed to the midweek wrestling bouts at Portsmouth's Guildhall, where I would see the great leotard-wearing women and men of the ring: Kendo Nagasaki, Bully Boy Muir, Mick McManus and the appalling Big Daddy. These were my people (apart from the hideous Big Daddy), and the wrestlers looked as mad as my dad.

If you know nothing about the British wrestling scene of the '70s and '80s, think of it as a world of super-unfit superheroes taking on super-unfit supervillains in tatty, draughty one-third-filled provincial halls of a Tuesday night. The heels (baddies): Giant Haystacks; 7 foot and 48 stone of troglodyte weirdness. Mick McManus – a tight swimming-cap of dyed black hair glued down on his head and 'the man you love to hate'. Mick began his career in

FREAKS DON'T WEAR SHORTS, THEY WEAR LEOTARDS

1947 and was still going strong in 1978. Marc 'Rollerball' Rocco, a tough-as-fuck Mancunian with a line in pseudo all-American bratty hot-dog bad dude vibes. Klondyke Kate, just fourteen when she started wrestling in 1977, and Brian Glover, the great actor, who transferred his roll as bully PE teacher from *Kes* onto the wrestling canvas as a baldie bully heel. Then there was the legendary Kendo Nagasaki, mighty masked man, and of course 'Exotic' Adrian Street.[4]

The blue-eyed boys, or 'good guys', were the granny's favourites and far less interesting than the heels; but for every debit you need a credit. Best of all were the Freaks: 'Beautiful' Bobby Barnes – who tag-teamed with Adrian Street as one half of the Hells Angels. Bobby Barnes' job was to mince and preen around the ring, interminably and carefully folding his silk dressing gown, and pouting defiantly at the cries of 'Poofter' from the front-row battleaxes. Finally, there was the mighty Catweazle, my favourite. Catweazle was a fighter who fell between the stools of heel and blue-eyed boy and landed firmly in the land of Freak. Catweazle (real name Gary Cooper) based his act on the marvellous Geoffrey Bayldon character from the early-1970s children's television show *Catweazle*, in which an eleventh-century

---

[4] Adrian Street was the wrestler that reignited my passion for this, the noblest of sports. One of my former outfits, Black Box Recorder, used a now-famous picture of Adrian Street in his full glam rock regalia down a mining shaft with his coal-miner father on the cover of our *England Made Me* elpee.

warlock ends up in 1970s rural England and grapples with such twentieth-century technology as the most righteously and accurately named 'elec-trickery' and the 'telling bone' (telephone). Catweazle the wrestler would climb into the ring, hair like Hawkwind's Nik Turner and beard like my dad, licking a hallucinogenic plastic frog.

Just like any medieval head.

Catweazle and Adrian Street had some kind of sporting kinship with rock 'n' roll. Just like a touring rock band, these bygone wrestlers would travel up and down the motorways of the UK, eat at the same service stations, even occasionally deal with the same promotors. By 2011, my whole childhood antipathy and 1990s loathing of 'sport' has coalesced into a concept album: *Nine and a Half Psychedelic Meditations on British Wrestling of the Late '70s and Early '80s*. The idea is simpler than the title, it's really just a good old-fashioned song cycle, or a series of meditations, on my beloved wrestlers that puts them into 'psychedelic situations': Les Kellett[5] goes through a *Heart of Darkness* epiphany after taking a microdot in his Bradford transport cafe. Kendo Nagasaki writes a rock opera about the theatre of cruelty that is the wrestling canvas, while Adrian Street rhapsodises about using his wife's head to step into the ring. It's all pretty basic stuff.

---

[5] Les Kellett was known as a phenomenally hard man, known for taking a hammer to his own hand to demonstrate his high pain threshold. Kellett ploughed his wrestling earnings into his dream: a transport cafe in Bradford. The cafe was known for its appalling food. Kellett kept hogs outside.

FREAKS DON'T WEAR SHORTS, THEY WEAR LEOTARDS

My dad by now is whiling away his final days in a care home; memory-less and loopy, his mind no longer able to take incoming traffic. He never hears the record, a record which is a tribute to him and my own 1970s childhood.

A year or so after the release of *Nine and a Half Psychedelic Meditations*, I am performing in the Hayward Gallery. The artist Jeremy Deller has made a film about 'Exotic' Adrian Street and has asked me to participate in an event. This is what we all get up to in the twenty-first century: events. All the artists and all the musicians and all the writers attend each other's 'events' and ask each other the same old questions. Round we all go, dilettante goldfish in the bowl. 'What inspired you to write this book/make this record/make this artwork?' It's all one big Q and A session until the end of time, until death.

At this particular event Jeremy and I are talking to Adrian and his wife Linda over the internet, they are speaking from Adrian's wrestling academy in Florida. My job, as always, is song and dance man. Jeremy asks me to serenade Linda with my song 'Linda's Head'. It doesn't take a genius to work out the double entendre. I sigh, and thank the stars that there are several thousand miles of Atlantic Ocean and cyberspace between me and the iron-head lock of Exotic Adrian Street. RIP.

I am forty-five. In my head I have evened the pitch. The final reckoning. The winners of sport can't go on for ever, but the 'losers' of rock 'n' roll can. Rock 'n' roll is for the Freaks, and sport is always a cunt's business.

CHAPTER 19

Dismantled teenage rock 'n' roll Pope

How post-punk happened before punk happened.

I don't often look back with shame or regret. I don't have any full skeletons in my closet. Just a leg bone here, a tibia there, and a jawbone up on the shelf. No terrible mortification. Just a few mutterings in the constant chase to be 'quotable'. You see, unfortunately, when I was in my twenties, other people in their twenties, who knew very little, chose to ask me questions about things that I too knew very little about. What a truly disastrous idea: young people talking to other young people and then printing the conversations. I am talking about my occasional forays into expressing opinions to the music press and sometimes the national press of the day, of which I am sometimes mildly embarrassed about whenever I have the misfortune to stumble across my juvenilia. I may be a Freak but I'm only human.

FREAKS OUT!

My true shame, though, is when as a teen – in the early '80s when the roolz were the roolz – I bowed to imagined peer pressure by getting shot of those records one really wasn't meant to listen to any more. So goodbye Led Zeppelin's *I–IV*. Goodbye Black Sabbath's *Master of Reality*. Goodbye Deep Purple's *In Rock* and *Machine Head*. And fuck off *Foxtrot* and *Selling England by the Pound*. Just to be sure, stick the Shadows' *20 Golden Greats* and the Beatles' *A Collection of Oldies . . . But Goldies* under the bed, or somewhere the imagined taste plod would never look. This was the real legacy of post-punk (and post-modernism).

Post-punk did not exist. The bits and the bobs, the knicks and the knacks of post-punk certainly existed, the lawnmower parts as Morrissey may have it. Post-punk did exist though before anyone called it 'post-punk'. Now, historians of rock will jump in at this point and they will say: 'No.' And I will counter and say: 'Okay, the term post-punk did crop up in 1978 to describe, er, the rock and roll that followed the blaze of punk, and yep, there is undeniable printed evidence of such atrocities taking place.' Paul Morley, or someone, may indeed have dibs on 'coining' such a phrase. However, dear punkas, there is a world of difference between a record being post-punk and an entire genre apparently being 'post-punk'.

If we are going to dismiss 'post-punk', which we are, then we have to place it within the context of post-modernism. This is when things start to get tricky for post-punky types. Post-modernism belongs somewhere within the forest of hi-art avant theory that has somehow entered the populist lexicon. Unless you have a Master of Fine Arts (MFA), you possibly won't understand hi-art theory. It's okay. It is not for you. You do not need to understand it. Music theorists have often claimed to understand post-modernism, in the same way that wealthy young couples watch TV programmes about 'building houses' in the mistaken belief that they understand minimalism; minimalism having its roots in complex art theory that has little to do with architecture save for the actual building – the Bauhaus School – whereupon Walter Gropius dreamt it up.

Post-modernism, as a misunderstood concept, became the template for the false flag op of post-punk. One could say this is just a shifting of the tectonic cultural plates; an evolving cultural language. Or one could say this was building a castle made of sand. I'd go further and say it's napalm-level horse shit and 'post-punk' was just New Wave, which was kind of a shit name but we all knew where we were with it at least. The only reason that New Wave didn't stick was because it had a built-in obsolescence, and the doctors and professors of rock really wanted something with more gravitas to pin pseudo academic theories on.

As we all know by now, I was grooving to the Shadows when punk came out of the traps. Punk didn't really hit the provinces – by the provinces I refer to me – until 1981/1982. I Was A Provincial Punk, in 1982. Too young for the original punk outburst and living in the wrong place anyway (have I told you about Portsmouth?). To be a provincial punk in 1982, you had to get everything wrong. Which as a fourteen-year-old was easy: a centre parting, with soap used in an attempt at punky spikiness. I was ginger anyway so no need to dye it: 'I look like Rat Scabies, do I not?' ('You do not'.) A leather motorbike jacket bought from Mr Clive (a leatherwear shop in Portsmouth), costing a mind-boggling £35. If you think there is any more ridiculous sight than a fourteen-year-old boy in a biker jacket with a spiky feather cut then you have not seen a fourteen-year-old boy in a biker jacket with a spiky feather cut. As a 1982 provincial punk you need to be getting every small detail wrong, and punk was very much about rights and wrongs.

After my expensive trip to Mr Clive I couldn't afford PIL's *First Issue* or *Metal Box*, so the contractually obligated live album, *Paris au Printemps*, it was. To top off this hormone-soaked battlefield of utter embarrassment, I wore an armband purchased from a day trip to Carnaby Street with the legend 'Smash It Up' written in punky graffito lettering. At the time I hated the fact that I was about six years too young for punk. Now I'm very glad, not just because of the natural fear of the slippage of time, but because it gave me the opportunity to get things very wrong.

Pop music in itself, however, can never be wrong or right, and if you love pop music, or the *idea* of pop music, then the pop music that you love can never be wrong or right. Only your attitude towards it. Oh, how we mocked the kids with centre partings, referring to them knowingly as '76ers' (this being a reference to the hairstyle that we assumed all people had in 1976 prior to some mutually agreed date when Punk Year Zero came into being). That we were wearing leather jackets had spiky hair and, God forgive me, a 'Smash It Up'

DISMANTLED TEENAGE ROCK 'N' ROLL POPE

armband, didn't really register. We were hitting the high nineties on the conformity barometer.

I fell hook and line for punk as a provincial suburban teen. I even abandoned my beloved Fall elpees for six months. Six months of most un-Freakish behaviour. I look back and realise I was going through an adolescent crisis of faith, like a dismantled teenage rock 'n' roll pope.

After me, it was prog rock that suffered the most from my wholehearted uptake of punkiness. We've all heard the battle lines before: self-indulgence, Post Syd Pink Floyd, ELP, Concept Albums on Ice, that famous one-word review of Yes in the *NME* ('No'). All of these critiques have their merits but they can rarely be aimed at one particular small cannon of work. Freaks and adepts, I present to you, the work of Genesis 1971–73: Britain's freakiest public-school arseholes.

On first glance, Genesis seem to have gone over their agreed overdraft in the Freak bank. Mike Rutherford, Tony Banks, Little Phil Collins and the other dude. Luckily, they had Top Freak Peter Gabriel. Despite these days coming across like some business advisor interested in ecologically sustainable investment, Gabriel was once one of Britain's weirdest motherfuckers, like Syd without mental illness. Where Genesis went, others could only hope to go.

By 1973, Pink Floyd, like all upper-class English males, had passive-aggressively in-fought their way into rejecting everything that made them good: Syd Barrett, 'space rock', sprawlingly flawed self-indulgent double albums. Cows. Songs without lyrics. Pretending to take drugs to keep the

FREAKS OUT!

stoners happy. In turn the Floyd embraced everything that made them, well, just crap: songs with lyrics by Roger Waters, and Roger Waters generally. What Big Rog didn't notice, as he was too busy pondering *The Dark Side of the Moon*, clogging up the album charts for ever, was that the real album of isolation, visionary political perception and class awareness had been recorded by the group who were seen as very much a 'junior', politer, gently eccentric version of the Floyd: Genesis, and their 1973 meditation on colonial excoriation, *Selling England by the Pound*.

Early '70s pop music tends to be measured in term of synaesthesia: the Kinks invented beige music with their late-'60s run of *Arthur* (the entire cover is beige) to 1971's *Muswell Hillbillies*, an album that reeks of stale ale and lunchtime drinking in beige pubs. Rock 'n' roll had moved into the age of beige: beige and gold. Glam was gold, and with a few exceptions – Third World War, Principal Edwards Magic Theatre, Hawkwind – rock 'n' roll was not getting political. Certainly not prog rock, and certainly not prog rock Freaks. But Genesis had already been there on their previous elpee, the weird-out wig-out classic, *Foxtrot*. Listen to Gabriel let fly on the papercuts sharp Rachman-proto-tenants-rights-drama, 'Get 'Em Out by Friday', and most famously, 'Supper's Ready', which beat Roger Waters' *Dark Side of the Moon* English-desperation-phantasmagoria at its own game.

So it was that *Selling England by the Pound* came to lacerate the UK like a prog rock Hogarth and provide a prophetic vision of 2016 Brexit Britain as well. In 1973, Britain had finally entered the European Common Market, and in the world of rock 'n' roll only Genesis seemed to notice; maybe it was that fiscally cautious public schooling of Charterhouse, an establishment more associated with financial markets than the classics, and maybe it ought not to have been surprising from a band whose keyboard player went on to make a solo album called *Bankstatement*. It's all there in the opening epic on *Selling England by the Pound*: 'Dancing With the Moonlight Night'. 'Can you tell me where my country lies?' asks something called a unifawn to a metaphorical lion, as the knights of the Green Shield Stamps have a tantrum.

The punks didn't care about *Selling England by the Pound*; well, maybe a few did but they would never admit it for fear of an amphetamine-crazed Tony Parsons attacking them with his Muji[1] slippers on the Circle line. Some of the post-punkers were listening. Swell Maps,[2] a band who'd been active in a variety of forms since as early as 1972, but were lumped in with the great post-punk rewrite, certainly knew their prog as well as they knew their Krautrock and their Marvin Gaye and their T. Rex. Post-punk, if we really have to go there, had little – musically and attitudinally – to do with punk. If we do have to have these categories then shouldn't post-punk really be post-prog?

---

[1] A somewhat niche joke based on the rumour that Tony Parsons practises Japanese Shoe Removal at home.
[2] I have a declared interest. I am currently a 'member' of Swell Maps C21, one of my favourite teenage bands.

FREAKS OUT!

But no one cares about categories any more. And in direct contradiction to all of the above, if anything then rock 'n' roll has become too eclectic. That's okay, rock 'n' roll being the great high folk art form can live with its own contradictions. If art has one purpose it is to acknowledge life's contradictions and embrace them. You can be anything you want, as long as it is sanctioned by someone. Unless you're a Freak. A true Freak cannot be sanctioned.

I claimed back my Genesis albums decades ago (along with Led Zeppelin, Deep Purple and, of course, Black Sabbath), and there they sit with the fuck tonne of rock 'n' roll that I've made and bought over the years. Now what about that Mike Oldfield guy? Strange character, another one who got involved in a cult.[3] Is Oldfield the true post-progger? Perhaps if Shy Mike had only come from Düsseldorf, Berlin or Munich we'd all be digging *Hergest Ridge* as much as we all dig *Tago Mago*.

---

[3] Exegesis, a UK 'therapy cult'.

CHAPTER 20

The Greatest Photograph of the Twentieth Century

In which we find the real 'Greatest Photograph of the Twentieth Century'.
The battle between Paul Morley and Jerry Garcia. Light entertainment Freaks, and the curious case of David Van Day.

The greatest photograph of the twentieth century, as proposed by the artist Jeremy Deller, is the image of 'glam rock' wrestler 'Exotic' Adrian Street, deep down in subterranea, preening to the camera in a Welsh coal mine, wearing his Ziggy boxing boots, wrapped in glam rock Bacofoil; shoulder-length platinum hair, just like Iggy's on the cover of *Raw Power*, and his Heavyweight World Championship belt given pride of place around his considerable buffed-up midriff. At Adrian's side is his coal-miner father, and in the rear of the picture are Adrian's father's workmates. Their coal-blackened faces a mixture of contempt and bemusement. Jeremy Deller first saw the photograph when one of my old outfits, Black Box

FREAKS OUT!

Recorder, used it on the cover of our 1998 album/state-of-the-nation address: *England Made Me*. Jeremy curated the photo and made the not unreasonable claim that it is the 'Greatest Photograph of the Twentieth Century'. We cannot include the photo here so I have provided an artist's impression of the 'Greatest Photograph of the Twentieth Century' (copyright J. Deller). I would, however, contend that the Greatest Photograph of the Twentieth Century is really only the Second Greatest Photograph of the Twentieth Century.

The *actual* 'Greatest Photograph of the Twentieth Century' (copyright L. Haines) is an image of an 'ageing' musician and a young gunslinger journalist. To my mind

Artist's impression: 'Adrian Street with his coal-miner father' (drawing by Mercy Millar, age six).

THE GREATEST PHOTOGRAPH

this particular image is the real Greatest Photograph of the Twentieth Century (copyright L. Haines) Once again, we will be unable to obtain permission to include a plate of the photograph in question. Once again, I have supplied an artist's impression of the photograph.

The musician in the photograph is Jerry Garcia, of the Grateful Dead, and the writer is Paul Morley. Not of the Grateful Dead. The subjects are staring straight into the lens, presumably post-interview. The photo was taken in 1981. Both men are waving peace-sign fingers at the camera. Morley has an ironic sneer on his face, with which he is signifying, 'Look at me, I'm giving it the peace sign and this sappy old hippie doesn't even know I'm taking

Artist's impression: 'Ageing musician and a young gunslinger' (drawing by Mercy Millar, age six), AKA the 'Greatest Photograph of the Twentieth Century' (copyright L. Haines).

the piss.' Garcia, an ancient thirty-nine years old at the time, is laughing. An avuncular weed head – well, okay, coke-head, smack-head, maximum-head – who's seen a bit of life. Garcia knows that Morley – in his early twenties at the time – is a pretender. As Queen Elizabeth II memorably said, 'Prime ministers come and go.' Jerry Garcia is thinking, 'Journalists, man, they come and go.'

Jerry Garcia looks groovy. Morley looks like a sixth former who thinks he might have got a good grade in his mock A-levels. The Morley/Garcia photo shows the young pretender thinking he is usurping the old man, but not realising he has totally failed. You see, Jerry G is a Freak. And his band (though you would be correct to dismiss much of their output as some of the least cosmic cocaine boogie ever wrung out by human hands) are the world's greatest Freak enablers. The Dead, for good or bad, have enabled their vast congregation of, well, 'Deadheads' to imagine some of the most righteous trips undertaken by human consciousness, despite being hindered by the utterly dire quality of 87 per cent of their music.

I digress. What the 'Greatest Photograph of the twentieth Century' is actually showing us is that Freakdom always wins out against irony. What Jerry's face tells us in the photograph is that when you are in the Grateful Dead, you know the universal truth: that we are all lying face down in fields upon fields of our own bullshit. Paul Morley would doubtless agree, but in his post-ironic heart he thinks that somehow he is not lying in a field of his own bullshit. The problem here is that Paul hasn't seen what Jerry has seen. Jerry has seen all

THE GREATEST PHOTOGRAPH

of the song and dance men and women throughout the ages, he has stood in every hall, every field and every cowpat that all the soldiers of heavy entertainment, medium entertainment and light entertainment have stood in, even though he has transcended them; he knows, as much as every Freak knows, that he is one of them. Paul Morley – Po Mo – has never been one of them. He does not know.

I like to ponder these equations and equivocations when I make my occasional journey from my provincial Travelodge to my date with destiny, to offer up my Freak wares to my Freak-appreciating public, be it local parish hall, a converted workingman's club, the upstairs room of a pub, or even somewhere on London's South Bank. Look at the posters on the wall; who played here a month ago? Who will be playing here in two months' time? Will it be Su Pollard? Someone who was briefly in Hawkwind? A hot young band getting their first excitable props on 6 Music? Vashti Bunyan? Or Jane McDonald? You see, the truth that Paul Morley thinks he knows, but Jerry Garcia *really* knew, is that, however much of a Freak we are, we are only treading a few boards short in the metaphorical feet of Jane McDonald.

It is quite possible that you, as a reader of, let's call it the 'classical' school of rock biography, may have no idea of who or what Jane McDonald is, let alone what her metaphorical feet are. Let's rewind to the great Covid lockdown.

March 2020. We all know what happened? Right? Right. If I have to remain inside for the foreseeable future, with only the making of two solo albums, a radio play, a second collaboration with Peter Buck (a double elpee) and finishing up a fuck-tonne of paintings for an art show, then I am going to need something to pass the time. I find it on the TV in *Cruising with Jane McDonald*, a programme about Jane, a Northern club crooner from Wakefield. Jane is a born entertainer, born to tread the boards. The boards she finds herself treading are the boards of the cabaret lounge of the good ship *Celebrity Galaxy*, no less, as it bobs around the Caribbean, with only the lusty tones of Jane's version of 'Lost in France' to propel its main sail. More prosaically, Jane McDonald is the singer on a luxury cruise ship. Channel 5 like Jane, and her earthy talk of Wakefield, and she becomes a huge star.[1]

I spend my lockdown evenings watching repeats of *Cruising with Jane McDonald*, in which Jane, in the pre-Covid world, cruised the oceans on luxury liners, got tiddly with the cruising public, sampled local fare, and ends each episode with a song, slightly relevant to whatever country she finds herself cruising around. Jane doesn't see herself as a Freak, of course. Neither do I, but the people who get to meet her onboard *Galaxy* do. They stare at her in admiration as she gets tipsy with them in the bar, while offering inanities, homilies and the occasional bit of slightly right-wing 'common' sense.

---

[1] Jane McDonald had a number-one album in 1998 off the back of earlier TV success in a BBC series called *The Cruise*.

THE GREATEST PHOTOGRAPH

How does one live the life of Jane? think the octogenarian cruisers, as they share a bit of Jane time, How come we are who we are, and Jane is who she is? they think. Their desire to be and have a bit of Jane bleeds out of their collagen-lifted faces. To them, Jane is a Freak. *Their* Freak.

Jane is in Vietnam now, she's cruising up the Mekong river, she's rhapsodising about the scenery of this 'beau-u-ti-fool country'. 'Of course, it's 'ad its problems,' says Jane, looking into the camera with pursed lips. 'But we won't dwell on that,' and she bursts into an enthusiastic mime of the Doors' 'Light My Fire'.

* * *

The Freaks are not entirely restricted to far-out music, cults, Morris troupes, the outer limits and orthodox rock 'n' roll. As we shall see, light entertainment can also be a haven for the Freak. Sometimes you find them miming to the Doors, and sometimes you find them hiding in plain sight, working their own burger vans in the lay-bys outside Worthing. These are the light entertainment Freaks of the public's 'mind politic'. Woah.

Rest easy, frendz. David Van Day; he walks among us.

David Van Day was the voice and face behind Dollar, the crystal-sharp pop duo who scored big at the dawn of the '80s with the smash hit 'Mirror Mirror'. Dollar were kind of cool in that hallucinogenic way, when the pre-med kicks in, just before the general anaesthetic, just as you are about to go under for major brain surgery.

FREAKS OUT!

Anti-Freak anti-hero Paul Morley (Po Mo) liked them so much that he (predictably) 'created' a genre for them: New Pop. Dollar should have conquered the world, but they were thwarted by a light entertainment behemoth: the horrific Bucks Fizz. Where Dollar were lean, moody and minimalist with sophisto Trevor Horn production, the Fizz were pure corn; the perpetual blocked bog in a Butlin's Pub & Kitchen.

Again, during my lockdown time-on-my hands (between the two solo albums, the collaborative album with Peter Buck, the radio play and the art show, etc.), I re-watched the BBC documentary *Trouble at the Top: Bucks Fizz Making Your Mind Up*. Along with *The Rock and Roll Singer*, *Trouble at the Top* is one of the most disturbing documentaries you will ever see. It is the story of the greatest coup d'état in history. How David Van Day took his vengeance and took control of Bucks Fizz.

Here's the skinny: By 1991 Bucks Fizz had gone flat. Original girl members Cheryl Baker and Jay Aston (Aston last seen standing and coming fifth as a candidate for the Brexit Party in Kensington) had long gone. Tour-bus-crash survivor Mike Nolan had also called it quits, resting control of the group with a gnomic mystical ex-builder: Bobby G. At the same time, Dollar were 'New Pop' toast. There is a terrible inevitability to what happened next.

On an overcast day in 1991, history was about to be written. At the Mitre pub in Hampton Court David Van Day and Bobby G were in talks, a kind of Warsaw Pact for men who had appeared on *Seaside Special*. It was agreed that Van

THE GREATEST PHOTOGRAPH

Day would join the Fizz. And from that moment onwards a bitter thermonuclear war broke out between these two titans of '80s pop.

The first rift, according to *Trouble at the Top*, was Van Day's not unreasonable assertion that he would only 'wear black', again not unreasonably, to 'hide his middle-age paunch'. And presumably because like Lee Van Cleef, David Van Day knew he was a bad guy, and as Minor Threat so wisely put it, 'Good Guys (Don't Wear White)'. Dave Van D. was at heart a rock 'n' roller. Just like Gene. Bobby G, however, was not the kind of guy to wear black. Black was not part of the Bucks Fizz aesthetic. Nor was Gene Vincent. Nor was performing old Dollar hits. Perhaps these problems were surmountable, but what happened next was not. The Fizz were controlled with a rod of iron by Bobby G and his girlfriend and now band member, Heidi Manton. This David St Hubbins and Jeanine situation clearly did not sit well with the maverick Van Day. In a NSFW scene from the *Trouble at the Top* documentary, Van Day accuses Heidi of 'having big ears'. Bobby's Zen iron dome shatters. David Van Day is out of the Fizz.

In a power snatch worthy of Idi Amin, Van Day coaxes original pretty boy Fizz-ter Mike Nolan over to his side. And here's the thing: Van Day and Nolan have not formed a new group. They have just instead formed a new, darker, sexier, meaner version of Bucks Fizz, called . . . Bucks Fizz. David Van Day, King of Scotland, Lord of All the Beasts of the Earth and Fishes of the Sea, and Conqueror of the British Empire. And of Bucks Fizz.

FREAKS OUT!

This is the point in *Trouble at the Top* when you realise what a force to be reckoned with is the former singer of Dollar. What could David Van Day achieve if he put the energy, ferocity and weird manipulative intelligence he applied to destroying and taking over Bucks Fizz? Surely he could annex half of Europe.

Trouble at the Top ends cheerfully enough for David Van Day in 2002, with our Freak hero punching the air after a court victory allowing him to carry on using the name Bucks Fizz. Bobby G and Heidi are seen gloomily setting up for a soundcheck, wondering how they can get back to the land of make-believe.

So Paul Morley was right about Dollar, as much as he was wrong about Jerry Garcia; they were indeed New Pop. Like a pop Venus flytrap gobbling up all enemies, taking their nutrients to become a better, stronger Dollar, and then a better, stronger, monstrous Bucks Fizz. More importantly, Van Day's High Court victory in being allowed to use the name Bucks Fizz perhaps opens the curtain to reveal a new autodidactic D. Van Day. Untethered and unyielding to contemporary whims and mores. A fully fledged post-classical Freak.

CHAPTER 21

Lou, John, Sterl, Mo Tucker and me

In which everyone is kindly advised to never, ever, 'get the old band back together'.

One thing that David Van Day demonstrates clearly: within the realm of rock and roll and truly committed Freakdom you have create your own monster, from time to time you will need this creature to fight off the non-Freaks. I know this, Van Day knows this and Lou Reed knows this.

I am fifteen years old. I am also a fucking sponge. Bend me shape me anyway you want me, baby. Every look, every put-down, and most importantly, every great record that I hear reinvents me. And, at fifteen years old there are a lot of great records ahead of me that I don't even know exist.

I've just picked up Lou Reed's *Take No Prisoners (Lou Reed Live)* from a market stall in Portsmouth's main shopping centre, just behind the Tricorn multi-storey car park and multi-level stabbing opportunity area. The record costs

FREAKS OUT!

£1.50, maybe reflecting Lou's lowly standing in the early 1980s, or maybe reflecting the album's battered cover. On the front is a terrible graffiti painting of a shaven-headed dude in suspenders and high heels, standing in a dark alley beside an upturned trash can. Spilling out of the trash can are make-up compacts, doll heads, and lots and lots of what I will learn to be 'drug-paraphernalia'. I understand that the cover is something of a play on Lou's public image. It is saying: 'You, the record buyer, think that Lou Reed is a cross-dressing junkie monster, so we are giving you this album sleeve to sate your pathetic imagination, which you won't even have to engage. Lou thinks you're all stupid, by the way.' I wonder about this in my fifteen-year-old brain. *Surely, Lou has created this image himself and has kind of run with it. Why does he think we're all stupid for believing him?* I will learn over the years that there is much of this double-thought to come when you invest a lot of time in pursuit of holy rock 'n' roll. The sleeve is possibly the worst album sleeve art-crime ever perpetrated. I don't have high hopes for this album, but still, it's Lou, and it cost pennies. Put the fucker on.

Enter Lou: *'Hello'* (long pause, mixture of audience boos and cheers).

'Sorry we were late, we were just tooning' (longer pause, and audible audience tension).

Lou starts talking to himself: *'It's rainin' out.'*

'Whadya mean it's rainin' out — we know it's fuckin' rainin',' goads Lou.

'Man, the guy who tightened this microphone is like . . . Godzilla, man . . . I need to either grow an inch or meet a boyfriend.'

(audience member with whiny New York accent): *'Meet a wha?'*

Lou Reed: *'Meet a boyfriend. Can'choo fuckin' hear? What's wrong wid choo?'*

Later on, Lou goes brilliantly schizoid, interviewing himself like two Lenny Bruces:

'Are you political, Lou?'

'Political about what?'

'Give me an issue, I'll give you a tissue . . . wipe my ass with it.'

And on it goes, for ninety-eight minutes. Lou Reed talks and talks and struts and insults everyone in New York. *Take No Prisoners* is a live album unlike any other. I've often thought about transcribing Lou's raps from this record and turning them into a one-man play/monologue.

Throughout the 1970s the live album became the *de rigueur* contractual obligation album for the artist, and for the punter, a cheap – they were usually doubles at single-elpee price – greatest hits bashed through jukebox. Think: *Kiss Alive*, *Frampton Comes Alive*, or the triple-album imperial statement of pop as a superpower that was *Wings Over America* (it's by Wings, you dumb motherfucker).[1] *Take No Prisoners* is none of these things. It is the anti-*Wings Over America*.

Recorded during a residency at the super-hip Bottom Line club in Greenwich Village (Andy Warhol and his entourage were in attendance) in a dirty New York in the '70s summer, *Take No Prisoners* sees Lou in 'playful' mood, destroying, deconstructing and bloating out his greatest songs. 'Playful'

---

[1] Said in the spirit of Lou Reed.

for Lou would be murderous for anyone else. Over a backing band comprising men who seem to mainly be called 'Marty', and sounding like an over-testosteroned E Street Band (if you don't like sax then you'll like it even less after listening to this album), Lou performs an exorcism upon himself.

If you enjoy audience baiting, then *Take No Prisoners* is just the album for you. Lou doesn't bother singing. He just harangues: the audience, the head of his record label, and most famously, *Village Voice* rock critic Robert Christgau, who Lou most righteously calls, 'A toe fucker'. Lou even has an argument with himself. It's a shame that old Lou Reed saddled himself with such a non-life-enhancing reputation. *Take No Prisoners* really is a blast in a New York wise guy punching himself (and everyone else) in the face kinda way.

It is 1993, my band – the Auteurs – are playing Glastonbury Festival for the first of four appearances over the years. Glastonbury is already taking baby steps towards becoming the mass media freebie and giant bowl of vegetable soup for the unimaginatively brain dead that it is today. This is not me saying, 'Glastonbury used to be great, it's really corporate now.' It's me saying, 'It was never great, it was always an overflowing pus bucket.' Sure, I can get down 'ideologically' with the early Glastonbury Fayre vibes, and it would have been groovy to see the Pink Fairies Marching Band, David doing his best song, 'Memory of a Free Festival', and Marc playing 'Elemental Child' on his eve of fame pomp. But would I actually have wanted to be there in the grass and in the world of worms? I would not.

LOU, JOHN, STERL, MO TUCKER AND ME

I am firmly of the belief that rock 'n' roll needs four walls, not four clouds. Simple science: sound bounces and reflects off walls. If there ain't no wall then the sound just kinda fizzles out and dies, plopping down next to a sleeping cow. Sleeping cows are not rock 'n' roll. Glastonbury has lots of cows. Dairy farmers are uncool, and Glastonbury is dead uncool.

The Auteurs play our mid-afternoon slot on some stage. Second stage? Third stage? Sheep-shearing stage? Face-painting stage? Who can say? It's okay. I don't particularly care, as I need walls and darkness and I won't find them here.

Glastonbury in 1993 is already becoming a career step. Up and onwards towards the next beacon of success. I'm not acutely aware of this. I suspect that Glastonbury is going to be full of 1990s Euro-hippies. It isn't. It seems to be populated with men in shorts. People from record companies have all put their shorts on. *NME* journalists have got their shorts on, and John Peel is wearing his shorts. If you like wearing shorts, Glastonbury will be right up your country footpath. As the reader will have gathered (see Chapter 18), I do not wear shorts and I don't consider them to be part of the rock armour.

The part of Glastonbury I am mainly interested in is the band on the main stage, just after our turn on 'some other stage'. The band is the Velvet Underground. You see the Velvet Underground have decided to re-form after an earlier re-formation in Paris. The original four-piece – minus Nico, obviously – have now agreed to do it again for a lap of honour whirl around the planet; 'unfinished business' or some other bullshit.

There's a school of thought that says that rock 'n' roll died in 1979. It's not true, incidentally, but the theory goes that 1979 was the first big revival (ze Mods!), and when there's a revival, the object of the revival is rendered null and void. It's just a theory, no need to lose your shit over it! And if the theory were true then surely Gene Vincent's 1968 tour – when Gene became his own tribute act – was the first shut-up-shop of beloved rock 'n' roll. Theories are for mathematicians and academics, and mathematicians and academics are not rock 'n' roll, sister. However, by the 1990s, British rock had puttered out into a kind of deadend conservatism. The future pop stars became cowards and collaborators. Self-evident years later, when your unreliable narrator was the only '90s survivor to stand up and say, 'Ah, fuck the *NME*, get over yourself.'

And you know what? Since I wrote my last screed on the 1990s, – *Bad Vibes: Britpop and My Part in Its Downfall* – almost every one of the bands mentioned in that book has now re-formed. What is a man to do? Did you not listen first time around? Did you not understand me? Are you all really so fucking dense?

Is it ever okay for the band to get back together? Absolutely not. The true Freak never even considers it. There is no unfinished business. The business finished when the goddamned band finished. The true Freak remains righteous in their search for holy rock 'n' roll. The big 'payday' is no excuse. If you really need money, show some dignity. Go and give hand jobs behind the railway station. No re-formed band has ever produced anything to rival their original glory days. To re-form is an act of artistic stagnation, an imagination fail. Why are you doing this if you have nothing to give? 'For the fans.' Gimme a break, Jake.

After the Auteurs Glastonbury set, the plan is to walk across the field and catch the Velvet Underground. That's *the* Velvet Underground. Here's a sketch of the Velvets in 1967 to get you in the mood: Andy, Lou, Nico, Cale looking like Satan. Moe looking like a Long Island secretary. Paul Morrissey being waspish. Ondine being nasty, Brigid Polk shooting speed into her butt. Amphetamine. Amphetamine, Amph,ph,ph,ph,ph, phetamine. The Silver Factory. 'Whip it on me, Jim, whip it on me, Jim, whip it on me, Jim, whip it on me, Jim.'

As it turns out, Glastonbury is a bit bigger than one field. Sadly, it is about 5,000 miles of fields (or perhaps 5,000 'acres', whatever these agricultural motherfuckers prefer). Tramp, tramp, tramp go my expensively Chelsea-booted feet, through grass, the grass and insects. Squish, squish, squish go the worms, the sworn enemies of the Freak. I arrive at the field of holiness. In the distance are the unmistakable forms of the four Velvets.

The Velvet Underground start playing. And they are shit. Can this really be happening? Could the greatest band of all time really be pissing like racehorses over their not inconsiderable chips like this? Is Lou really serious? 'Shiny, shiny, shiny, oh wooah, shiny boots of leather,' he goes. Oh! Lou.

FREAKS OUT!

Do you really think that 'Venus in Furs' could be improved by giving it a little late-'80s cocaine boogie? Even the Grateful Dead never stooped to this. You can kind of feel Cale's palpable embarrassment. To make matters considerably worse, the guitar Lou is playing is most certainly not his famed Gretsch Country Gent 'Ostrich' guitar. No, it is one of those stupid Steinberger guitars, the ones with the cut-off head. The great signifiers of the end of the terrible 1980s. For that is when it happened: the unthinkable . . .

When Buzzcocks re-formed in 1989 there was a palpable feeling of excitement – for they were among the very first groups to saddle up the re-formation horse – and also a feeling of dread. Should this be happening? Are groups allowed to re-form? There were rules about these things back then within the strict orthodoxy of the times. It was seen as at worst: a cop-out. At best: there is no best. Others followed tentatively in their footsteps. Gradually, perfectly good groups started serving themselves up with chips (self-seasoned with their own piss), trussed and basted. The chickens in their own baskets, on the chicken and basket re-formation circuit. That's meta-sucking.

Back in the field of 1993. Heads are down. Thousands of faces scan the grass, looking for solace. The lads who have heard the Velvets because Primal Scream like them have lost interest, and the girls who like 'Transformer' wander off, curiosity exhausted, to go and listen to some up-and-coming Britpoppers. After fifteen minutes I don't think I can take any more, so I walk back, another thousand miles, across more fields, mud, rivers and lakes, and worms; squish, squish, squish. This isn't really what the Velvet Underground were meant to be all about, is it? The VU don't belong in a field full of cowpats. The VU need Uptight A-Men. Andy, the Coney Island Steeplechase, 'Heroin', Black Angels, Jackie Curtis, Candy Darling and Holly Woodlawn. Jim Carroll – one of the stars of my *New York in the '70s* album – trying to score Tuinals at Max's Kansas City. The Chelsea Hotel. Scary transvestites who live on the streets. The Velvets need Freaks, and Glastonbury – and re-forming – is not for Freaks.

I didn't listen to the Velvets for years after Apocalypse Glastonbury. They had pissed all over their immaculate myth and like a tramp's shoes could never quite shake off the stench. Many others wandered off down the same path as heritage rock became a new currency, working on the premise that all the great bands have gone, so here they are re-formed, reissued, repackaged, reheated, and if it was working for the great bands, could it not work for the not-so-great bands? Hell, yeah. Well, sort of. There were a couple of snags: the great bands were no longer great, and the not-so-great bands remained not so great.

CHAPTER 22

The three Fs

In which some very important 'Rules' are discussed.

Rock 'n' roll is all about the Fs: the Big F: F for Freak (where have you been, for Chrissakes?), F and Non-F, and Freak Enablers (FE). As we have previously established, F is also for the Fall, and F is for fortissimo or double fortissimo; that is 'loud' and even 'louder' (remember when records used to print the legend 'To Be Played Loud' on the back cover?). We can proceed no further in our search for the holy without addressing the three Fs:

1) F = I wanna fuck you, and I hope you wanna fuck me.
2) F = I'm fucked-up. Do you wanna get fucked-up with me?
3) F = Fuck you, I'm an outlier on the rock 'n' roll horse riding around the city gates. You won't let me in. Fuck off and Fuck you.

FREAKS OUT!

Even if you're not a Freak, you can possibly blag your way near to the shrine if you can invoke the three Fs. Warning: if you're not a Freak, you'll eventually be found out, so enjoy the ride while it lasts.

The first F is perhaps the easiest to gain purchase over. Everybody wants to be loved. With a few very rare exceptions: Charles Manson, Hitler, Morrissey. And everyone wants to get laid, perhaps with a few exceptions: Hitler. Morrissey. Now, getting laid can be problematic for the Freak. At least that's what the football lads wanted me to believe. Until I found my inner Freak and laid my Freak balls out on the table. If you wanna score, take a hotty back to your Freak pad and play her your Sun City Girls albums and your Doors albums, and if you've got any Radiohead records, hide them under the bed.

The Fabs knew the power of the first F, perhaps more than anyone who followed in their wake (the sexual carnage they left in their wake is well documented). Others seemed to exist merely to fuck their way around the world, and boy, did it get dark out there when the spotlights of the twenty-first century shone upon the 1960s and '70s' carnal night rally.

'I wanna fuck you, do you wanna fuck me?' It still stands, and always will. Humans for all their innate contradictions, sophistication, stupidity, insignificance, capabilities of inspired strangeness will always want to say to each other, in so many ways, 'I wanna fuck you, do you wanna fuck me?' You want evidence? Just turn on the radio to any channel, or if you want specifics, just stick on your original Fly

Records 45 of T. Rex's 'Get It On', and listen to Marc Bolan singing. Sure, he's singing about 'eagles' and 'hubcaps' but it really translates as: 'I wanna fuck you, do you wanna fuck me?' To which the answer from a few million '70s teenagers was, 'Yes, Marc, we do.' What Marc knew, and many others who came from the stars and actually *saw* the world through enlightened eyes also knew, was that the first F levelled the playing field for the Freak. How we savoured the look on the football dunces' faces, how we rubbed their faces in the dog shit, how we made them look up and stare in disbelief as they watched the misfits inherit the earth and get the girl.

The second F: 'I'm fucked-up' is the easiest of the Fs to attain. In truth, 'I'm fucked' is hardly righteous and tends to fall into the Male Genius Bohemian Myth, as outlined in Chapter 12. Dubious as it is, it undoubtably has its place on the rock 'n' roll menu and, sorrowfully, we've all played that hand a little. For every fucked-up David Crosby, there is a Pete Doherty. For every junkie dull Pete Doherty and his body count, there is a throng of adoring male music journalists who cannot get over their Nick Kent habit and their need to watch young men throwing up in wastepaper bins. It is not going anywhere anytime soon but one day it will, and we will wonder what this spectacle of the fuck-up was all about.

The true Freak doesn't need to announce that they are 'fucked-up'. It should be self-evident. Freakery is the currency, not smack or crack or whack or gak. Morrissey knows this and Tod Browning knew it, too. It's a much harder sell though; as every journalist knows, it's easier to write about the ongoing updates in Pete Doherty's drug diary than it is to write about Wesley Willis.

The third F: 'Fuck you/fuck off' is perhaps the hardest of the Fs to achieve and yet it is ultimately the most wholesome and worthwhile. This is the one that seemed to vanish in the 1990s. As the gates of the city opened up to the eeny-meany Brit guitar bands and the money lenders beckoned. Once the bucks were laid out upon the table and the white lines were racked out, unsurprisingly 'Fuck you' changed to 'Thank you'. My own generation very much sold themselves out at the drop of a pork-pie hat. You can blame any one or all of the players of the era. The loaded lads. The record companies. All complicit of course, but you'd be looking in the wrong place. It was all the fault of the musicians who just rolled over and took it. To fully embrace the 'fuck you' of pop, you must ask yourself one question: Have I ever listened to *Metal Machine Music* in full, more than once? You know the correct answer.

In my first excellent book – you know the one – I wrote about the Britpop years and the re-adoption of the Union Jack. At the time of writing (2009), the Union Jack just seemed a mindless co-opting of an old pop-art signifier. When culture first rehashed the Union flag it was a symbol of modish reclamation, and less than two decades after the end of the Second World War, sharp girls and boys were wearing T-shirts and mini-skirts that incorporated designs using the flag that represented the freedoms that their mams and dads had fought for. When *Select* magazine put it on the cover of a 1993 issue, it represented nothing

THE THREE FS

but nationalism.[1] From then on, the flag was omnipresent, not once representing any kind of subversion, just mindless and rampant conformity.

In 2016, the British public were sold the dummy in the pack when 52 per cent of the electorate voted out of the European Union. Whether that was or wasn't the right decision is not what this book is about (you'll have to guess which way I voted), but did the proliferation of mindless 'Cool Britannia' a decade and a half earlier have an impact on the psyche of the population – all those late-teens and twenty-somethings grooving to Noel G. with his Union Jack Epiphone guitar at Maine Road? Fifteen years later and they are approaching middle age and only just realising that they had been sold the dummy back in the 1990s. What to do? When you've bought the dummy once and it wasn't even hiding in plain sight, you're only going to be a repeat offender. Did *Select* magazine inadvertently play a part in Brexit? You can bet your bottom Euro it did. Fuck you, indeed.

---

[1] As has been the case since. The disaster of that *Select* cover was very much the result of hacks and halfwit designers not understanding how to apply pop-art concepts.

CHAPTER 23

We have to talk about Steve, Part Two

In which we talk about Steve. Not Steve Peregrin Took, that other Steve.

Every year on 26 December in Clovis, New Mexico, a pageant takes place. It is known as the Real Feast of St Stephen. Hundreds of bequiffed, bespectacled young men wibble-wobble through the streets astride punctured bicycles. The four-eyed bike riders are followed by a group of worried cultural commentators in blackface wearing huge platform boots. The cultural commentators stop every thirty seconds, get down on one knee and perform a finger-wagging ritual aimed at the bequiffed bicycle lads. A Mariachi band made up entirely of Yootha Joyce, Viv Nicholson and Myra Hindley lookalikes run breathlessly alongside. Their yellow plastic macs throb like man-made lightning in the refried New Mexico heat. After much yodelling and preening and chanting

FREAKS OUT!

of frightful statements about the Chinese and Brexit, the procession settles down for a vegan feast. The food bearers (Ronnie Kray and Freddie Mills lookalikes) set down the grub on trestle tables. The pageanters give the food a sniff and a let out a collective 'Nah' for there are more important things to dwell on than nut sundaes. The evening will bring on the annual sacrifice: The Burning of the Spare Parts of a Lawnmower Ceremony.

The above was how I started a review[1] on the Talkhouse website of Morrissey's rather excellent 2014 album, *World Peace is None of Your Business*. Morrissey: a man who understood the heathen and yet holy power of the quiff from a very young age. Morrissey: a man who rescued our great hero, Johnnie Ray, when few others would not have shed a single tear for him. To you, little Morrissey fan, La Moz has one thing to say: 'Frankly, *I* am none of your business.' Frendz, you may not want to, but we have to talk about Steven.

It is early 1983, I am fifteen, I'm in a band. I'm beginning to feel like I understand what it is to be hip. I've got weird. I am no longer the lanky, uncool, ginger-haired, gap-toothed kid at school. (I am of course still all these things but now I can style it out.) Other kids, some of whom may even be the *real* cool kids, think I know stuff. More than them, perhaps? And I kind of do, because I'm checking *everything* out. My

---

[1] I added in the reference to 'Brexit' in this edit. Morrissey being a supporter of leaving the EU and a fan of chanting, 'Brexit, Brexit, Brexit' at his live shows of the period.

style and thinking is getting more militant. I've got the sus on the shit that's going down.

The band who are several feet in front of me in the half-full Portsmouth Polytechnic hall (younger readers should be advised that polytechnics were universities for kids that went to state school. If you went to a 'private' school it was illegal to attend a polytechnic. All true) are causing ructions. There have been rumours about how good they are from those in the know. They are the band with the quiffy singer who minces around with beads and daffs. The rumours are not incorrect.

To see the Smiths in 1983 was to see a band imperial (three years before their official imperial phase), imperious and fully formed. Also, what tends to get forgotten is that no British band dared to wear those '60s influences quite so boldly – in the early '80s world of Cabaret Voltaire, the Human League and Soft Cell – as the Smiths once did. For that one night the Smiths were perfect. They seemed to have only seven songs, some of which they maybe played more than once. Whether they had recorded that famous first Peel session I do not remember. Whether their first single had even been released, again, 'I dunno'. What was certain was the hold they already had on their strange skin-heady audience. Morrissey, the lead singer, was clearly an actual Freak, and he was already – to the audience – a very special Freak.

Despite all of the above, I didn't carry that night with me as much as you might think. Much as I thought the Smiths were fantastic, Morrissey never ever spoke for me. I didn't need a spokesman and I didn't feel his brand of outsider-dom. I recognised the heraldry of his own particular Freak flag, but mine was different colours which didn't manifest around Morrissey's kitchen sink despair.

The records didn't really do it for me either. While 'Reel Around the Fountain' sounded like it was beamed in from another world when it was first set free in BBC-session format on the *John Peel Show*, by the time it showed up late on the Smiths' debut album, it just sounded like it had been beamed in from 'the record producers' conference', today's seminar being, 'How to fuck up a really great band' (answer: overdub a crappy chocolate-box piano). From then on, each album was a diminished experience, as the producer worked their tragic un-magick and every great song got mired in the sound of the terrible 1980s. The Smiths broke up, as bands do, and sensitive young people cried. Not I though. Morrissey did what singers do and went solo. It was then supposed to get dull. But it didn't. It got weird. And the cakes got hotter, and the cakes got a bit racist.

Of all the strange statements Morrissey has made, his 1984 'Reggae is vile' comment (this is the one that laid the foundations for the case 'against' him) is the one that affected me the most. In 1984, I might have even agreed with it, having only really experienced reggae as something of an annoying distraction on the *John Peel Show* between records by the Three Johns, the Nightingales and the Birthday Party, what I considered to be at the time 'the proper stuff'.

My only experience of reggae at this time was via the Clash (bless me and bless the Clash). There are many reasons to laugh at the Clash and their weepy sentimental army of old bloke fans, but the Rock-Action-Men's efforts to bring reggae to the punk kids is not one of them. I would look at the label of 'Complete Control' and wonder 'If this Lee Perry dude is a Rasta and this is what reggae sounds like, then it can't be too bad.'[2] By the same token I'd put on the Clash's club-footed cover of Junior Murvin's immortal 'Police and Thieves', squint and pretend it wasn't 'well, a bit long and boring'. Then there was the line in 'Safe European Home', a great song and one of the few where the group drop their Palitoy hardman stance. It's all about the time that Clash manager Bernie Rhodes sent Joe and Mick off to write songs in Jamaica and get some Rasta-man vibrations from the island of their heroes. Joe and Mick, as it happened, found Jamaica a bit, er, too heavy, and found themselves re-writing 'Dreadlock Holiday': 'I went to the place where every white face is an invitation to robbery'. Yikes, Joe, this is not in the script. Never mind, you can always hide out at the hotel bar. Oh no, you can't, because the Sheraton is full of dreads. Shit, man.

The Sheraton Hotel, Kingston, Jamaica. One of the dreads who helped build the Sheraton in 1962 was one Manley Augustus Buchanan. Better known as the seriously mighty Big Youth. Remember the question? Bob Marley or Big Youth? Well, the answer is always Big Youth.

---

[2] How much of Lee Perry's production remains on the finished 'Complete Control' is up for grabs. The record doesn't exactly sound like a Lee Perry production. The record does bear a Lee Perry production credit though.

FREAKS OUT!

It took me until my late twenties to really get it. Until my own *Baader-Meinhof* album. Up until then I really was a music-of-white-origin unforward-thinking motherfucker. Maybe it was all the flag waving of the Britpop era or maybe it was just the 'Freddie and the Dreamers on *Blue Peter*' vibes of that era that were giving me the white man collywobbles, but pretty soon, thank God, I'd fallen for reggae pretty hard. The harder they come, the harder they fall.

By 1998, one of my old outfits – Black Box Recorder – have even recorded a reggae cover version: Althea and Donna's deathless pop reggae attitude classic, 'Uptown Top Ranking' (Joe Strummer didn't like pop reggae, remember). Okay, so it's built around a sample of Peter Wyngarde's ultra-creep-out 'Rape', but it's the thought that counts, right? And my next thought was to go full tilt and do a reggae covers EP. Leading off with Big Youth's dread warning meditation, 'Wolf in Sheep's Clothing'. I'm voted down on this by our tragically democratic group.

The Youth's *Natty Cultural Dread* was my first reggae album. It's the one with 'Wolf in Sheep's Clothing' on. And the one with 'Genetic, stenetic, remote control'. You've heard it being sampled – to Big Youth's considerable chagrin – by the far less imaginative. There he is on the front cover of *Natty Cultural Dread*, in lurid mustard yellow, gold teeth, kids' sunglasses, and the biggest – put you on the fucking floor after you've spun round the ceiling one hundred times – spliff hanging the fuck out of his gob. Woah! What an album cover.

WE HAVE TO TALK ABOUT STEVE

The year 1976 was peak Big Youth time, and he was battling it out with Bob Marley to be JA's greatest reggae star. At one point the Youth had seven singles in the Jamaican top ten. But Bob, perhaps more ambitious and perhaps less of a – you guessed it – Freak, was the one to go international.

However, by the 1980s, Manley Augustus Buchanan's star was diminished as reggae changed. Big Youth's considerable style just didn't chime with the new digital-recording techniques. The vibes were changing.

In the late '80s and early '90s, Steven Patrick Morrissey's star was waning as his fans grew a little wiser, a little slower and a little older. The vibes were changing and Morrissey was at odds with the less-bad vibes of the Britpopping throng. He was starting to come over like a fellow living alone in the woods too long, who's started to cook up roadkill (obviously not roadkill, let's go with fallen fruit).

Lone woodsman Morrissey, a kind of effete Raoul Moat, was now playing a strange game of truth or dare with his increasingly baffled fanbase. There were the misfiring songs: 'Bengali in Platforms', 'Asian Rut' and the excellent but wildly misunderstood 'National Front Disco', which would have been a lot less misunderstood had Steve not laid the groundwork of suspicion with the two grievous precedents.

At some point around this time, it looks as though Morrissey self-actualised again, lost in his best fantasy: as the third guest at Judy Garland's fifth wedding to Mickey Deans. Lest we forget, the only other guest was Judy's pal at the dipso disco: poor old Johnnie Ray. Judy and Johnnie were the only double act in the world without a straight man. But in his dreams, Big Steve was the gooseberry.

In the 2000s, Morrissey wrote his autobiography; it's a fabulous book and Morrissey gives himself full props for a life strangely lived. Here are some words I wrote at the time of publication:

'Throughout his teenage years young women seem to throw themselves at our author and teenage boys readily become confidants and mentors. Throughout Morrissey remains resolutely lonely.'

And there it is. He wants adulation and when he gets it, he must reject it. I would take a wild swing and say that, perhaps, Moz has never felt the pain of being jilted. Chucked. He wouldn't let it happen and besides he's far too handsome. So it is that Steven Morrissey must do the jilting. To each and every one of his fans, on a grand scale, he is the emperor of the dump. It is who he is, it is what he has made himself, it is how he must die.

Morrissey can never be a national treasure, as Morrissey fully knows he has to always be in opposition, and as our Jarv knows, once you're the Queen Mother of Pop then you are never going to be in opposition again.

Like the hard leftist politician who can never lead a mainstream political party in a country as socially conservative as Great Britain, Morrissey tries on a rum 'point of view' in the mirror of his Sunset Boulevard Gloria Swanson mansion, or by the pool in LA, drinking a pornstar martini (we must never know), and wonders whether this is the opinion that will finally lose him that last four-eyed bicycle-riding fan last seen at the beginning of this chapter. And it will, because the four-eyed fans have all changed: they have jobs, they do proper things, they have – *quelle horreur* – careers, and, ooh, hiss it with pursed lips like a disgusted Morrissey, 'they have families'; they help people, they help others, and they help themselves. Morrissey never helps himself, or anyone else. Unlike you four eyes, he's a proper un-grown-up Freak.

In the 2000s, Big Youth could be found restoring his famous mural on Orange Street. Murals and statues; remember Scott King's efforts to build a 300-foot statue of Lee Brilleaux in Southend-on-Sea? Well, you don't get a mural or a statue unless you're the devil or an angel, or are holy and righteous, and we know which one Manley Augustus Buchanan is. That Big Youth's mural is being removed is an act of sacrilege. Just like removing Morrissey, devil or angel, is an act of sacrilege.

CHAPTER 24

Weasels (slight return)

*In which we finally get around to discussing
the Incredible String Band.*

It is 2016. I am in a pub basement with my friend Caroline. Caroline is an actress on a couple of ITV1 shows: the one about the doctor who lives in a tiny village in Cornwall, and one about detectives in Leeds, or somewhere like that. Caroline is very successful in the world of telly and acting. She has another life in righteousness. She is a film director and has directed a film about the marvellous Jesse Hector[1]

---

[1] Jesse Hector first emerged as the eleven-year-old leader of the Rock and Roll Trio, playing at the Cliff Richard-bothered 2i's Coffee Bar. Jesse's perhaps best-known groups were the excellently named Crushed Butler and Hammersmith Gorillas. Musically, Jesse maintained (and continues to this day) an orthodox bovver boot/glam aesthetic. His Freak aesthetic is best realised in his hirsute heyday of him wearing three haircuts simultaneously.

and is working on a film about everyone's fave Radiophonic Workshop heroine: Delia Derbyshire. This evening, in rainy north London, we are in a small folk club cellar in Crouch End waiting for Robin Williamson – one time co-leader of the extraordinary Incredible String Band – to take the stage, in front of fifty ageing heads.

I've been wanting to see Robin for a while. The expectations in mine and Caroline's minds are heading skywards. If you've ever seen the BBC documentary about the Incredible String Band, *Retying the Knot*, you'll understand why. There is one scene where the great man, in his 1968 pomp, berobed and bearded like a William Blake vision of a hippie Christ, wanders up to the camera, smiles and introduces himself: 'Robin Williamson, Genius of this Parish', and here we are tonight, Caroline and I, awaiting the 'Genius of this Parish'.

I'd first heard the Incredible String Band in 1986. 'Heard' is a stretch. I'd picked up the sleeve to their 1968 masterpiece, *The Hangman's Beautiful Daughter*, out of my friend David Westlake's record collection. I took in the image on the wild front sleeve: a scene of rural witchy bad trippery, where the String Band look like a Scottish version of the Manson Family. I put the needle on the plastic, gave it a minute, and then took the fucker off.

'Jesus, what is this weak hippie shit?' It's fair to say that I do not fall in love with the Incredible String Band on first meeting.

Around three decades later and the ISB shilling has finally dropped. So much so, that on my own 2016

WEASELS (SLIGHT RETURN)

Smash the System elpee I write a sincere campfire sing-song tribute to these mad Scottish motherfuckers. Let's take it verse by verse and break it in easy for you:

> *The Incredible String Band were an unholy act*
> *They sang like a couple of weasels trapped in sack*
> *Mike and Robin*
> *Rose and Likky*
> *Then there was Malcolm and Clive, if you're gonna get picky.*

So there was Mike: Mike Heron, handsome and a wee bit McCartney-like in both looks and musicality. Mike was *that* guy in the songwriting partnership. The *other* songwriter, who wrote the more melodic and on-the-surface-easier tunes. The one the fans don't like as much as the guy they really dig. The 'genius' (myth) one. In this case, Robin Williamson. Then there was Malcolm and Clive, who – for the sake of my own song – I am a little disingenuous towards: Clive Palmer: founder member and dyed-in-the-wool folkie. Clive left after the first eponymous *ISB* album in 1966. He looked a bit like a provincial bank manager gone slightly to seed and was an original beatnik, extremely cool and a true Freak. For him, the Incredible String Band were teetering too much on their original folk axis and wobbling into a new heady psychedelic world. Like the true excellent hippie he was, Clive hopped it to Morocco. Malcolm. Sorry, Malcolm. Malcolm Le Maistre. Joined later, he was an intuitive dancer in the head troupe Stone Monkey: a Vibe guy. It was always going to be tough for Malcolm to be 'cool' (see Chapter 6) when Robin Williamson was floating around like an angel.

And of course, Rose and Likky, oh my word, yes. Rose Simpson was Mike's girlfriend, and the only non-Scot of the imperial phase Incredibles Fab-Four line-up. Rose,[2] by her own admission, was not a musician; she was a traveller in the spirit of the age, happy to join in, learn the bass, and in her own words, 'bang things'.

Perhaps most importantly, there was the talismanic Likky: Christina 'Licorice' McKechnie. The toothless fan favourite. Licorice was very much the cosmic essence of the Incredible String Band. Along with her main recorded contributions, whispering 'Amoebas are very small' on the epic classic 'A Very Cellular Song', and some otherworldly glass-bothering witchy vocals, Licorice is perhaps best known for being a missing person since 1987. She was 'last seen in 1987 hitchhiking across the Arizona Desert'.[3]

And then there was one: Robin Williamson. The Craig Scanlon to Mike Heron's Martin Bramah. The Robert Forster to Mike's Grant McLennan. All songwriting duos must have this dynamic, by holy decree of the Royal Fraternity of *Mojo* magazine. Robin and Likky were also a couple, and as a couple they were certainly Freak royalty.

---

[2] In 1994, Rose became Lady Mayoress of Aberystwyth, Wales.
[3] Mark Ellen writing in *Mojo* magazine. Licorice is thought to be living in sheltered housing somewhere in California.

WEASELS (SLIGHT RETURN)

So, Robin Williamson, Genius of this Parish, for sure. But were Robin and Licorice the only Freaks in the ISB?

> *They've got songs about caterpillars*
> *Hedgehogs and death*
> *They even had a song about a . . .*
> *dude with no head*

By late 1968, on the ISBs third masterpiece, the sprawling *Wee Tam and the Big Huge,* Mike Heron was entering into his Paulie Mac, 'Helter Skelter'/'Why Don't We Do It in the Road?' phase. That is to say, Mike was getting really weird. The song about caterpillars? That was 'Cousin Caterpillar', a simple children's song about metamorphosis. All straightforward enough, except that it's about a fucking caterpillar. But then Heron, who would later undersell himself somewhat as 'just a boring old songwriter', unleashes one of the greatest and strangest songs let loose on the world outside of a Wesley Willis cassette: 'Douglas Traherne Harding', it is indeed a song about a dude with no head.

Long ago, when pop stars used to read books (or at least pretend to read books), Mike Heron read a book about the seventeenth-century theologian, metaphysical poet and visionary, Thomas Traherne. Traherne had an almost child-like view of God, nature and animals. His strange works had languished until he was rediscovered in the late nineteenth century. Mike was friends with an English visionary: Douglas Harding. Harding explained to Mike how, like Traherne, he had experienced life as a man with no head.[4] That is, 'living with all thought fallen away, as if having no head'. Or, as Mike put it in the first line of the song, 'When I was born I had no head.' There would have to be room in the parish now for an extra Freak and two 'Genius' of the Parish'.

Then one day Joe Boyd came along
and he didn't see.
Some dude lurking in the shadows
From the Church of Scientology.

Received wisdom tells us that the Incredible String Band peaked around 1968, after the colossal *Wee Tam and the Big Huge*. As we all know, received wisdom tends to be handed down by dull apes. Hairy hand to hairy hand. In this case our hairy-handed frendz may have a point. By the end of 1969, Mike and Robin had split with their girlfriends, Rose and Licorice, joined forces with Stone Monkey and moved up to a commune, first in a freezing house in Penwern, Wales, then to a row of freezing cottages in Innerleithen, Scotland. The good vibes pipes burst and turned to bad vibes.

---

[4] Out of our heads; the countercultural generation, self-styled heads, took losing one's head seriously. Joey Mellen, author of trepanation pulp classic memoir *Bore Hole*, spent much of the late '60s under the influence of Dutch psychonaut Dr Bart Hughes, attempting (and eventually succeeding) to trepan himself in a bid to 'stay permanently high'. His wife, Amanda Feilding, made a film of her own trepanation, *Heartbeat in a Brain* (1970). Don't watch it.

WEASELS (SLIGHT RETURN)

The keen imbiber of freakery will have noted that this book takes a light-hearted approach to cults and cultish tomfoolery, and in general gives a cheery thumbs-up up to cutting oneself off from one's family, giving away one's possessions and surrendering any self-sovereignty to megalomaniacal creepy types with a death wish (see Chapter 16). I cannot, however, endorse the Church of Scientology in any way. The main problem with the Church is that they do not seem to have taken the most cursory of butchers at the *How to Be a Cult* handbook. There appears to be no drug abuse, no hairy motherfuckers, no Volkswagen campervans in Texas, no Death Valley, and most catastrophically, no all-encompassing doomsday prophesy. What a mob of hopelessly un-fun dunces the Scientologists are, and it is the Church of Scientology that we must blame for (partially) ruining the Incredible String Band. Having listened to their manager Joe Boyd regaling them with tales of L. Ron Hubbard in a New York City restaurant, the Fab Four were gone. Hook, line and sinker, saucer-eyed, clutching tightly on to the dummy hand, and they were never quite the same again.

That's the script at least, and there would seem to be some truth in it. But perhaps it was also a bit of misplaced careerism on manager Joe Boyd's behalf that scuppered the Increds.

In the summer of '69, Boyd, as much of a businessman as an excellent record producer, convinced the Incredibles to appear at the Woodstock Festival. The appearance was, oddly, not a success. The String Band refused to perform in the rain and the heads got 'pissed' at them. Woah, downer! If the ISB – God's greatest Freaks – could 'flop' at Woodstock, then where *can* a Freak go and fly their flag high? After the Woodstock bummer, their reputation never quite recovered and the once-luminous quasar of the Incredible String Band dimmed unstoppably.

This dimstar period of the ISB proved how fantastic a prospect they were, and that despite being programmed up to the gills with Scientology codswallop, they could still crack out reliably nutzoid elpees. None more so than the 1970 parable *U*, which perhaps the Residents based their entire career upon. *U* may be the true test of anyone wishing to go deep (there really is no other way) with the Increds. A two-hour double-album soundtrack (recorded in just two days) of the ISB's demented and epic Scientology pantomime, with live dancing from Stone Monkey, the plot of which concerns an End Times paradise planet called 'El Wool'– where people are free to 'invent' water and unicycles. There is also some stuff about cowboys. Where once the ISB could do no wrong, now it seemed that was all they could do. The critics savaged *U*.

The Incredible String Band split with Joe Boyd in 1970, after the critical and financial catastrophe of *U*, leaving the talismanic Electra record label and signing with Island Records. A year later, Rose Simpson left to be replaced by poor old Malcolm Le Maistre as a full-time member. And then . . . and then . . . well, the ISB made some more records that were cool, but it was the '70s and sitars were out (and so were the String Band). In came electric guitars (scoundrels),

WEASELS (SLIGHT RETURN)

possibly a wee bit too much Malcolm for the diehards (Malcolm!), and full drumkits (privateers! Plutocrats!), all of which made our beloved heroes sound like ... a normal rock band. Speaking on the *Retying the Knot* documentary about this later line-up, Joe Boyd puts it bluntly: 'Those other guys were good but they weren't great. If you're not great, get off the stage. And Mike and Robin were both great. Malcolm wasn't.' Poor Malcolm.[5]

In Crouch End, in the folk club, Robin and his wife Bina, who accompanies the Genius of this Parish by plucking homemade instruments out of a carrier bag and enthusiastically making some horrible and some not-quite-so-horrible sounds are packing down their gear. Caroline, being gregarious, says that we should introduce ourselves to Robin. I go along for the ride.

'Hi,' says Caroline, at Robin. 'This is my friend Luke, he's a huge admir—' But before the sentence finishes, Robin peers attentively at Caroline over his wire-rimmed granny glasses.

'It's you, isn't it?' says the Genius of this Parish. 'You're on *Doc Martin* on the TV, aren't you?'

Caroline, a little taken aback, confirms that she is indeed the suspect.

'We love that show,' says the man who wrote 'Witches Hat'.

'We love it so much,' agrees Bina.

---

[5] *Earthspan* (1972) is Malcolm's most prominent ISB album, and at this point, all the better for it. Malcolm conjures up the fab 'My Father Was A Lighthouse Keeper' and ... it's great! So, Joe Boyd was wrong.

'Would you like me to help you load up your car?' I ask Robin, boldly inserting myself into the conversation.

'Yes, please,' says Robin. Matter-of-factly un-inserting me from the conversation.

So I leave them chatting about ITV1. I walk up the staircase with Robin's guitar in my hand. I wait by an old estate car that will carry Robin and Bina back to their home in Cardiff. I am the new roadie for the Incredible String Band. I am not famous. Robin's not famous any more either. Soon, nobody will be famous any more.

Postscript

I am checking the master for my latest elpee, *Smash the System*, in the modern way, on my phone, while walking round a supermarket in the north of England. My tribute song, 'The Incredible String Band' song, is just about to start up. I notice someone. Who's that man by the bananas?

I am holding a singular earplug up to Mike Heron's ear. He's a bit baffled, he just wanted to buy some bananas; he didn't want to listen to a song about his old band. He makes little acknowledgement that there is a song that is all about him now being poured into one side of his head. After less than a minute he smiles. 'Quite nice,' he says. Then he walks off. And so do I.

CHAPTER 25

In the future nobody will be famous for fifteen minutes

In which we find out that Andy Warhol was right and is now wrong.

He said it, Andy Warhol that is, in 1968. The famous, 'In the future, everybody will be famous for fifteen minutes' quote. The most prescient line of the twentieth century. Except he, that is, Andy Warhol, didn't say it, as any first-year art student used to know. It was Allen Midgette who came up with the gold. Midgette was a brief Warhol superstar, who had appeared in the Warhol movie, *The Nude Restaurant*, in 1967, and would later horse around in the high-camp – and actually pretty funny – *Lonesome Cowboys*.

In 1968, Andy had been shot by part headbanger, part visionary and Freak immense, Valerie Solanas. Allen Midgette – with Andy's blessing – put on Andy's silver powdered fright-wig and pale-face make-up and was sent out as 'Andy Warhol' on a university lecture tour. It was a classic Warhol pop-art put-on, made even better when somewhere along the line Allen improvised out of thin air the immortal quote: 'In the future, everybody will be famous for fifteen minutes.'[1] In the end it didn't matter who said it, Allen Midgette guessed it was the kind of thing that Andy might have said and he was right. Who cares if Andy didn't actually speak his most famous line? Who cares if he didn't actually make all the films that he put his name on? Who cares if he got assistants to do the screen-printing and some of the paintings? Who cares?

As rock 'n' roll head-butted the impasse of the early twenty-first century, a boatload of young and suspiciously well-to-do New York City groups – the Strokes, Yeah Yeah Yeahs, the Bravery, the Moldy Peaches – acted out a pageant in homage to the original New York in the '70s, and the kids were distracted briefly, but did it really stick? It did not. This time the revival didn't really feel like one of those revivals where some old dudes (me) might say, 'It's just a revival, so it must be the end of pop music.' It just felt like it was a revival for the sake of a revival. No old dudes actually said, 'This is the end of pop music,' because it clearly wasn't. Pop music was just going to go on like this. For ever. Who cares?

---

[1] This quote – possibly the greatest line of the twentieth century – is also attributed to Pontus Hultén, director of the Moderna Museet in Stockholm. Hultén was writing the programme for a 1968 Warhol show. In the programme the quote appeared supposedly from a box of writings by Warhol. When checking, no one could confirm the source. Hultén's response was: 'If he [Warhol] didn't say it, he could very well have said it. Let's put it in.'

IN THE FUTURE NOBODY WILL BE FAMOUS

I was already contemplating my full Freak vision at this point. After a few solo albums, I sat down to write my first book. I decided the only way to write a memoir was as if I was writing a diary that was never meant to be seen, but which ultimately would be seen! Then hopefully I would be finished. My business all done. Banished to the badlands and cast out of the city walls for ever. That is where I wanted to be. It's where I always am anyway. Who cares?

Then it occurred to me: what if in the future, Warhol/Allen Midgette's maxim was reversed? What if nobody wanted to be famous at all? Let alone for fifteen minutes. Think of the fun to be had in a world where people were just too smart to fall for it. Think of the last dwindling stars, who didn't get the memo, grimly hanging on to 'fame' that no one else wants and rattling around their huge mansions, peering anxiously from behind the curtains, wondering where the paparazzi are. Imagine the gates of the city crashing to the ground. *Big Brother* contestants going into the Big Brother house for ten weeks or forever and not being filmed. Future generation after future generation after future generation wondering what all the screaming was about. And, in retrospect, the screaming and the parasocial arrangement of fame will seem stranger. What *was* the screaming about? Were they screaming for God? How come they were screaming for God if they don't believe in God? If God cannot be defined, how can they not believe in God? Why did Shakin' Stevens make a concept album about Cornish tin mining? Why was Luke Haines still bothering to make records for a tiny audience?

FREAKS OUT!

Did he think he was going to be famous? What a dick. Can you still get Kim Wilde's album about aliens? How come Hall & Oates were seen to be as influential as the Velvet Underground? Why did Kurt Cobain kill himself? Who were Joy Division? Were they famous or not famous? We don't understand.

It's so vast that it's almost impossible to define and describe; this future where nobody is famous. But it will come upon us, and the Freaks will rise up, and wander across this un-famous land — lay preachers, preaching anonymity on the side of the road. Philip Larkin knew it, and so did Ivor Cutler, as he went up and down on the bus.

CHAPTER 26

The empty seat on the bus

*A bus journey with Ivor Cutler and
his very dependable hat.*

By the early 2000s, more by luck than judgement, I lived in one of the leafy areas of London that I was not welcome in, or even knew existed, back in the mid-1980s. My old neighbours were beginning to be 'replaced' by actors. Not actors playing the parts of the old neighbours, but actors playing the parts of new neighbours. One of the old neighbours was Ivor Cutler, the poet, singer, teacher and man on the C11 bus – final destination: Brent Cross. They were trying to replace Ivor with some actors, no doubt. They were also trying to replace me.

I had first encountered Ivor Cutler, like most who had bothered to encounter Ivor, via the *John Peel* radio show. Ivor was old, even in the early '80s, but he was one of those whose age didn't matter. Captain Beefheart sounded as if he was as old as God. John Betjeman not only sounded like he was as old as God's grandfather, he really was as old as God's grandfather. Betjeman's *Banana Blush* and *Late Flowering Love* were, and still should be, Freak favourites, and for the true Freak, age does not matter.

Isadore Cutler was born in 1923, in Govan, Glasgow, to a middle-class Jewish family. Isadore joined the RAF in the Second World War. What was it about the Air Force? Bob Calvert, Bruce Lacey (although he ended up in the Royal Navy) and Ivor all had a thing about being up in the skies – the flying Freaks! As seems to be the pattern, these aerial fantasies never last long, and Ivor was grounded for 'dreaminess' and sketching clouds mid-air.

By the 1950s, having given up teaching due to his dislike of corporal punishment, Ivor began writing songs for the BBC Home Service, cutting a couple of EPs for uncool Decca records. As ever, Big Paulie Mac's deely-boppers were on high-alert setting and he cast dear Ivor in *Magical Mystery Tour*, the Fabs' wildest, weirdest and loosest film. Ivor was given the scene-stealing role of the strange and drained bus conductor Buster Bloodvessel, who lusts after Ringo's Aunt Jessie.

From *Magical Mystery Tour* onwards, Ivor gained his hip audience. Peel gave him umpteen sessions, to the point that in the 1980s Ivor seemed so omnipresent that he might have even got the odd illicit inward groan from teenage me.

I didn't know Ivor, when we were neighbours, though we often shared the same bus (Freaks do not take taxis). Ivor would sit near the front of the bus, with his little Sufi hat

THE EMPTY SEAT ON THE BUS

on. Staring ahead. The seat next to him was often vacant. People would rather sit somewhere else if available than sit next to the weird guy in the Sufi hat.

Mid-afternoon, 2010. I am on the C11 bus with Ivor. I am sat a couple of seats behind him. This was nothing unusual. Ivor was often on the bus and so was I. Heading into the north London suburbs. A bunch of school-uniformed kids get on. A large boy, about fourteen years old, sits in the empty seat next to Ivor. The big kid looks at Ivor and smiles. I'm watching. There is no sense of malevolence but I'm wary that the kid might get cheeky with Mr Cutler. I don't want this to happen. The kid starts talking to Ivor:

'Excuse me, sir, I like your hat,' says the kid.

'Thank you,' says Ivor, dreamily.

'What kind of hat is it?' continues the kid, genuinely interested.

'It's a poet's hat,' says Ivor, now becoming engaged.

'Woah, are you a poet?' The kid is pretty enthused.

'It's a very dependable hat. You need a dependable hat if you are a poet,' says Mr Cutler, sagely.

'Where could I get one?' the kid shoots back.

I have to get off the bus, so I leave Ivor chatting away happily to his new friend. Perhaps the kid went home and listened to *Life in a Scotch Sitting Room, Vol. 2* on Spotify.

A decade later, in the midst of Covid, I made an album called *Setting the Dogs on the Post Punk Postman*. I had written a song about Ivor called, naturally enough, 'Ivor on the Bus', a tribute to my old neighbour and the old neighbours in general of my neighbourhood, who were getting replaced by red-trouser-wearing hoorays, actors and brigades of North London Human Rights Lawyers. I had included the conversation that I had witnessed in the song, but that wasn't really the point. The real point was about the empty seat on the bus. I'd noticed in the intervening years that I was no longer a young person. I was now the weird fucker on the bus, with facial hair and a hat and clothes that bore no resemblance to contemporary style or, God help me, fashion. I was either the guy you dreaded coming to sit next to you, or I was the guy you wouldn't sit next to.

Ivor on the Bus

Singing a song with Ivor on the bus
Singing a song with Ivor on the bus
It's been years since he passed
time doesn't fly by fast . . .
when you're singing a song with Ivor on the bus
'Excuse me, sir, can I ask for some advice?'
A Sufi hat and a three-piece suit and tie
I used to be the tour guide
but that was a different life
Now I'm singing a song with Ivor on the bus
Singing a song with Ivor on the bus
a wheezing harmonium and an old-age pensioner pass
I could try to sing . . .
but I'm no Phyllis King
I'm just sitting next to Ivor on the bus

THE EMPTY SEAT ON THE BUS

'Can I tell you Mr. Cutler, how much I admire your hat?'
'It's the headdress of a poet – it's a very dependable hat . . .'
In the Church of England John Tavener plays 'The Lamb'
On the top deck of the bus lovers hold hands
Now I'm the freak, nobody wants to sit next to me . . .
I'm just singing a song with Ivor on the bus.

The question is: 'Wherever you are meeting your maker, is the seat on the bus empty?' If the answer is yes, then you are a Freak, and your place at the top table is assured.

CHAPTER 27

Fifty dead Taylor Swifts

Taylor Swift is dead. Neil Young is Dead.
AI is dead as well. To create, you have to destroy.

I was going to call this chapter – and it was going to be the final chapter of this book – Neil Young is Dead. You see, Neil Young is Dead has got a cool agit-pop ring to it for the ageing hipster, and it's a bit annoying to middle-aged rockers and those serious old rock scribes. It's good to annoy these people; you never know, they might have a heart attack. Hell, if I'd seen some fucker had written a think-piece called Neil Young is Dead, I might even find it quite annoying, too. It's the stuff of the professional controversialist.[1] It's iconoclastic.[2]

---

[1] I have doubtless been accused of this terrible crime. I can assure the reader that I am resolutely unprofessional in all of my undertakings.
[2] Iconoclastic is one of those words that stupid people tend to use, often given as a positive attribute. It implies much but has no nuance. 'Pretentious' is another word that stupid people use as a derogatory *j'accuse*. Again, it is without nuance.

FREAKS OUT!

Let me clarify: this chapter is about a fictional version of Neil Young, called Neil Young, who dies. By the time this book comes out the real Neil Young may have died (I really hope not), in which case you will have to substitute the fictional Neil Young in this chapter for a real character who is of a similar age to the real Neil and then fictionalise him, i.e. put him into the situations that I am putting fictional Neil Young into. Fictional Neil is just a kind of placeholder, so it's cool. This chapter is also about fictional Taylor Swift as well as fictional Neil Young. That is why I decided to name the chapter Fifty Dead Taylor Swifts. You'll see why there are fifty Taylors – and they are all dead – in a few paragraphs' time. Hold on, tiger!

If the real Taylor Swift dies before this book comes out (again, I really hope not), then you will have to substitute the fictional Taylor Swift for a real character who is a similar age to Taylor and then fictionalise her, i.e. put her into the situation that I am putting fictional Taylor Swift into. Taylor is just a kind of placeholder, so it's cool. Is real Taylor Swift just a placeholder anyway? Just like Neil Young? Perhaps all the pop stars since Johnnie Ray at the beginning of this book are just placeholders? Placeholders for the great revolution of the non-famous, as prophesied in Chapter 25. Ah.

In this chapter, it is 2044. That's two decades from now. The only music that really survives is the music of the Beatles, Taylor Swift and Neil Young, the latter of whom is still liked by some very old people, though they have mainly forgotten what his music sounds like. Other than that, not much has changed and the brave new world of 2044 is largely not that much different to our brave new world of 2024, which, when you really gnaw down on the bone, was not that different to the world of Elvis impressing Gene Vincent on a country radio show in 1955. We have many of the same fears: teenagers, sex, pending nuclear oblivion, stupid war, famine; people are still arseholes, and technology still frightens us as we get older. The frightening new technology of the Elvis '50s was the weaponising of the atom, and the weaponising of the telly. The frightening new tech of 2023 is artificial intelligence.

By 2044, AI has been put to the sword and largely found to be a fucking dud. Sure, the Beatles corporation have managed to dig up a hundred acoustic demos, by deceased solo Beatles, mysteriously found once a year in attics, skips and Yoko's garbage disposal chute, treated with AI 'separation' and guaranteeing enough brand spanking-new Fabs Christmas number ones for the next century. In 2044, AI was also integrated into the general domestic tableaux of the Western world but was soon dropped in favour of those old faves: hard labour and general human misery. Most people in 2044 just found AI, well, a bit fucking boring.

At various time zones in mid-August 2044 in fifty world city airports, a squadron of planes is about to take off. This is the bi-annual tour of the Fifty Taylor Swifts. Some time in around 2037 it was tacitly decided – by an increasingly jaundiced, bedazzled and deeply confused 'over-under-culture'– that Taylor Swift pretty much provided all cultural entertainment needs for most of the populace, that part of the populace at least that was still buying into 'culture'. Swift being an early and confused adopter of AI, conceived of a plan where she could essentially become a World Domination Pop-Star (her own branding) by having multitudes of AI versions of herself on tour simultaneously. Swift was a smart onion, and knew how to max out productivity/consumer happiness/marketing opportunities and the exponentially expanding new arms exporting/Outer Space domination interface sector.[3]

The terrible news came over throughout the day of 16 August 2044. Five planes departing from LAX airport dove into the Atlantic Ocean en route to mainland Europe. Hour by hour, more planes crashed and more AI Taylor Swifts plunged to their deaths. No one knew at the time the cause of this simultaneous multiple air carnage. It was probably AI-related. Most things were. That's why many people had got tired of the artificial overlord (apart from Taylor Swift, that is).

The bad news carried on through the next twenty-four hours. Another airplane down. Another Taylor Swift gone. The real (non AI) Taylor Swift had no doubt met her own tragic plane crash death as well. She was a grafter and liked to muck in with her AI self(s). By 6 a.m. the next morning,

---

[3] T. S. had maxed out her weapons selling commercial portfolio when she had [three?] of her AI selfs marry three arms dealers. The AI Taylors and the non-AI arms dealers opened up a non-AI missile expo hotel in the Eritrean coastal desert where weapons – grade hotshots literally made a killing.

the last of the squadron of fifty luxury Swift jets had immolated in the skies. Swifties – young and old – were naturally a bit sad for a few days, but life went back to normal, and to many, it occurred that perhaps the death of the fifty Taylor Swifts was not such a bad thing after all. I mean, how much Taylor Swift does anyone really need?

Neil Young, now impossibly and improbably old, sat in his high-tech studio barn watching the news. He didn't really understand AI, much in the same way that he didn't really understand Spotify. He guessed that the fifty dead Taylor Swifts must all be sisters. 'I think they must be some kind of very high-order, multiple-birth phenomenon,' squeaked Neil to his ever-faithful Crazy Horse rhythm guitarist, Frank 'Poncho' Sampedro (retired), who was busy restringing Neil's faithful Les Paul, 'Ol' Black'.

'Yeah, Shakey,' growled Poncho. 'It sure is some motherfuckin' fucked-up shit.'

'Ponch,' whined Neil.

'Yes, boss?' wheezed Frank.

'We gotta come out of retirement after a respectful period of mourning for the fifty dead Taylor Swifts. Y'see, we, as the last warriors of rock, have gotta step up to the plate. The kids need their rock 'n' roll. It's time for the Horse to rise up.'

'What about the Fabs?' asked Frank.

'They're all dead,' said Shakey, sadly. 'They only exist as a branding commodity useful in keeping their own considerable cultural worth relevant to every future generation.'

'I see,' said Poncho, wisely.

FREAKS OUT!

The great Crazy Horse comeback tour was a slow burner. Since Neil's retirement five years earlier his works had been largely forgotten. His old fanbase were, in the main, senile, dribbling, demented or, frankly, dead. An unwillingness to embrace 'digital platforms' on Young's part and a genuine and earnest dislike of the high-pitched-voiced singer's canon from younger generations meant that many so-called 'Gen Zers' mainly remembered Neil because of something that happened to Kurt Cobain. The Gen Zers tended towards the opinion that Nirvana's relatively small body of work was superior to Neil's shockingly bloated oeuvre of which only about five albums were any good.[4] After all, Nirvana had made three albums and only two sucked. Their one good album, *Nevermind*,[5] had all the bloat and pomp and angst that a Gen Zer could relate to. Who gave a fuck if Kurt hated himself and wanted to die? Nuance had died out long before the era of the Fifty Taylor Swifts.

Neil, Poncho and the other two fuckers in Crazy Horse started playing small venues. The audiences, such as they were, didn't like a lot of Neil's terrible country music, but they did like a couple of his rock 'n' roll songs. Soon enough, the Horse dropped the country shit (some of Neil's long-term fans wished that this had happened long before

---

[4] Keep in mind that this chapter is largely fictitious. I actually think that Neil Young has made far more than five decent albums.

[5] Once again, this chapter is largely fictitious. I don't really think that *Nevermind* is Nirvana's only decent album. It's great of course, but *Bleach* and *In Utero* are better.

the death of the fifty Taylor Swifts) and stuck to grinding out the pure Crazy Horse moronic rock 'n' roll that several generations of fans, mostly deceased, had come to love. One of the songs they liked most was the one that Kurt Cobain quoted in his suicide note. Unfortunately, no one could quite remember exactly what Kurt had written, as by 2044 most music writing had been destroyed due to the adverse effect it had been having on ageing men. In doing this the suicide rates of males of eighty-plus had dropped astonishingly. Although, in truth, this was nothing much to write home about.

Neil Young, who was naturally enough struggling with his ancient and grizzled short-term memory, couldn't quite remember all the words to the song he'd written that Kurt Cobain liked so much that he killed himself. After all, he had taken all of his songs off Spotify sometime in the 2000s and he'd lost all the master tapes to his old recordings on that night when Poncho accidentally burned down Neil's barn with an enormous joint.

'My, my, hey, hey,' sang Neil Young to a nearly full baseball stadium. Stuck in a loop. Tonight's loop had gone on for forty-five minutes. This was part of a ritual that Crazy Horse and their fans now had no control over. Neil would sing 'My, my' and the fans would sing back the answer, 'Hey, hey,' and then it would go back to Neil to do his bit. A typical Crazy Horse gig from 2044 would go like this:

Neil: 'My, my.'
Audience: 'Hey, hey.'
Neil: 'My, my.'

Audience: 'Hey, hey.'
Neil: 'My, my.'
Audience: 'Hey, hey.'
Neil: 'My, my.'
Audience: 'Hey, hey.'
Neil: 'My, my.'
Audience: 'Hey, hey.'
Neil: 'My, my.'
Audience: 'Hey, hey.'
Neil: 'My, my.'
Audience: 'Hey, hey.'
Neil: 'My, my.'
Audience: 'Hey, hey.'
Neil: 'My, my.'
Audience: 'Hey, hey.'
Neil: 'My, my.'
Audience: 'Hey, hey.'
Neil: 'My, my.'
Audience: 'Hey, hey.'
Neil: 'My, my.'
Audience: 'Hey, hey.'

This would go on for twenty minutes or so, occasionally to be broken by:
Neil: 'My, my.'
Audience: 'Hey, hey.'
Neil: 'My, my.'
Audience: 'Hey, hey.'
Neil: 'Hey, does anyone remember the next line, man?'
Audience: 'Woooooh. Allriiiight. Neeeeeeiiiiiillllll.'
Neil: 'Heh, heh, heh. My, my.'
Audience: 'Hey, hey.'

This would go on for another two hours.

As rock 'n' roll rituals went, it was no dumber than many that came before, until one day it happened.

Neil: 'My, my.'

Audience: 'Hey, hey.'

Neil: 'My, my.'

Audience: 'Hey, hey.'

This continues for thirty-eight minutes.

Neil: 'My, my.'

Audience: 'Hey, hey.'

Neil: 'Hey, does anyone remember the next line, man?'

Audience: 'Woooooh. Allriiiight. Neeeeeeiiiiillllll.'

Neil: 'Uh . . . huh . . . oh man, it's coming back to me . . . Rock and roll is here to stay.'

Neil had finally remembered the next line! A shocked Neil Young turned to an even more shocked Frank 'Poncho' Sampedro, and in a state of beatific epiphany at this most moronic of revelations, Neil Young and Frank 'Poncho' Sampedro both dropped dead.

No one was that shocked at the death of Neil Young. All of his generation of 'rockers' had pegged out in the previous decade. There were no tribute nights as no one could remember any songs apart from the 'My my, Hey, hey' number, which had taken on a mythical status, especially after the 'death stage' revelation from Neil that the next line was 'Rock 'n' Roll Will Never Die'.

Mystical revelations in the mid-twenty-first century happily lead to conspiracy theories and the 'Rock 'n' Roll Will Never Die' cult grew stronger as word of mouth travelled via nomadic sects, lay preachers and travelling puppet shows, who acted out pageants based upon misunderstood legends of the hedonistic early- to mid-'70s Crosby, Stills, Nash & Young tours, to shiftless peasants in the car parks of abandoned supermarkets. It goes without saying that the internet had long gone by 2051, after a collusion of Western governments proposed a referendum: Vote 'Yes'! if you think the internet is stupid. Vote 'No' if you think it's alright. The 'Yes' vote won and the internet was deemed to be 'stupid', thus it was abandoned. However, some information regarding the 'Rock 'n' Roll Will Never Die' mythos did pass over from dissident Russian internet providers, giving the believers more fragments of bones and guts to fashion the new God out of.

Over the coming years, the years that became known as 'the time before the hearing aid', cultists joined forces with academics to slowly reconstruct a new fable. As had happened in the old times, when seekers would look for signs of UFOs in the desert, now they would look for clues to the 'Rock 'n' Roll Will Never Die' codex. A fine velvet-collared garment with razor blades sown into the collar was found in a suitcase secreted in a ruined amusement arcade in Shoeburyness (along with plans for a statue of a giant man called Lee Brilleaux). Various rare, intact and playable 'vinyl' records were also found around the south of England (most vinyl records had been destroyed in the Record Store Day massacres of 2029). These historical vinyl artefacts, one by the Wild Angels and the other by a minstrel troupe called

FIFTY DEAD TAYLOR SWIFTS

the Hersham Boys, were found in an old boathouse in Walton-on-Thames, Surrey, England.

The archaeological diggings moved across the globe to Jamaica, where a mural of a man with gold teeth was found to be perfectly preserved on what was once Orange Street in the old capital of Kingston. A holy credo seemed inevitable, as inevitable as the final righteous excavations in New Mexico, which were held up for six months by the unearthing of some kind of warhead which had the face of one of the fifty dead Taylor Swifts printed on its rusting fuselage. After a military intervention, when it was eventually confirmed that the warhead with the face of one of the fifty dead Taylor Swifts was actually a damp squib, the digging continued.

The final revelation of the 'Rock 'n' Roll Will Never Die' mythos was also found in New Mexico, in Clovis, a few hundred miles from the fifty dead Taylor Swifts' squib. In a prehistory cave, an altar stood in front of a fresco. On top of the altar rested a tea mug with a picture of a moustached man, looking like some kind of English aristocrat from the twentieth century; the mug bore the legend 'National Disgrace'. Inside the mug was a carefully rolled-up piece of paper. A scroll, if you will; a printout from an old internet review, by some unknown scribe, Luke Hain . . . the print had faded in time. The text that was still legible spoke of 'Punctured bicycles', 'Ugly dudes' flagellating themselves in something called 'blackface'. Then, a name, 'Moriss? Moriss? Who is Moriss?' The brave adventurers and diggers could only guess who this 'Moriss' was as the paper was torn at the edge. Most diabolically, at the bottom of this printed page was a reference to some kind of neo-pagan ceremony: 'The Spare Parts of a Lawn Mower!' The fresco which the cup was placed in front of bore an inscription, a scrawled signature that seemed to read:

Johnnie ----
Painted by Jack Good

The word after 'Johnnie' was long lost to time. The fresco was startling enough though: a man with hair fashioned into some kind of horn, bent double in some extraordinary invocation of hysteria. From the idols' eyes there were tears, and in his saintly ears what had become known from previous archaeological digs as 'hearing aids'.

The new gospel travelled and word spread from brother number one to brother number two. Soon, there were a thousand brothers (and some sisters too). By the end of the twenty-first century, the brothers and the smattering of sisters amassed beyond cultishness. This was a holy crusade. Soon, a name for the hair horn on the fresco was found: The Quiff. The Spare Parts of the Lawn Mower ceremony had also gradually changed and due to the political mores of the times had become more commonly known as: 'The Ceremony of the Reborn Freak'. And the name of this new God of freakery: Johnny Morris.

CHAPTER 28

Billie Eilish is alive and kicking – and she's gonna make us all freaks, baby

In which Billie Eilish saves the day.

Billie saves the day. Not once but twice. The first time a Billie saved the day was way back at the beginning of the twentieth century, when she was a singer called Billie Piper. Billie Piper had a brief career as a successful teen singer with a couple of big provincial hits: 'Because We Want To', an excellent bit of concocted teens-against-the-man fodder (essentially an update of Sham's 'I Don't Wanna') and the even better 'Honey to the Bee', a horny 'swingbeat' (some sort of genre popular briefly in the early 2000s) classic. At the time, one of my outfits, Black Box Recorder, were looking for a hit, for the first and only time, and we found the juju in Billie's marvellous 'Honey to the Bee'. And why would a Freak like your unreliable narrator be after a bit of chart how's yer father? It was all a matter of vindication and chivalry most noble, you see, befitting a world-class Freak. I've told the story many times, not least in my second classic memoir, *Post Everything – Outsider Rock 'n' Roll, 2000–2010*, so if you need a recap, you know where to go. We got our hit and the world moved on. This final instalment of *Freaks Out* is about the second time that Billie saved the day: Billie Eilish.

Ephebiphobia: fear of youth. The Mancunian master author Anthony Burgess knew about ephebiphobia, the thorn in his side and his failure. It's all in his *Enderby* series of books. Wherein a young fogey poet, F. X. Enderby, convinced of his imperious genius, farcically wrestles with the end of Western civilisation. The end of Eastern civilisation for Enderby is actually the end of post-war austerity Britain and the terrible dawning of the permissive new age. Enderby is forced into foreign travel, comes across teenagers and has to endure exotic foreign fare such as spaghetti. Burgess's fear of the youth was all there in Enderby's predecessor, and the author's greatest folly, *A Clockwork Orange*, published in 1962, pre-Beatle England. It is the ultimate screed against the young. When Stanley Kubrick turned *A Clockwork Orange* into a movie in 1972, he also brilliantly turned the movie against the novel, and almost made it into an attack on Burgess's original idea. Burgess may have feared young people but he didn't hate them, except in their four-headed hydra form: the Beatles. He even proposed a death fantasy for the beloved Fabs:

'They should be bound to a white hot turntable (45 rpm for ever and ever) stuck all over with blunt and rusty acoustic needles, each tooth hollowed to the raw nerve and filled with a micro-transistor (thirty-two several pop stations blaring through all eternity thirty-two worn flip sides into their sinuses), an eternal Ringo battering the tympanic membrane.'

It is not known whether Anthony Burgess ever listened to Wings.

Never fear the young. Just because your youth was over three or four decades ago doesn't mean you must fear your replacements. Make a funeral pyre out of all those magazines that you've hoarded. You don't need to read about the Byrds any more. You can even chuck this book into the fire when you've finished it.

The previous chapter was going to be the final chapter of this book, but God has intervened and now this is last chapter. I'm glad that the last chapter, which for the those losing short-term memory – and let's be honest, a few people reading this may be approaching that stage – was called Fifty dead Taylor Swifts, is not the last chapter. With this new last chapter I have a chance to explain the last chapter. Let's face it, with a chapter title like Fifty dead Taylor Swifts, I could be laying myself open to charges of, a) Misogyny, and b) Ephebiphobia. Although, remember, I set Fifty dead Taylor Swifts in the year 2044, so Taylor Swift would be fifty-four years old at the time of her fictitious death in her fictitious future. So, the second charge wouldn't have stood. As for misogyny, I think I had that one sorted out with my ardent fanboy worship of the Manson Girls in Chapter 16.

FREAKS OUT!

So how did God intervene? Well, while I was keeping busy by happily recording my solo albums in the post business 'music business', where with my Freak self in full formation, I could do what I fucking liked, God had also been busy. God, you see, has invented something called TikTok. TikTok is a video-sharing website, where the kids, the real kids, share bits and bobs of songs with each other. This poses a very important question: Who are these Real Kids?

The slightly facetious and somewhat literal answer to this ageless question is: Well, the Real Kids were a short-lived power pop band from Boston, led by John Felice. Felice was also in the original Modern Lovers. As every motherfucker Freak, or even non-Freak, probably knows: Jonathan Richman's Modern Lovers were up there in the history of world-changing righteous events that didn't actually change the world but kind of did but should have changed it even more. *The Original Modern Lovers* elpee, produced by John Cale, was and is essentially heavy Mass for the Freak, extolling the virtues of self-education, health food, anti-hippie ideals, anti-drugs, eschewing the middlebrow and the mediocre, dropping out of college and discovering high art – and most importantly: staying out all night, listening to rock 'n' roll.

John Felice was Jonathan Richman's friend and neighbour, and together they formed the Modern Lovers in 1970, but by 1972, Felice had formed his own band: the Real Kids. Now the Real Kids came across even more militantly than the Modern Lovers and failed perhaps even more spectacularly in their mission to 'save' the kids.

So, if the Real Kids were not *the real kids*, then who and where were *the real kids*?

The real kids had been hiding in plain sight for years. They'd been trapped in the pages of *Look In*. I'm not sure they were ever in the all-too-knowing and smug pages of *Smash Hits*, much as *Smash Hits* longed for them to be. They certainly weren't in the pages of the weekly inky music press in the 1980s and 1990s. I think I saw them in the genuine teenage rampage of some of those early Suede gigs in 1992, when my band the Auteurs supported, but that was my only oblique glimpse of these 'real kids'. Quite rightly, I'd long forgotten about the Real Kids.

Then, while writing this book something happened: one of my old songs got discovered. Not re-discovered or re-appraised, but discovered for the first time by young people: the Real Kids. It all comes down to the eternal question: What came first? The TikTok viral hit or Billie Eilish?

In late 2022, I got an email from an old record label, Chrysalis Records. The email informed us that an old Black Box Recorder song, 'Child Psychology', had gone viral on video-sharing social media site TikTok. That's cool, I thought. Then I saw what was going on: millions of teenage girls were making short twenty-second clips of themselves miming to the chorus of our old song:

Life is Unfair
Kill Yourself or Get Over It.

Be careful what you wish for. Things could get grim.

FREAKS OUT!

Those two lines were written a quarter of a century ago. The words of a 29-year-old cynic (that's me), a rejoinder — or chorus — to verses of a song about a little girl who'd given up speaking. I liked the verses (written by John Moore) but I intuitively wanted to spike the song. Shoot some junk into its veins. Give it some bad shit. So I did. The other band members liked my chorus. A bit. Well, they laughed. And made 'Are you fucking joking?' comments. To which I may have said, 'Yes, kind of . . . and no.' It was a long time ago. All I remember is that we recorded it and it sounded great.

Much to our surprise our record label thought it would make a good first single to promote our first album, *England Made Me*. Once again we went into convulsions of giggling and adopted our collective 'are you fucking joking?' mode. And so 'Child Psychology' was released as the first Black Box Recorder single in early 1998, and the BBC banned it.

At some point Billie Eilish enters this improbable tale. Billie Eilish, born in 2001, three years after 'Child Psychology' was first released, and a year after Black Box Recorder's song 'The Facts of Life' became our only proper hit. Whether Billie E picked up 'Child Psychology' from TikTok or whether she originally posted it on the video-sharing site, no one knows. What is known is that every time she posts the song, it accumulates a few more million streams.

I don't know about that chorus any more. I'm not sure that life is unfair either. Life, if it is anything, is indifferent — the death of my friend Cathal Coughlan proved that. Make God laugh — tell him your plans and other well-worn micro philosophies. Anyway, 'life is indifferent, kill yourself or get over it' really doesn't scan as well as 'life is unfair, kill yourself or get over it', and as a songwriter, one's duty is to the song and not the truth. The kids who have picked up on this ancient screed are the children of social media. I hope they're alright. At least they've got a Fuck U, and 'Fuck U' is the most important of the 'The Three Fs'.

As for Billie Eilish, she has nailed her colours to the internet. She flies her Freak flag high. When I started this book, it was in remembrance to what I thought of as the lost cause and birthright of anyone who picked up a guitar, uttered some mad poetry, or just hobbled across the stage in the belief that, whether they had everything or nothing to say, they were gonna goddamned say it anyway. Now, as I write these last words, it's maybe correct to quote Lou Reed:

'Now we're coming out – out of our closets – out on the streets.'

Grow old, bring the noise and don't dis the young. They have Billie Eilish as their leader and the Freaks are once again out.

Epilogue

*A handy incomplete index of just who is a Freak (F) and who is
not Freak (Non-F), and who is a Freak Enabler (FE).
Add your own in the margin. This is not a list.
Remember: lists are for shoppers, not Freaks and rockers.*[1]

F

Vince Taylor
Lee Brilleaux
Karen Carpenter
Richard Carpenter
George Clinton
Eddie Hazel
Marshall Allen

---

[1] The reader will notice that I have borrowed the U and Non-U format from terrible aristo snob Nancy Mitford. Within Mitford's original framework it was estimated that 7 per cent of the populace were U and the remaining 93 per cent were Non-U. I think this figure represents my own Freak configuration: F and Non-F.

FREAKS OUT!

Lemon Kittens
Lana Del Rey
Alan Vega
Nik Turner
Robert Calvert
David Tibet
Lady June Campbell
Russ Conway
Kurt Cobain
Ian Dury
Ritchie Blackmore
Pose Group/Bruce McLean
Gong
Jimi Hendrix
Jarvis Cocker
Russell Senior
Johnny Moped
Wilko Johnson
June Tyson
Poly Styrene
Courtney Love
Rose McDowall
The cover of 'A Trip to Marineville' by Swell Maps
Danielle Dax
The Stranglers
Roland Kirk
Clive Palmer
Robin Williamson
Mike Heron

EPILOGUE

Licorice McKechnie
Phil Ochs
Here and Now
Martin Degville
Rat Scabies
Captain Sensible
Robert Wyatt
Mike Ratledge
Kevin Ayers
Pauline Murray
Bruce Lacey
Nina Hagen
Billy Idol
Arthur Brown
Slimy Toad
Jacko Pistorius
Rock and Roll Robot
Cow on the front of *Atom Heart Mother*
Tiny Tim
Dave Gilmour's hair on *Ummagumma*
Steve Ignorant
Ron and Scott Asheton
Siouxsie Sioux
John Tavener
Pink Fairies
David Johansen
Killer Cane
Hasil Adkins
Poison Ivy Rorschach

FREAKS OUT!

Arthur Russell
Bryan Gregory
Jonathan Richman
Eric Felice
Link Wray
Lou Reed
John Cale
Nico
Sun Ra

Non-F

Nick Cave
Bill Callahan
Viv Albertine
Ian Dury
Johnny Ramone
Cosey Fanni Tutti
Genesis P-Orridge
Kraftwerk
Mark Fisher
Bob Dylan
Stereolab
Nick Drake
The Ukelele Orchestra of Great Britain
Michael Eavis
Emily Eavis
The 1975
Dave Gilmour's hair post-*Ummagumma*
Nick Land

EPILOGUE

Frank Zappa
Jaco Pastorius
Brix Smith
Chrissie Hynde
Brian Eno
Steely Dan
Roger Waters
Tony James
ABBA
Will Oldham
Cat Power
David Bowie
John Densmore
James Williamson
Tony Banks
Mike Rutherford
Blixa Bargeld
Jerry Harrison
David Byrne
Cows at Glastonbury Festival

FE

MC5
Larry Williams
David Bowie
Iggy Pop
The Residents
Sterling Morrison
Moe Tucker

FREAKS OUT!

Billy Yule
Rose Simpson
Can
Rose Stone
Paul Hanley
Steve Hanley
Lee Perry
Ian Hunter
Mickey Finn
Doug Yule
Tommy Ramone
Johnny Ramone
Johnny Marr
Mick Farren
Paul Cook
Glen Matlock
Thurston Moore
Hank B. Marvin
Don Letts
Billie Eilish
Ray Manzarek
Robby Krieger
Syd Barrett
Peter Gabriel
Phil Collins
Kay Carroll

Discography, bibliography, miscellany

Chapter 1
Discography

The Fall – *Dragnet* (LP)
The Fall – *Early Fall 77–79* (LP)
Various Artists – *Earcom 2: Contradiction* (12-inch EP) – This was listened to as it was considerably cheaper than most parts of the Joy Division canon. We also thought that Basczax and Thursdays might be good . . .
Magazine – *Real Life* (LP)
Magazine – *Secondhand Daylight* (LP)
Magazine – *The Correct Use of Soap* (LP) – At the time Magazine seemed more important to us than Joy Division.
Bauhaus – 'Terror Couple Kill Colonel' (45)
Bauhaus – *In the Flat Field* (LP). Bauhaus are better than you'd forgotten.
Lemon Kittens – *We Buy a Hammer for Daddy* (LP)

Lives Of Angels – *Elevator to Eden* (Cassette)
Virgin Prunes – *A New Form of Beauty*, parts one to four (45, 10-inch EP, 12-inch EP, Cassette)
Virgin Prunes – 'Pagan Love Song/Dave-Id is Dead' (45)
Virgin Prunes – *If I Die, I Die* (LP). The importance of the Virgin Prunes cannot be underestimated in this period. We adored them. I rarely played them after the mid-1980s when I moved to London. I dug out the records again on writing this book. They still sound utterly uncanny.

Chapter 2

Discography

Gene Vincent and the Blue Caps – 'Be-Bop-A-Lula/Woman Love' (45)
Gene Vincent and the Blue Caps – 'Race With the Devil' (45)
Gene Vincent and the Blue Caps – *Bluejean Bop*. The greatest album ever recorded? (LP)
Gene Vincent and the Blue Caps – *Gene Vincent and the Blue Caps* (LP). Cliff Gallup came back to record this follow-up. Even better than the first LP.
Gene Vincent – *I'm Back and I'm Proud* (LP). Not great but contextually interesting latter-day Gene-goes-country album.
Eddie Cochran – 'C'mon Everybody' (45)
Eddie Cochran – 'Somethin' Else' (45)
Eddie Cochran – 'Summertime Blues' (45). Any version, it's goddamned tank-proof, un-fucking ruinable. Mick Farren's take is fantastic.
The Wild Angels – *Live at the Revolution* (LP). Orthodox rock 'n' roll for non-short-trouser wearers.

DISCOGRAPHY, BIBLIOGRAPHY, MISCELLANY

Ian Dury – 'Sweet Gene Vincent' (45)

Sham 69 – *That's Life* (LP). Genuinely great and original concept album that actually follows the concept.

Sham 69 – 'Hersham Boys' (45). One of only two songs to namecheck the Walton Hop.

Jerry Lee Lewis – *Live at the Star-Club* (LP). Hands down greatest live album ever recorded. Breach no discussion.

The Nashville Teens – *Tobacco Road* (LP)

Suicide – *Suicide* (LP). Essentially art-synth Gene Vincent.

Johnny Kidd and the Pirates – 'Shakin' All Over' (45). The original Johnny Kidd version of the Pirates had a few fantastic 45s, but you really need to hear the later Mick Green hard-rock version of the Pirates.

Bibliography

J. G. Ballard – *The Unlimited Dream Company*

Susan Van Hecke – *Race with the Devil*

Mick Farren – *Gene Vincent – There's One in Every Town*

Jonathan Green – *Days in the Life*. Extremely funny account of the London counterculture from those that were there.

Miscellany

Jon Ronson – 'The Fall Of A Pop Impresario'. *Observer* magazine

The Gene Vincent Foundation (online)

'Be Bop A Lula' – The History of Rock In 500 Songs (online)

The Rock and Roll Singer – Thames TV documentary.

Chapter 3

Discography

Luke Haines – *New York in the '70s* (LP)

The real New York in the '70s selection

The Ramones – first two albums. Obviously.
Suicide – *Suicide* (LP). The second Suicide album is under-listened to as well.
New York Dolls – Both albums, of course.
Television – 'Little Johnny Jewel' (45)
Television – *Marquee Moon* (LP). Would be too contrarian even for me to omit.
Johnny Thunders and the Heartbreakers – *LAMF* (LP)
Johnny Thunders – *So Alone* (LP). This, and as many of Johnny's fucked-up albums as you like – read the Male Genius Myth chapter before you go into Thunders' more esoteric/damaged work.
You don't have to be an eagle-eyed reader to notice that I haven't included Blondie in this chapter. Never dug them too much.
Sad Café – 'Everyday Hurts' (45). Ubiquitous and no greater signifier of the drab side of the 1970s.
Smokie – Ditto.
Look Back in Anger – 'Flowers' (45). Archetypal Banshees provincial punk from the early '80s. Again, there was one in every town.
Emptifish – No records to recommend. Omnipresent local psychobilly low-level pests. Probably still going.

Chapter 4
Discography

The Alberts – *By Jingo It's . . . British Rubbish* (LP). Great compilation of singles.

Bruce Lacey – *The Spacey Bruce Lacey* (LP). Cool homemade primitive synth and voltage generator recordings.

Johnnie Ray – 'Cry' (45)

Johnnie Ray – 'Little White Cloud' (45)

Johnnie Ray – 'Walking in the Rain' (45)

Elvis Presley – *The Sun Sessions* (LP). 'Nuff said.

Tiny Tim – *God Bless Tiny Tim* (LP). Worth it for a groovy version of Biff Rose's 'Fill Your Heart'.

The Beatles 1968 Christmas Fan Club record (7-inch single). Features Tiny Tim performing a ukulele version of 'Nowhere Man'. Recorded by George Harrison. Presumably to piss off John and Paul.

Mojo Nixon and Skid Roper – *Bo-Day Shus!!!* (LP). There are two righteous Mojos: Mojo Nixon and Mr Mojo Rising. Accept no imitations.

The Wizard of Oz (LP). Original motion picture soundtrack.

Dexys Midnight Runners – *To Rye Aye* (LP). Under-liked. Much better than the over-liked *Don't Stand Me Down*.

Bibliography

Justin Martell and Alanna Wray – *Eternal Troubadour: The Improbable Life of Tiny Tim*. This book should come with a 'trigger warning'. Read at your peril, but Tiny is not a pleasant dude.

FREAKS OUT!

Jonny Whiteside – *Cry: The Johnnie Ray Story*
Richard Hall – *UFO: Flying Saucers from Other Worlds*
Nicholas Redfern – *Mind Control Oswald and JFK*

Chapter 5

Discography

H. Villa Lobos – *Five Preludes*

Isaac Albéniz – Asturios. Much ripped off. Check the Doors' 'Spanish Caravan' and my own *Setting the Dogs on the Post Punk Postman*.

Danny La Rue – 'On Mother Kelly's Doorstep' (45). Golden age light entertainment about a money lender.

The Shadows – *20 Golden Greats* (LP). Peerless. Top tracks: all of them, except maybe 'Guitar Tango' and 'Foot-tapper'. I've kept Cliff out of this, even in the face of creeping revisionism.

Tomorrow – 'My White Bicycle' (45)

Keith West – 'Excerpt from a Teenage Opera' (45). Epic Tomorrow-related smash-hit psychedelia. Did Big Dave Bowie base much of his early career on this? The missing link between 'Rubber Band' and 'Wild Eyed Boy from Freecloud'? Stick with the single, the re-imagined 'lost' album by Mark Wirtz, like most of these things is hard work.

The Move – 'Fire Brigade' (45). Or anything else for that matter. Don't listen to the likes of D. Hepworth, who had the Move down as also-rans. They were nothing of the sort and by far the leaders of the pack, plus Carl Wayne looked less like a psychedelic waif and more like a Bullring pub fighter. Highly recommended.

Pink Floyd – *The Piper at the Gates Of Dawn* (LP). As obvious as night and day but would be churlish not to include it. Still rules.

Chapter 6

Discography

Nat King Cole – 'Nature Boy' (45)

The Beatles – *Live at the Star-Club in Hamburg* (LP). One day Giles Martin will do an 'AI' job on this one. Will Billy Childish still like it, though?

The Beatles – *A Collection of Oldies . . . But Goldies* (LP). If one was being disputatious there's a reasonable argument to say that this is all you need. One for the pub, eh, lads?

The Beatles – *With the Beatles* (LP). Oh, go on then. Just one more.

The Beatles – 'Revolution 9' (album track). And another.

Parliament – *Chocolate City* (LP). Play it to the Prince fan in your life.

Sun Ra – Where do you start? Well, you don't start. As befitting such a high order priest of jazz – guh, there is no beginning and no end. A thousand Ra recordings seem to be unearthed every day. My own excavations into this world are meagre compared to those shit deep in Ra. But listen to these:

The Heliocentric Worlds of Sun Ra Vols 1-3 – Serious and intense explorations into free jazz futurism. Vol. 2 is my fave. Big with the Ra purists.

Atlantis – Side 1 = very odd minimalist broken 'Casio' keyboard sub-melodies accompanied by extremely 'outsider' rhythmic hand percussion. Most people would think a lot before even recording this let alone releasing it. Much has been written about the all-out assault title track. It's all great.

Cosmic Tones for Mental Therapy – Early experiment in echo plates, super primitive keyboards and (again) care in the community percussion. Totally radical, nothing like it before or since.

Astro Black – In which the Arkestra may or may not have been listening to George Clinton. The title track with regular singer June Tyson is an under-heard classic.

Space Is the Place – It's Sun Ra's *Abbey Road*, or *Dark Side of the Moon*, or *Catch a Fire*. The Sun Ra album for the Radiohead fan in your life. Hey, don't rag on me for my musical elitism. If we're gonna get down and dirty with the Sun Ra catalogue then accusations of musical snobbery are the last of your worries.

Cosmos
Lanquidity
On Jupiter
Sleeping Beauty
A Fireside Chat with Lucifer

Larry Williams – *The Specialty Recordings* (LP). Fantastic, though many of the covers of Bad Boy Larry improved upon the originals.

Larry Williams and Johnny Guitar Watson – *Live* (LP). What do they say? Smokin' hot, that is what they say.

Bibliography

Countless Beatle books and Beatle writings, also Derek Taylor's memoir *As Tears Go By* – simply one of the greatest memoirs of a period of time.

Samuel Beckett – *Murphy*
Colin MacInnes – *Absolute Beginners*
Terry Taylor – *Barons Court – All Change*. Super-early proto-beat mod novel. The inspiration for MacInnes.
Robert Irwin – *Memoirs of a Dervish*
Robert Irwin – *Satan Wants Me*
Sean Martin – *The Cathars*

Chapter 7
Discography

Tyrannosaurus Rex – Complete discography, *Unicorn* and *A Beard of Stars* in particular. I've been listening to these albums for forty-plus years now, they never fail to blow my mind.

T. Rex – Complete discography. The obvious suspects are immense. So is *Zinc Alloy and the Hidden Riders of Tomorrow – A Creamed Cage in August*.

Shagrat – *Lone Star* (LP). Took's best post-Ty Rex jams. The fact that it has been mastered slightly slower than the correct speed just improves the Mandrax fucked-up vibes.

Steve Peregrin Took – *Crazy Diamond* (LP). So-called to reel in the Syd fanatics and because Syd Barrett (perhaps) appears somewhere in the murk.

Steve Took's Horns – *Further Adventures* (LP). A few great 'Horns' tracks and some fairly pointless remixes to buff up an EP into something longer.

Robert Calvert – *Captain Lockheed and the Starfighters* (LP). Every home should have this album. If you think you're a Freak, yet you don't own this record then you ain't a Freak.

Various Artists – *Voltage '78* (LP). Includes the Dodgems and their major classic, 'Lord Lucan is Missing'.

Pere Ubu and pals – *Terminal Drive* (LP). A compilation of Pere Ubu-related rarities, including Electric Eels, 'Jaguar Ride', and David Thomas and Peter Laughner's original band Rocket from the Tombs. Pere Ubu could have featured more in this book; D. Thomas, though, would probably be appalled at the suggestion he is a most righteous Freak. Much as I sometimes adore early Ubu, they haven't impacted my life hugely, so for that reason they remain a footnote.

Bibliography

Mark Paytress – *Bolan: The Rise and Fall of a 20-century Superstar.* Definitive words on Marc.

Paul Rowland – *The Marc Bolan Story.* Early biography, interesting as it presents some of Marc's more fanciful flights as fact.

Fee Warner – *A Trip Through Ladbroke Grove. The Life And Times Of Underground 'Hero' Steve Peregrin Took.* Wild self-published screed. The author doesn't like Paytress or Roland much, which is good fun. For all the, er, looseness of the prose, this book is an invaluable source of Steve Took info. Good work, Fee.

Mick Farren – *Give the Anarchist a Cigarette.* Hilarious, pompous, idiotic and highly readable autobiography by Mick. Great on Gene Vincent.

Miscellany

Seventies school playground joke.

Chapter 8

Discography

Luke Haines – *Rock And Roll Animals* (LP)
The Deviants – *Ptooff!* (LP)
The Deviants – *Disposable* (LP)
The Deviants – *The Deviants* (LP)

If you really want to go there, then *Ptooff* is the best Deviants' album. *Disposable* does have the Rachman influenced 'Slum Lord'.

Twink – *Think Pink* (LP)
Pink Fairies – *Never, Never Land* (LP)
Pink Fairies – *What A Bunch of Sweeties* (LP)
Pink Fairies – *Kings of Oblivion* (LP)

I feel that the Pink Fairies' history has been fairly well covered elsewhere and I really wanted to get my thoughts about Steve Took, Twink and Mick Farren across without going into the even more convoluted cross paths of everything that was going on at the time. The original core trio of Pink Fairies' albums are all 24-carat Freak gold, of course. The second album, perhaps seen as the lesser of the three, is the most interesting to me. This was essentially a band with no songs, relying on the secret weapon of Paul Rudolph and his over-amplified Gibson SG. This is the album that sounds closest to my imagination of what the dwindling UK Freak scene would have sounded like in 1972. From the hopelessly dated and almost gloriously unfunny 'Pigs of Uranus' skits to the lude downer protest of 'Right On Fight On' and the grimy 'Portobello Shuffle'. *What a Bunch of Sweeties*, with its inside photos of the band looking consumptively green, is almost enough to make any head go and get a job in straight land. Almost.

Bibliography

Shirley Green – *Rachman*
Rich Deakin – *Keep It Together! Cosmic Boogie with the Deviants and the Pink Fairies*

Miscellany

David Frost Show – Frost versus the Yippies. You can find this on YouTube. Lots of shouting and pointing from Mick Farren. Jerry Rubin lights a joint. Phil Ochs is in the audience and Frost comes across as a world-class dick.

Chapter 9

Discography

Hawkwind – *In Search of Space* (LP). I dig Hawkwind's self-titled debut as much as the next Head, but this is the one where shit gets real. Worth it for Calvert's metaphysical avant-concept alone.

Hawkwind – *The Space Ritual* (LP). Look, so many words have been wasted on this wasted splurge of sheer nothingness and it really doesn't need words. If you don't know this motherfucker, then get to know it sharpish. If you do know it, then what are you doing reading this? Turn it the fuck on.

DISCOGRAPHY, BIBLIOGRAPHY, MISCELLANY

Hawkwind – *Quark, Strangeness and Charm* (LP). *Astounding Sounds, Amazing Music*, the first of the Bob as lead singer Hawk albums, was a bit of a hit 'n' miss dud; *Quark* is not. It's hard to imagine how Hawkwind made such an off-road turn to produce this 'power pop' masterpiece, but they did, and that is the marvel of this almighty group.

Hawklords – *25 Years On* (LP). Hawkwind in everything but name. In the late 1970s, Hawkwind were reinventing at a rate that made Big David Bowie look damned slouchy. No one noticed until years later. This is my favourite Calvert album.

Robert Calvert – *Captain Lockheed and the Starfighters* (LP). Calvert's best-known solo album. Much of the music was written by an uncredited Paul Rudolph.

Robert Calvert – *Freq* (LP). Bob's most consistent – if consistent is something you want from a Calvert product – solo album. Electro-pop concept piece recorded during and about the 1984 miners' strike.

Miscellany

Mildred Edie Brady – 'The New Cult of Sex and Anarchy', *Harper's* magazine, April 1947.

Chapter 10

Discography

The North Sea Scrolls – *The North Sea Scrolls* (LP). Don't be a lightweight, dive into the 'full show' version of this extremely heavy motherfucker.

FREAKS OUT!

Groundhogs – *Split* (LP)

Groundhogs – *Thank Christ for the Bomb* (LP). Everything by the 'hogs is wholly righteous. You should then do yourself the favour of listening to *The Two Sides of Tony McPhee*.

Edgar Broughton Band – 'Out Demons Out' (album track on *As Was*). Essential rallying cry. Up there with the Fairies' 'Do It'.

Fairport Convention – *Liege and Lief* (LP). With reluctance. If you have to get all Fairports then stick with Judy (Dyble) and Sandy (Denny); after that yer 'ports get too much like a real ale pub quiz team, specialist subject: the weight of dart flights. Not groovy.

Morris On and sequels (LPs). Depending how deep you can take it.

Strawbs – *Hero and Heroine* (LP). Strawbs are briefly mentioned in this chapter for context. This album isn't. As Strawbs' most prog album it is worth hearing. If 'Strawbs' and 'Prog' in one sentence doesn't float in your moat, then you probably shouldn't be reading this book.

Luke Haines – *Smash the System* (LP)

Bibliography

Gordon Carr – *The Angry Brigade: A History of Britain's First Urban Guerrilla Group*

Tom Vague – *Anarchy in the UK: The Angry Brigade*

Miscellany

Way of the Morris – Morris documentary directed by Tim Plester and Rob Curry.

Women in the Morris – online.

Chapter 11

Discography

Microdisney – *We Hate You South African Bastards!* (LP)

Microdisney – 'Singer's Hampstead Home' (45). Of course it should have been massive. On the other hand 'who cares'? I happily strummed along, accompanying the great man when we encored with this lovely bit of pop spite directed at Boy George.

Fatima Mansions – 'Only Losers Take the Bus' (45)

Fatima Mansions – 'Blues for Ceausescu' (45)

Fatima Mansions – *Viva Dead Ponies* (LP)

Fatima Mansions – *Bertie's Brochures* (EP). 'In rainy Ireland in the '50s . . .' states Cathal at the beginning of the title track, summing up a world view.

Telefís (LPs). The two Telefís albums are Cathal's finest hours, but a tough listen for me.

Chapter 12

Discography

Nick Drake – *Pink Moon* (LP). The Male Genius canon is overstuffed. Big Nick is not really my thing.

Joy Division – *Closer* (LP). It's fantastic of course, as is almost everything they recorded, but I haven't listened to Joy Division since the early 1990s.

Syd Barrett – *Barrett*. Syd's best and, sadly, most disturbed solo album. Much of the acid dislocated quirk of *Madcap* has been, er, lost and a fog of mandies and ludes has descended over the woods, where Syd has sought shelter in a thicket of mad words and worlds. Frightening and brilliant.

John Lennon – *Plastic Ono Band* (LP)

Nirvana – *In Utero* (LP). Along with *John Lennon/Plastic Ono Band*, two established Male Genius screeds, from two Freak lords. The Nirvana record is their best.

Bibliography

Peter Ackroyd – *Chatterton*

Various writers – *From Gothic to Romantic: Thomas Chatterton's Bristol*

William Blake – *Songs of Innocence* and *Songs of Experience*

Thomas De Quincey – Don't bother

Arthur Rimbaud, Paul Verlaine – Don't bother, listen to Patti Smith or Bob Dylan instead (if you must). Better still, listen to great New Zealand band the Verlaines' 'Death and the Maiden' *('Do you like Paul Verlaine? Is it gonna rain today/ We'll have our photo taken/ We'll look like Death and the Maiden/ Verlaine, Verlaine/ Verlaine /Verlaine/ Verlaine/ Verlaine/ Verlaaaaiiine!*

Deborah Curtis – *Touching from a Distance*

Charles R. Cross – *Heavier Than Heaven*. The terrible life of Kurt Cobain.

Rob Chapman – *A Very Irregular Head: The Life of Syd Barrett*. There are many books about Syd. This is the best.

Chapter 13

Discography

The Jam – All the albums are chock full of wing-dingers.

Rema-Rema – 'Rema-Rema' (45). Marco Pirroni's short-lived Dr. Mix/Mary Chain pre-empting tribal noise manifesto. Covered by Big Black.

Adam and the Ants – *Dirk Wears White Sox* (LP). Sure, *Kings of the Wild Frontier* is a pop Freak wipe-out and one in which Marco gets to go imperial (a great thing). However, I have to go for *Dirk Wears White Sox* and its surrounding singles: 'Deutscher Girls', 'Zerox', 'Young Parisians' and Adam's greatest moment: 'Car-trouble'. Few albums are so over-burdened with ideas and underwhelmed by recording budget and ability. Keep your feet off the upholstery, Ronnie! A major triumph.

The Fall – 'The Container Drivers' (album track)

Earl Brutus – 'East' (album track)

Luke Haines – *Adventures in Dementia* (EP)

Bibliography

Scott King – *The Debrist Manifesto*

Scott King – *Art Works*

Max Schaefer – *Children of the Sun*. Interesting fiction with appearances from various far-right headbangers: Savitri Devi, Ian Stuart Donaldson and Nazi skinhead pinup Nicky Crane.

Miscellany

Alan S. C. Ross – Bulletin de la Société Néo-philogique
Nancy Mitford – 'U and Non U', 'The English Aristocracy', *Encounter* magazine

Chapter 14
Discography

All the Go-Betweens' albums – their debut, *Send Me a Lullaby*, is often dismissed as a 'work in progress'. As one of the strangest documents of the early '80s, it might be their best record. My own favourite remains *Tallulah*, just because . . .

The Apartments – *The Evening Visits . . . And Stays for Years* (LP)

The Modern Lovers – John Cale produced debut LP

The Original Modern Lovers – Kim Fowley produced early recordings.

David Westlake – *Westlake* – Mini album. Re-released in 2023 as full album: David Westlake, *D87*

Felt – *Forever Breathes the Lonely Word* (LP)

Felt – *Poem of the River* (Mini LP)

Felt – *Me and a Monkey on the Moon* (LP)

The Triffids – *Born Sandy Devotional* (LP). Sounds rather grandiose in 2024. Hobbled by disastrous '80s production technology. Nevertheless, an important record at the time.

Ed Kuepper – *Today Wonder* (LP). Non-cost-effective task of sorting through Ed's mass production machine, but this album seems emblematic of the time. Maybe Ed's best solo album. Enormous stereo acoustic guitar and drums. Wild.

Chapter 15
Discography

The Chills – 'Doledrums' (45). 'In the dole-drums, on the dole.' Everyone loved the Chills, didn't they?
The Puddle – *Pop Lib* (LP). Fantastic and hard to find from superbly outsider New Zealand band.
Sleaford Mods – 'Jobseeker' (45). Hardly contemporaneous of the chapter, but some things are timeless.
Luke Haines – 'Never Work' (Album track)
Servants – *Reserved* (LP). Compilation of all the Servants singles, 1985–88.
The Auteurs – *New Wave* (LP)

Bibliography

Harry Thompson – *Peter Cook: A Biography*. A Bible for the disinclined.
Andrew Hussey – *Speaking East – The Strange and Enchanted Life of Isidore Isou*. Old Testament for the disinclined.

Miscellany

Viz – Comic started by Chris Donald on the Enterprise Allowance Scheme. Forget Amis, M., the best writing of the 1980s can be found in *Viz*. Big David Bowie knew this.

Chapter 16

Discography

Servants – *Disinterest* (LP). Rarer than an original thought in Brian Eno's head. If you can score one of these, then congratulations, you may well be the tenth person to own this record.

Sun City Girls – Get anything and everything you can by these Super-Freaks. My favourite is *Jacks Creek*, a largely spoken-word disturbing hillbilly concept album apparently about the three dumbest people in the Appalachian Mountains.

Les Rallizes Dénudés – There are many, many Rallizes' albums. Buy them all if you are insane. If not then: *Heavier Than a Death in the Family* and *Blind Baby Has Its Mother Eyes*.

Trees Community – *The Christ Tree* (LP).

YaHoWha 13 – *Magnificence in the Memory* (LP). Worth it for the terrifying 'Camp of the Gypsies'.

The Manson Family – *Family Jams* (LP). The Family, well the ones who weren't on Death Row, sing the songs of Charles Manson. Undeniably great record.

Bibliography

Jenny Fabian – *Groupie*. The fictitious group 'Relation' in the book are Family. Family's first two albums, *Music From a Dolls House* and *Family Entertainment*, are well worth anyone's attention. The group don't come out of the book too well.

Julian Cope – *Japrocksampler*. Go here for Julian's usual boisterous writing on Les Rallizes Dénudés (which is the source of much of the Les Rallizes material in this book), J. A. Caesar, Flower Travellin' Band, Speed Glue and Shinki. Purists may gripe that there are inaccuracies. Who cares? It's a fuck tonne of fun.

There are many words written about the Ant Hill Kids. Approach with extreme caution.

Ditto Charles Manson and the Manson Family – *Helter Skelter* by Victor Bugliosi is the standard text but comes with a very pro-Bugliosi agenda. *Chaos: The Truth Behind the Manson Murders, the CIA and the Secret History of the Sixties* is good and addresses the problems with the *Helter Skelter* book. The best of the Manson books is Ed Sanders' *The Family*, written at the time of the trial. Genuinely creeped out.

Miscellany

Isis Aquarian/Source – *The Source: The Untold Story of Father Yod and the Source Family*

Chapter 17

Discography

Sparks – *Kimono My House* (45). You can have all the Island albums and pick any of the remaining oeuvre. My pick for off-menu under-acclaimed Sparks LP goes to *In Outer Space*.

Suzi Quatro – 'Devil Gate Drive', 'Can the Can'. Supercool Suzi 45s.

The Sweet – *Desolation Boulevard* (LP)

Gary Glitter – Deep breath: The following singles are all unreasonably tainted by greatness: 'Hello, Hello, I'm Back Again', 'Leader of the Gang I Am', 'Rock and Roll' (parts 1 and 2), 'I Love You Love Me Love'. If you can still get these old Bell Records' singles for 15p in charity shops, then buy 'em. You won't be paying any royalties so it's between you and your ears.

Gene Vincent – 'Over the Rainbow' (45)

John Tavener – *The Lamb*

Chapter 18

Discography

Roy Harper – *Stormcock* (LP)

Roy Harper – *HQ* (LP). Worth it for 'When an Old Cricketer Leaves the Crease'.

Adrian Street – *Shake, Wrestle, and Rock 'n' Roll with the Pile Drivers* (LP). Exotic Adrian Street goes Dick Emery. Okay, it's a lot of fun to hear once.

Luke Haines – *Nine and a Half Psychedelic Meditations on British Wrestling from the Late '70s to the Early '80s* (LP)

Bibliography

Simon Garfield – *The Wrestling*. Definitive account of British wrestling, 1950s–80s.

Jackie Pallo – *You Grunt, I'll Groan: The Inside Story of Wresting*. Less-than-definitive memoir from 'heel' Jackie Pallo.

Kendo Nagasaki – *The Grapple Manual*

Jim Fry – *A Licence to Rock and Pop: An Inventory of Attitude*.

DISCOGRAPHY, BIBLIOGRAPHY, MISCELLANY

Chapter 19

Discography

Genesis – *Trespass, Nursery Cryme, Foxtrot, Selling England by the Pound, The Lamb Lies Down on Broadway*. The five (six) albums with Big Pete have more to do with John Tavener and Women's Institute cake competitions than Yes or other less transgressive loons. Everybody knows this now, but it's taken a while.

Peter Gabriel – first three albums. Go no further.

Pink Floyd – Post-Syd, I would leave it at *Atom Heart Mother*, which has the Post Really Groovy Floyd at their pleasingly epic and disastrous best.

Principle Edwards Magic Theatre – *Assamoto Band* (LP). I can't fully recommend the sub, sub, ISB Principles (as no one on earth has ever called them), but their second album is worth some of your time. A concept album about the corporate takeover of Kidderminster by the McAlpine construction company. Really.

Swell Maps – *A Trip to Marineville* (LP)

Swell Maps – *Jane From Occupied Europe* (LP)

Swell Maps – 'Let's Build a Car' (45). The T. Rex side of the Maps. Fab cacophony.

Swell Maps C21 – *Polar Regions* (LP)

Bibliography

It's hard to recommend any reading on the post-punk period as most of these books labour under one single misapprehension. Jowe Head's own history of Swell Maps, *Swell Maps (1972–1980)*, is far better.

Chapter 20

Discography

The Grateful Dead – *American Beauty* (LP)

The Grateful Dead – *Working Man's Dead* (LP). In my non-expert, un-dead-head view there are four versions of the Dead. These two albums are by the second version, let's call it the 'Alt country' Dead.

The Grateful Dead – *Anthems for the Sun* (LP)

The Grateful Dead – *Aoxomoxoa* (LP). This one and *Anthems for the Sun* are from the first period of the Dead: the psychedelic Grateful Dead. These are the only albums that sound how British people think the Dead should sound. *Anthems of the Sun* is a dud. *Aoxomoxoa* is a creeped-out masterpiece.

The Grateful Dead – *Mars Hotel* (LP). This is version three of the Dead: Cocaine Boogie Dead. Some of this album is fantastic, some of it isn't. Tony Blair pretends to be a fan.

The Grateful Dead – *Live Dead* (LP). The fourth version of the Grateful Dead: Live. Be very careful, or you may be gone a long, long time.

And we jump, almost seemlessly, to Bucks Fizz and David Van Day.

Bucks Fizz – *The Land of Make Believe* (45). Their one luminous moment. A scabrous attack on the '80s Thatcher government. As powerful as Crass. I ain't kidding.

Dollar – *Shooting Stars* (LP). Starts with an excellent Todd Rundgren, *A Wizard a True Star* – like 'Overture' with a co-writing credit to Van Day. Superb.

Dollar – *The Paris Collection* (LP). Did David Van Day suss that 'The Land of Make Believe' was about Thatcher and then did he set out to avenge the honour of his beloved Lady Thatcher?

Miscellany

Cruising with Jane McDonald – Channel 5 travel show.

Chapter 21
Discography

The Velvet Underground – self-titled third album, the closet mix is the one you need. The transgressive nature of the Velvets' two Cale albums obviously overshadows the Yule Brothers, but hey, the Yules are cool. If not exactly Freaks.

Lou Reed – *Take No Prisoners – Lou Reed Live* (LP)
Buzzcocks – *Another Music in a Different Kitchen* (LP)
Buzzcocks – *Love Bites* (LP)
Buzzcocks – *A Different Kind of Tension* (LP)
Buzzcocks – *Singles Going Steady* (LP). The four original albums, and that lethal run of actual hit singles compilation. If any group have pissed on their legacy by re-forming then it is this lot.

Chapter 22
Discography

T. Rex. 'Get it On' (45). Marc Bolan encapsulated in four minutes and twenty-four seconds.

The B-side 'Raw Ramp' is even better. My fave Bolan song.

Wesley Willis – *Greatest Hits* (LP). Jello Biafra compiled. The Fab One: The Wez. There is never a bad time to break out the Wesley Willis – his *Rock 'n' Roll Will Never Die* LP is one of my all-time big hits. Marvel, as I do, to Wesley's tributes to Kurt C. and Hootie & the Blowfish.

Lou Reed – *Metal Machine Music* (LP). Listen at volume extreme, and listen at low volume, where it actually works best.

Bibliography

Luke Haines – *Bad Vibes: Britpop and My Part in Its Downfall*. Standard text. Classic.

Chapter 23

Discography

Althea and Donna – 'Uptown Top Ranking' (45)

Black Box Recorder – 'Uptown Top Ranking'. From the Don Letts album, *Version Excursion*. This 'version' is a remix that improves upon BBR group's original cover. That no one asked permission to remix is academic. We will let it slide as the result is pretty groovy, and it's a blast to be on an album with Dennis Bovell. Which is more – and possibly not a thing – than Morrissey can or would want to say.

The Clash – Must we? Okay. Cast your Action Man eagle eyes upon their second album (you know it), easily their best and really funny.

Lee Perry – You could get everything. Or if you don't want to spend the rest of your life 'in dub' then go for:

The Mighty Upsetter – *Kung Fu Meets the Dragon* (LP)
Upsetters – *Super Ape* (LP). The 'Pet Sounds'/'Sgt. P' of '70s dub reggae.
Lee Perry – *Roast Fish Collie Weed & Corn Bread* (LP). Perry at his eccentric best before the eccentricities got too self-conscious.
Morrissey – All the solo albums are great. Who cares about Johnny Marr when you've got Boz Boorer? A man who truly knows the importance of Mick Green over Roger McGuinn. The earlier Morrissey band sound twee. I accept I am in the minority.
Big Youth – Again, get as much of this Freak as you can track down. Listen on vinyl. Reggae works better that way. For starters:
Screaming Target (LP)
Natty Cultural Dread (LP)
Dreadlocks Dread (LP)
Reggae Phenomenon (LP)

Bibliography

George Melly – *Revolt Into Style*
Morrissey – *Autobiography*

Miscellany

Billy Wilder – *Sunset Boulevard*, 1950

Chapter 24
Discography

Luke Haines – *Smash the System* (LP)

FREAKS OUT!

The Incredible String Band. Of course, you should own all of their records. The first self-titled album (the only one with Clive Palmer) has many great moments but is more of an orthodox mid-1960s folk album than anything else that the ISB ever released. Their post *Wee Tam and the Big Huge* albums are a lot better than some will have you believe, and surely the measure of pure freakery is whether you dig *U* (of course I do). I tend to stop at *Earthspan*, which is a wonderful thing.

C.O.B (Clive's Original Band). Clive's great post-ISB group. *Spirit Of Love* and *Moyshe McStiff and the Tartan Lancers of the Sacred Heart*, combine 'Clive-ness' with spook-out weirdness. Much better than the foundation-course 'artiness' of Comus.

Joe Boyd – *White Bicycles*. Bone-ash dry memoir that fulfils tin requirements from the man who produced the Floyd's 'Arnold Layne'.

Rose Simpson – *Muse, Odalisque, Handmaiden: A Girl's Life in the Incredible String Band*. Memoir by Rose.

Adrian Whittaker (ed.) – *Be Glad for the Song Has No Ending: An Incredible String Band Compendium*. All ISB info is here. Essential.

Miscellany

Be Glad the Song Has No Ending. Incredible Omnibus film made by the Incredibles throughout 1968–69. Features the fab five, six, seven, eight . . . ? (at this point) getting heavy on their Welsh commune. Unmissable.

The Incredible String Band Retying the Knot – excellent BBC documentary that contains the 'Genius of this Parish'.

Chapter 25

Obviously, there is no discography for this chapter, so instead you should make your own music, or your own piece of art. Or perhaps a poem or even a manifesto. The most important thing is not to show or play what you have created; keep it for the length it takes to read the chapter, then bury it somewhere it can be found by a future generation.

Chapter 26
Discography

Ivor Cutler – *An Elpee and Two Epees* (LP)
Ivor Cutler – *Dandruff* (LP)
Ivor Cutler – *Life in a Scotch Living Room Volume Two* (LP)
Sir John Betjeman – *Banana Blush* (LP)
Sir John Betjeman – *Late Flowering Love* (LP) This and *Banana Blush* are the best of the Poet Laureate's late soft-focus psychedelic phase. Can be played quite happily alongside Syd Barrett's solo masterpieces. 'The Liquorice Fields of Pontefract' (from *Late Flowering Love*) comes on like 1969 Velvet Underground jamming with the Black Dyke Band.
The Beatles – *Magical Mystery Tour* (EP)
Robert Wyatt – *Rock Bottom* (LP)
Luke Haines – *Setting the Dogs on the Post Punk Postman* (LP)

Bibliography

Ivor Cutler – *Is That Your Flap, Jack?*
Ivor Cutler – *Life in a Scotch Sitting Room*

Chapter 27

Discography

Neil Young – *Rust Never Sleeps* (LP). Argue among yerselves.

Chapter 28

Discography

Kevin Junior – *Ruins* (LP). Get everything you can that Kevin recorded. This album has his version of the Real Kids' 'Common at Noon'. You need this in your life, and you will thank me.
Black Box Recorder – 'The Facts of Life' (45). Chart smash.
Black Box Recorder – 'Child Psychology' (45). Spotify smash hit.

About the author

Luke Haines is a London-based writer, visual artist, singer-songwriter and founder member of the Auteurs and Black Box Recorder.

A prolific artist, he has released nineteen albums in the twenty-first century, most recently his 2022 collaboration with R.E.M.'s Peter Buck – *All the Kids Are Super Bummed Out*.

He writes a regular monthly column for *Record Collector* and is the author of two critically acclaimed autobiographical books: *Bad Vibes* (2009) and *Post Everything* (2011).